DRUG ABUSE IN SOCIETY

A Reference Handbook

DRUG ABUSE IN SOCIETY

A Reference Handbook

Geraldine Woods

CONTEMPORARY WORLD ISSUES

ABC-CLIO

Santa Barbara, California
Denver, Colorado
Oxford, England

Copyright © 1993 by Geraldine Woods

Library of Congress Cataloging-in-Publication Data

Woods, Geraldine.
    Drug abuse in society : a reference handbook / Geraldine Woods.
        p. cm.—(Contemporary world issues)
    Includes bibliographical references and index.
    1. Drug abuse—United States.   2. Narcotic habit—United States.
    I. Title.   II. Series.
    HV5825.W5746   1993   362.29′0973—dc20   93-11858

ISBN 0-87436-720-4

99 98 97 96 95 94 93   10 9 8 7 6 5 4 3 2 1

ABC-CLIO, Inc.
130 Cremona Drive, P.O. Box 1911
Santa Barbara, California 93116-1911

Contents

Preface

There are a few clear areas in which we as a society must rise up united and express our intolerance. The most obvious now is drugs. When that first cocaine was smuggled in on a ship, it may as well have been a deadly bacteria, so much has it hurt the body, the soul of our country. There is much to be done and to be said, but take my word for it: This scourge will stop.[1]

With this promise, made to the nation during his inaugural address on 20 January 1989, George Bush became the latest in a series of presidents to take aim at drug abuse in the United States. Richard Nixon first declared a war on drugs in the early 1970s, and a few years later he announced that victory was at hand. In the 1980s Ronald Reagan set a crusade in motion, and he too noted progress. George Bush's inaugural optimism was typical, and so were the tactics of his administration. Like his predecessors, President Bush committed more federal funds to anti-drug efforts, pressed for stricter drug legislation, and made reduction of the supply of drugs from overseas a key element of his foreign policy.

Now the 1990s are here, and despite a slight decline in usage, drug abuse is still rampant. Cocaine, heroin, LSD, speed—all these old elements are still with us. New forms of drug abuse—designer drugs, crack cocaine, smokeable heroin, Ecstasy—have only deepened the problem.

The effects of drug abuse on society are horrifying. An elementary school principal searching for one of his students is caught in the cross fire between rival drug pushers and is fatally wounded. An elderly widow is strangled by an intruder seeking money to buy crack. A once-respected judge, popping tranquilizers even while on the bench, is arrested for extortion. A promising athlete dies after snorting cocaine. A man and woman are arrested while attempting to trade their baby for crack.

Those who take drugs may believe that they harm only themselves and those who care about them, but the fact is that drug abuse harms all of us. Our institutions are overwhelmed. Courts are glutted with drug cases, and prison construction is, unfortunately, one of the country's fastest growing industries. The nation's health care system—and health insurance system—are also burdened by drug abuse. In addition to the risk of overdose and the side effects of drugs, drug abuse brings increased rates of AIDS (Acquired Immune Deficiency Syndrome), other sexually transmitted diseases (STDs), and tuberculosis, presenting a public health threat.

Drugs have torn the fabric of our neighborhoods and families. Social workers report an enormous rise in child abuse cases and an increasing number of no-parent families, in which both parents have succumbed to drugs. The foster care system in many large U.S. cities simply cannot keep up with the demand. Schools too are struggling; thousands of children who were born addicted now experience learning problems. Other young people cannot concentrate because they live with violence and fear, in some cases in their own school hallways. Many children lack appropriate role models because they see wealth flow not to hardworking, honest adults, but to the local drug pushers.

Most Americans favor strict controls on psychoactive drugs— drugs that affect the mind—and support an intense federal effort to counter drug abuse in the United States. In fact, in the 1992 presidential campaign the war on drugs was one of the few issues on which all three candidates (President Bush, William Clinton, and Ross Perot) agreed. This agreement, however, encompasses only the general concept; when specific tactics are discussed, fierce arguments arise. Should all workers be subject to random drug tests? To what extent should the armed forces be involved in efforts to stop drug sales? What is the best treatment for drug addiction? How should treatment be funded? Should marijuana be subject to the same controls as heroin?

This book explores these questions and many other drug-related issues. Chapter 1 presents an overview of the effects of drugs in U.S. society. In Chapter 2, the history of psychoactive drug use and regulation, including important court cases, is detailed. Chapter 3 provides capsule biographies of major figures in the field. Chapter 4 explores facts and statistics on past and present drug use, the relationship between drugs and crime, health care, drug testing, drugs in the workplace, accidents, international efforts, and treatment. Chapter 4 also contains original documents, including presidential speeches, and the drug policies of major sports organizations. Federal, state, and private agencies combatting drug abuse are listed in Chapter 5. Chapter 6 provides an annotated bibliography, with books and articles organized by topic, for further research. Chapter 7 lists films that have proved helpful in drug prevention and education, particularly for young people. Finally, there is a glossary of terms from the field of drug abuse.

My interest in this topic springs from my work as a teacher. As I talk with young people, I sense their feelings of powerlessness in the face of what appears to be an insurmountable problem. My commitment to teaching is a result of my belief that knowledge itself confers power. The issue of drug abuse is crucial because the United States has not won the war on drugs. Instead, too many Americans have become casualties of the war that drugs have made against our society. I hope this book will help readers gain insight and practical knowledge so that they can begin to fight back.

Note

1. George Bush, "The Inaugural Address" (U.S. Department of State, Washington, D.C., April 1989, bulletin), 3.

1

Overview

CHEWING ON AN ALMOST RAW PORK CHOP, Rose sits on the stoop in front of her apartment building. She probably has not had any cocaine yet today because she is not expressing the paranoia that pours out of her when she is high: The government is following her, foreign agents threaten to kill her, and the police want to tow her car away. Today she is slumped over, absorbed in a music tape and in her troubles. "Don't ask me how I'm doing," she says. "I don't have anything good to say."

Rose sees danger in every passing police car, yet she does not consider herself a criminal, even though she breaks the law every day. Cocaine is a controlled substance, as are marijuana, heroin, hallucinogens, barbiturates, amphetamines, and many other drugs. Controlled substances are strictly regulated, even for medical professionals. Their possession, use, and sale are subject to stringent laws. When she snorts cocaine, Rose risks arrest. So does the executive who swallows black-market uppers (amphetamines) to get through a meeting, the housewife who puffs marijuana when she is bored, and the underage teen who buys a six-pack of beer with fake proof of age.

None of these people—even Rose, who lives in a fashionable block on New York's Upper East Side—fits the media's stereotype of a criminal. In fact, not all, or even most, drug abusers are tough, inner-city thugs. Racial stereotypes do not hold either. At most, poor African Americans account for 20 percent of the $100 billion yearly drug habit in the United States.[1] The lion's share belongs to the white middle class, but drug users are part of every

1

economic, social, and ethnic group. Americans currently consume more psychoactive drugs than any other nation in the world. We spend more on these drugs than we do on food, and drugs are our biggest import, tipping the balance of trade away from American industry and seriously harming our economy.[2]

The term *drug* in this book refers to illegal, psychoactive drugs such as heroin, cocaine, hallucinogens, marijuana, and inhalants. It also applies to legal drugs (e.g., sedatives and amphetamines) taken improperly, without prescription, or contrary to a doctor's orders. Lastly, it includes alcohol and tobacco. Alcohol is a psychoactive drug with the potential for addiction in some users. Nicotine, an active ingredient found in cigarettes and other tobacco products, is one of the most addictive substances known; about 80 percent of those who smoke become smokers, that is, addicts.[3] The nation's war on drugs generally excludes alcohol and tobacco because they are legal for adults. These drugs, however, have an enormous impact on society, and therefore they will be discussed in this book.

Addiction is another term that needs to be defined. For a long time doctors distinguished between a person's physical and psychological needs for drugs, as if the body and the mind were distinct entities. Much research was designed to discover whether a drug was physically addictive or simply led to a mental craving. This was a fairly useless effort, because the mind and body are intertwined, not separate elements. It does not matter whether an addict's body or an addict's mind needs the drug. The *addict* needs it. In recent years, many scientists have adopted the term *dependence,* which they use to encompass both physical and mental needs, and others have continued to use the term *addiction.* In 1965 the World Health Organization adopted the term *drug dependence* and defined it as "a state, psychic and sometimes also physical, resulting from the interaction between a living organism and a drug, characterized by behavioral and other responses that always include a compulsion to take the drug on a continuous or periodic basis in order to experience its psychic effects, and sometimes to avoid the discomfort of its absence."[4]

The Scope of the Problem

Exactly how many Americans abuse drugs, and why do they do it? These questions are not easy to answer. By its nature illicit (illegal) drug use is a secret activity; people who break the law are not usually anxious to advertise their behavior. As Professor Mark Kleiman of Harvard University's Kennedy School of Government said, "A lot of people just won't tell the nice man from the government that they smoked crack recently."[5] Confidential surveys alleviate this problem in some cases, but not all. Drug testing of urine or blood gives more accurate statistics than questionnaires, but tests are not administered to the population at large.

That brings us to another question: Who is being surveyed? For several years the government has sponsored a confidential national survey of high school seniors to track drug trends. The results do not include school dropouts, a group that may have a higher rate of drug abuse than those who remain in school. Similarly, an annual survey of households questions representative Americans, recording how many drugs are used in each residence. Until 1991, homeless people were not represented in these numbers, nor were military personnel or jail inmates. The best way to interpret statistics on drug use, therefore, is to consider them, as the National Institute on Drug Abuse (NIDA) does, "as accurate as the sources from which they were drawn."[6]

With these factors in mind, NIDA estimates that about 26 million Americans—one in every ten—sampled an illicit drug at least once during 1991, and more than 72 million have tried an illicit drug at some time in their lives.[7] More than 1 million Americans inject heroin, cocaine, and amphetamines intravenously[8] and more than 10 million are alcoholics.[9] About 55 million Americans smoke tobacco products.[10] Furthermore, an increasing portion of those who abuse drugs are cross-addicted. That is, they take more than one type of drug.

Surveys show, however, that overall drug use declined slightly during most of the 1980s,[11] particularly among more educated or casual users. Casual users take only a small fraction of the total amount of drugs produced. For example, about 80 percent of all cocaine and alcohol is consumed by addicts and alcoholics.[12] Rates of drug use in the inner cities have also increased, as have the number of addicts requesting treatment for heroin emergencies and cocaine problems. Dr. Mitchell Rosenthal, president of the drug treatment organization Phoenix House, explained that these numbers indicate that "this chronic problem that we have been dealing with is in fact deepening" and "that we have not halted drug abuse in the most vulnerable, most disadvantaged population."[13]

Nearly all heroin is consumed in inner cities. PCP and speedballs (a combination of heroin and cocaine) are also urban.[14]

Alcohol, marijuana, cocaine, and many other drugs cross city/ suburban lines. Crack cocaine took hold in 1986 as an inner-city phenomenon, but by 1988, according to a nationwide cocaine helpline, users were almost as likely to live in the suburbs as in the city.[15] As New York State Lieutenant Governor Stan Lundine commented, "For a long time, particularly after the advent of crack, it was felt that this [drug abuse] was primarily a city problem. Now we know that the incidence of drug use is at least as high and may be higher outside the city than it is in the city."[16]

Patterns of Drug Use

Some historians believe that drug use follows a cyclical pattern. On the upswing of the cycle, drugs become popular and many marvelous claims are made for them: They are safe, they are thrilling (or calming), they solve all sorts of problems and create none. Then comes the slide. Word spreads about users who have medical problems or whose lives have slipped out of control. Deaths and property damage occur as a result of drug abuse. The media trumpet drugs as a menace or a plague. Society declares war on drugs and usage drops. Then what many observers call historical amnesia sets in. Finally, drugs are rediscovered. They are hailed as safe, thrilling (or calming), the answer to all problems! The cycle begins again.[17]

Although this model is somewhat simplistic, both the post–Civil War period (1866–1900) and the Vietnam War era (1966–1975) did see a boom in drug use. The early twentieth century and the post-Vietnam era were characterized by tightened restrictions on drugs and a drop in their use.[18]

Individual drugs, such as LSD, may also follow this pattern. This hallucinogen was first synthesized in 1938 by the Swiss chemist Albert Hoffman and first used on humans in 1943. LSD remained rare until the early 1960s when it was praised as mind-expanding and consciousness-raising. The media reported on such figures as Ken Kesey's Merry Pranksters, a group that traveled across the country on a psychedelically painted bus, dropping acid (LSD) like Johnny Appleseeds of chemistry. During the 1960s and early 1970s, LSD and organic hallucinogens such as peyote and mescaline grew in popularity, as did other drugs. Then tales of bad trips (bad reactions to drugs) circulated. Every hippie knew of someone who had, in the slang of the day, freaked out and ended up in trouble when using LSD. The media reported a growing list of tragedies, such as young people who had tried to fly and fallen to their deaths and the like. Use declined and gradually people forgot about LSD. A generation not even born during its heyday had no fears of the drug. Now, according to Robert Bonner, head of the U.S. Drug Enforcement Administration (DEA), "LSD is the fastest growing drug of abuse among the under-20 age group."[19]

Individual drug abuse follows a less predictable pattern. Certain drugs seem to act as gateways. That is, they are the first psychoactive drugs taken before a person uses other, more potent substances, or they provide the entry to addiction. Tobacco, alcohol, and marijuana are the primary gateway drugs, and in the inner city crack is often a gateway drug.[20]

Though not everyone who uses a psychoactive drug walks through the gateway and enters a life of addiction, there is no way to tell who will become addicted. People may become dependent after many months, even years, of use of a drug and sometimes after the very first dose. One study followed 660 men of all economic backgrounds from 1940 to 1980, from their adolescence to middle age. The researchers concluded that there was no personality type that predicts alcoholism.[21] On the other hand, other studies have identified some factors that seem to increase risk of drug abuse. According to the National Academy of Science, "Addicts are more likely to have low self esteem, to be depressed, to be alienated, to behave compulsively and unconventionally, to have difficulty in forming long term goals, and to cope less effectively with stress."[22] Of course, those personality characteristics may be a result, rather than a contributing cause, of drug abuse.

Genetics is also a factor. Scientists do not believe that anyone inherits alcoholism or drug abuse, but the child of an alcoholic parent is four to five times more likely to develop the disease than the general population, even if he or she is raised by adoptive parents.[23] Clearly there is an inherited predisposition to alcoholism and perhaps to abuse of other drugs.

Some studies conclude that the condition of the community may also be conducive to drug abuse. Poor, high-crime neighborhoods with intense gang activity appear to present increased risk.[24] Experts stress, however, that no matter how many risk factors one faces, drug abuse is not a predetermined fate. It is not the environment, but how a person chooses to respond to it, that determines whether he or she becomes a drug addict.

The earlier the age at which a person begins to take drugs, the more likely he or she is to become addicted. In a study of smokers, for example, men who began to smoke during their teens were twice as likely to smoke more than two packs a day as an adult as those who started after the age of 20. Similar statistics apply to women smokers.[25] Furthermore, most people who use psycho-active drugs begin when they are very young. The most vulnerable years for first use are 12 to 20, with the peak year being 15 for most users, and even younger for dropouts and inner-city children. Of those who try drugs, the greatest number first sample cigarettes in the sixth or seventh grade, alcohol in the ninth, and cocaine in the eleventh. Almost no use of alcohol, tobacco, or illicit drugs (except cocaine) begins after age 25. Overall, peak consumption of psychoactive drugs occurs between ages 18 and 25.[26]

Drugs and Sports

A glance at today's newspaper headlines might lead one to believe that athletes run the highest risk of drug abuse. Len Bias, the college basketball star who died from the effects of cocaine; Dexter Manley, the Washington Redskins football player who was suspended for use of the same drug; Billy Martin, the former New York Yankees manager who died in an auto accident after an evening of drinking—the list goes on and on. Professional athletes are targeted by drug dealers because today's athletes have large incomes and a stressful life-style that puts them on the road, away from stabilizing influences, for long periods of time. They are also under great pressure to perform, and their failures on the court or field are always public.

Whether athletes have a greater rate of drug abuse than the general population is not known. Their problems become widely publicized, however, and because athletes tend to be role models for young people, the frailty of these heroes is particularly painful. Moreover, major league sports organizations have recognized that drug abuse among athletes represents a special kind of threat: Players dependent on drug pushers are open to blackmail and might be tempted to throw a game in order to earn their next dose or to maintain their secrets. For these and other reasons, the governing bodies of many sports have formulated strict anti-drug policies that entail testing, suspension, and even expulsion from the sport. (An explanation of each sport's drug policy appears in Chapter 4.) Several leagues have also designed prevention programs. The National Basketball Association's (NBA) Rookie Orientation Program, for example, discusses drugs as well as other temptations.[27]

Drugs and Crime

Users of drugs often refer to their behavior as a matter of personal choice, and they may criticize drug laws as prosecuting what they call victimless crimes. On the contrary, it is clear that individual activity has an intense effect on society and on other citizens. Once a radio talk-show guest discussing the sociology of crack users was angrily attacked by a caller: "Don't talk to me about those people," she virtually screamed. "I don't want to understand why they are taking drugs. I want them off my block! Since my neighbor started dealing crack, there have been two fires in my apartment building, and I don't know how many murders in front of my house. *I've had it.*"

A lot of Americans would agree, partly because so-called victimless drug crimes often lead to other crimes. As addicts burrow more deeply into their drug habits, they often sell drugs to earn money. Other drug users prostitute themselves or steal; muggings, car thefts, and purse snatchings finance drug use. While not life-threatening, petty crimes erode the quality of American life. Poet Ishmael Reed wrote of returning to his home in Oakland, California, shortly after crack became popular. He reported that four car break-ins and four burglaries occurred in less than a month. Reed attributed these crimes to the Living Dead, crack addicts whose days revolve around using drugs and financing their habits.[28] Even addicts with full-time, legitimate jobs may turn to crime. With a $1,000-a-month cocaine bill, a worker who earns $25,000 a year will have trouble making ends meet. Stolen products, faked time sheets, and embezzled funds may fill the gap.

Violence also accompanies the use of many drugs. In one survey of college students who had confessed to violent crimes on or near their campuses, more than half said they were high on drugs when they broke the law, as were almost half of the victims.[29] There are literally thousands of stories: The high school student in Fairfax County, Virginia, who shot a police officer, allegedly after taking six or more hits of LSD, and the Washington, D.C., honor student who was murdered by a stranger under the influence of PCP are only two examples. In a survey by the national cocaine hotline, (800) COCAINE, 25 percent of the callers said they had had violent arguments while on crack, and 83 percent said they believed that the drug caused violence. A frightening 17 percent said they carried guns because of their drug use.[30]

Even more destructive is the violence that accompanies the drug trade. Alex Kotlowitz, in his book *There Are No Children Here,* describes an urban nightmare: a 12-year-old boy named Layfeyette huddled in an apartment hallway for hours, trying to avoid bullets that might stray through the windows as rival gangs fight for turf. When asked about his future the boy replies, "If I grow up, I'd like to be a bus driver."[31] Layfeyette already knows a truth that defines his life in the inner city: As drug use spreads, so do gangs and gang warfare.

At one time the Mafia's crime organization controlled much of the illegal drug traffic in the United States. After several successful prosecutions in the 1980s (dubbed the Pizza Connection and Pizza Connection II by the media), the Mafia's hold on the drug business loosened. New and even more ruthless groups entered the market. In the 1980s, gangs called *posses* from the island country of Jamaica began emigrating to the eastern United States, gradually moving to the heartland. About the same time, Asian gangs, as well as established Californian gangs like the Bloods and the Crips, moved from the West Coast inward. Each territorial inroad has been marked by furious gun battles between the local gangs and the newcomers. The invaders, armed with paramilitary weapons like Uzis, AK-47s, and semiautomatic pistols, have generally prevailed.

The criminals are not the only ones hurt by this violence; exchanges of gunfire and drive-by shootings, in which bullets spray as a car speeds past the target, have killed many bystanders, including children. The drug world calls these victims mushrooms because they sprout up in the line of fire. As former President Bush commented, drugs "are turning our cities into battle zones and murdering our children."[32]

Confident of their power, drug traffickers have also instituted a reign of terror against those who oppose them. Maria and Carlos Hernandez, for example, challenged drug dealers who had moved onto their street in Brooklyn, New York. The couple reported drug dealers to the police and rallied neighbors to their cause. Early one morning in August 1989, as Maria was dressing for work, shots blasted through the window, killing her. Similarly Lee Arthur Lawrence, a storekeeper in Miami, was shot 30 times because he tried to force drug dealers away from his neighborhood. Even those in the law are vulnerable. In 1992, a federal attorney known for her tough prosecutions of Asian drug gangs was given a briefcase booby-trapped with a sawed-off rifle. Fortunately, she discovered the gun before it went off.[33]

The Justice System Responds

Not surprisingly, law-abiding citizens have cried out for justice and a return of peace to their streets. The police have responded: Drug arrests have skyrocketed in the last two decades, mostly because of the apprehension of users and low-level dealers. In many high-crime areas, the police have organized special squads to sweep neighborhoods clean of drug dealing. In New York City, the Tactical Narcotics Team (TNT) flooded a neighborhood in southeastern Queens for nine months, using undercover buy-and-bust operations as well as visible street patrols. The drug trade, however, has proved to be a balloon: Punch it in one spot and it bulges in another. Remove the pressure and it swells to its previous size. In southeastern Queens the dealers returned only two weeks after the TNT was withdrawn.[34]

Another problem is police corruption. The profits in the drug business are almost unimaginably high, and they match the violence the dealers are willing to employ. Imagine a police officer, earning perhaps $30,000 a year, chasing a criminal who offers him a choice between $100,000 and sudden death. Most law enforcement officials are honest and committed to the work they do, but it is not surprising that some succumb to temptation. Drug Enforcement Agency official Edward O'Brien, a 20-year veteran who helped break the famous French Connection case, was arrested when he tried to deliver 62 pounds of cocaine to an informant.[35] In 1992, the New York City Police Department was rocked by arrests of several officers for cocaine trafficking.[36]

A recent weapon in the drug war, one that actually dates to the 1700s when it was used to catch pirates, is being employed to even the odds somewhat against anti-drug forces. The law of forfeiture allows police to confiscate property involved in a crime. A house used to store drugs, a car that transports them, and cash that was paid for drugs can be seized. The proceeds of forfeiture are returned to the police to help cover law enforcement expenses. Using the law of forfeiture, the government has appropriated huge amounts of assets from drug traffickers—about a billion dollars in 1990 alone.

This tactic is effective, but it is not without danger. Legally the property is accused of a crime, not the person, so constitutional protections of civil rights do not apply. If the government has made a mistake, the person who has lost the property must sue to get it back, and the burden of proof is on the plaintiff, that is, the person who sues. He or she must show that the property was seized unjustly. The government does not have to prove anything. (This is the opposite of criminal cases in which the burden of proof is on the prosecutor, and the accused is innocent until proven guilty.) A person may actually be found not guilty of a crime and still lose his or her property.[37]

Anyone who brings suit is in for a long wait. The increase in drug prosecutions has overburdened the nation's criminal justice system, which has in turn expanded, adding judges, prosecutors, and jail space, only to see still another rise in arrests and a continuing shortage of criminal justice resources. The United States now has a larger percentage of its citizens behind bars than any other country in the world.[38]

Pregnancy Prosecutions

In spite of prison overcrowding, some prosecutors, concerned about drug-addicted babies, have expanded their arrest targets to include pregnant addicts. In 1989, a Florida court became the first in the nation to prosecute a woman for delivering drugs to her two children through the umbilical cord. Jennifer Johnson, a crack addict, used the drug frequently while pregnant. When she sought treatment, she could find no program that accepted pregnant women. (A survey that year found that 54 percent of drug treatment programs refused to admit pregnant addicts, and 87 percent refused pregnant crack addicts on Medicaid, the federal program that pays for treatment for most low-income people.)

Johnson's newborn babies each tested positive for cocaine. Since Florida law does not recognize the fetus as a separate person, the prosecutor based his case on the 60 to 90 seconds after birth in which the umbilical cord remains attached, circulating drugs from the mother through the child's body. Johnson was found guilty and sentenced to 15 years, 1 year of drug treatment and 14 on probation. The Florida Supreme Court later overturned her conviction. Since 1989, 160 other pregnant women have been prosecuted on similar grounds, and one was prosecuted for passing drugs to her baby through breast milk.[39]

These prosecutions are extremely controversial. Opponents believe that jailing pregnant women and nursing mothers discourages addicted mothers from seeking help. With so few options for treatment, critics point out that society tells addicts to ask for help and, when they do so, answers no and provides a jail cell instead of a hospital room. Civil rights advocates also worry that the law is applied unevenly. Studies show that women of all races take illegal drugs during pregnancy at about the same rate. Women of color, however, are much more likely to be tested for drugs after they give birth, and thus are more frequently prosecuted. Also, while certain drugs affect the sperm and therefore any pregnancies that result from the father's use of drugs, no men have been prosecuted for harm to their children under these laws.

Should Drugs Be Legalized?

In the current climate of drug crisis, pregnancy prosecutions are likely to continue. So are all types of get-tough anti-drug measures, such as those that provide special penalties for selling drugs to minors or in the vicinity of schools. Some laws mandate penalties up to and including life imprisonment, and even require the death penalty in certain circumstances. Even this does not satisfy some critics, such as former New York City Mayor Ed Koch, who called for shooting drug dealers on the spot, or former federal drug czar William Bennett, who advocated beheading them. It is unlikely that these officials were speaking literally, but their frustration is evident.

A growing number of politicians and social commentators from all parts of the political spectrum have come up with another answer. Conservative economist Milton Friedman, newspaper columnist Russell Baker, conservative leader William F. Buckley, former New York City Police Commissioner Patrick Murphy, Baltimore Mayor Kurt Schmoke, and others believe that the United States should just say no—not to drugs but to drug laws. They cite the example of Prohibition (1918–1933), in which sale of alcohol was illegal in the United States, and which was accompanied by bootlegging, widespread disobedience to the law, and mob violence by the likes of Al Capone. Proponents of drug legalization believe that banning drugs ultimately creates more problems than it solves. As U.S. District Judge James C. Paine of Miami commented, "Alcohol did not cause the high crime rates of the 20s and 30s. Prohibition did. And drugs do not cause today's alarming crime rates, but drug prohibition does."[40]

Those who favor legalization do not favor the use of psychoactive drugs. They simply believe that drug addiction is a medical problem, not a law enforcement matter. As George P. Shultz, a member of both the Nixon and the Reagan cabinets, put it, "It seems to me that we are not really going to get anywhere until we can take the criminality out of the drug business and the incentives for criminality out of it."[41] Shultz proposed that addicts be able to "buy drugs at some regulated place at a price that approximates their cost. When you do that, you wipe out the criminal incentives, including the incentives that the drug pushers have to go around and get kids addicted."[42]

Proponents of legalization believe that the drug war cannot be won; they see it as a kind of chemical Vietnam. Three presidents have declared a national war on drugs. The first was Richard Nixon, who in 1971 took aim at heroin traffickers from Turkey. The outcome illustrates the pitfalls of many anti-drug initiatives. Seizures of heroin rose, the number of acres in poppy cultivation fell, and the amount of heroin on American streets dwindled. Victory! declared Nixon in 1973. Then the law of supply and demand took over. The price of heroin skyrocketed, as did crimes to pay for it. Attracted by high prices, enterprising cartels in Iran, Afghanistan, and Pakistan (the Golden Crescent of opium or heroin production) and criminals in Southeast Asia (the Golden Triangle of Burma, Laos, and Thailand) entered the market.

Opponents of current U.S. drug policy also believe that our drug laws actually encourage the use of more dangerous drugs. Fifty thousand dollars worth of cocaine weighs about 5 pounds. Fifty thousand dollars worth of marijuana weighs 150 pounds and has more bulk. Someone seeking to get high might feel there is less danger in the more concentrated substance, even though cocaine causes many more problems than marijuana. One thing is certain: U.S. success in the international drug war has encouraged the domestic production of drugs. Underground chemists in the United States produce many designer drugs, man-ufactured forms of organic opiates, hallucinogens, and so forth. Marijuana is now a major American crop.

Another concern is civil liberties. In Operation Clean Sweep, the Chicago Housing Authority sealed off a public housing project and conducted house-to-house inspections without warrants. When criticized, the authority replied, "We are not infringing on rights; we are restoring residents' rights to a safe and decent en-vironment."[43] In Lawrence, Massachusetts, police issued passes to residents in a four-block area where drugs are often sold and then set up roadblocks. Motorists are routinely stopped and their passes are checked. Nonresident drivers receive a letter saying that their cars have been seen in a drug-selling center. The roadblocks and passes may discourage drug dealing, but they also inhibit a traditional freedom of American life, the freedom of movement.[44]

Most Americans support strict drug laws. In a recent poll, 62 percent of respondents said that they would be willing to give up some constitutional freedoms in order to fight drugs.[45] Many Americans would agree with former Mayor Koch, who compared legalization of drugs to fighting fire with napalm (a bomb material widely used in the Vietnam War). Supporters of current drug policy believe that the difficulty of fighting the drug war is no reason to abandon it. They fear that legalization would send the message that psychoactive drugs are not dangerous, and that mes-sage, coupled with availability, would increase demand. To sup-port this view, opponents of legalization cite the fact that the most abused drugs in the United States today are precisely those that are legal: alcohol and tobacco. Robert Peterson, former deputy attorney general of Pennsylvania, wrote, "By removing legal sanc-tions and lowering drug cost, a broader and more frequent de-mand for drugs will be created."[46]

Drugs and Health

His future was shining with promise. Len Bias, star basketball player from the University of Maryland, had just become the Boston Celtics' first-round pick in the 1986 NBA draft. He could look forward to a contract worth $2 million or more. It was time to celebrate. At a party, Len tried cocaine. A few hours later, the young, superbly conditioned athlete was dead.

How could this happen? All too easily. The drugs that many people think are safe kill every day: Thousands of Americans die each year as a direct result of the illicit drugs they have taken. Death comes for many reasons. Drugs, even when medically necessary, are dangerous substances. Doctors who prescribe drugs apply years of knowledge to determine the proper drug and dose. Dealers do not. Doctors also examine their patients carefully to see how the drug will affect the particular physiology of each individual. Kids who sniff glue or aerosol propellant have no idea how the chemical will interact with their bodies. Legitimate pharmacies and drug-manufacturing plants undergo rigorous inspections to ensure cleanliness and purity. Underground labs do not. In fact, dealers often cut, or mix, their products with other substances in order to make more money. There is no quality control, and a difference of just a few degrees when cooking, or making, the designer drug MDMA can result in a different chemical entirely, one as lethal as cyanide. If a user asks, How strong is this hit of cocaine?, What's in this shot of heroin?, or What will this capsule do to me?, the answer is, Who knows?

Illicit drug use is also linked to other ills. AIDS, for example, is transmitted through bodily fluids including blood. Before addicts inject heroin or cocaine, they often draw a little of their own blood into the needle to mix it with the drug. Since they share needles with other addicts, if one addict has AIDS, those who share the needle will probably soon have it also. Nationwide, about one-quarter of all intravenous (IV) drug users have AIDS. About one-third of the 40,000 Americans who are infected each year with HIV, the virus that causes AIDS, can trace their illness to IV drug use.[47] Shared needles also spread hepatitis and other life-threatening illnesses.

To stem the spread of AIDS, some cities have begun needle-exchange programs in which addicts trade their used syringes for sterile replacements. Opponents of needle exchange argue that such actions sanction drug use. "Our goal should be to eliminate drug abuse, not to find a cleaner, safer way to do it," said Congressman Charles B. Rangel, D-N.Y., chairman of the House Select Committee on Narcotics Abuse and Control.[48] Critics also charge that the programs are ineffective. Addicts are too disorganized to participate in a regulated program, they say. They add that needle sharing is a ritual, a kind of bonding between addicts. Even addicts with clean works (needles) may share a dirty needle with a friend. Supporters of needle-exchange programs, however, believe that AIDS must be fought by every means possible. In many cities where possession of a syringe is illegal without a prescription, AIDS activists have set up needle swaps in defiance of the law.

Uninhibited while under the influence of drugs, addicts are also unlikely to practice safe sex. According to one study, only 9 percent of male and 7 percent of female IV drug users said they used condoms every time they had sex, and only 27 percent used condoms sometimes.[49] Add to this the fact that many addicts work as prostitutes with dozens of sexual partners in order to finance their habits, and it is easy to see why IV drug users and their sexual partners are a fast-growing segment of the AIDS population. Syphilis, another potentially lethal sexually transmitted disease, is also on the rise because of crack and other drugs. One survey revealed an increase in syphilis cases of 132 percent between 1986 (when crack hit the streets) and 1990.[50] Crack has also helped to bring back an old enemy, tuberculosis, perhaps because of drug-induced lung damage and unhealthy life-styles.[51]

Two drugs legal for adults—tobacco and alcohol—cause the most health problems in the United States today. The link between smoking and increased risk of cancer, heart disease, and lung disease is well established. Recently, scientists have also documented the risks that smoking poses to nonsmokers who inhale someone else's smoke. Sidestream or secondhand smoke increases the risk of serious respiratory illness in children, and nonsmokers who live with smokers have a 30 percent greater risk of heart attacks. Passive smoking is blamed for 5,000 lung cancer deaths in nonsmokers each year.[52] Alcohol, in moderation, is not particularly harmful to adults, but heavy drinking raises the risk of cancer of the liver, stomach, colon, larynx, esophagus, and breast. Alcohol can damage the brain, pancreas, and kidneys, and contribute to heart disease, strokes, hepatitis, and cirrhosis. About a quarter of all hospital admissions are alcohol-related.[53] About 100,000 Americans die each year from alcohol.[54] Smoking kills 434,000 Americans each year, more than alcohol, illegal drugs, homicide, suicide, car accidents, fire, and AIDS combined.[55]

The medical bill for drug abuse, even excluding tobacco, is high. According to the Institute for a Drug-Free Workplace, employed drug users incur medical expenses that are 300 percent higher than those of nonusers.[56] Officials of the U.S. Alcohol, Drug Abuse, and Mental Health Administration estimate that the nation's doctor bill for substance abuse was about $150 billion in a recent year, even though many users of illicit drugs carry no health insurance and receive minimal care.[57]

Drug Babies

The most tragic result of drug addiction is the effect on the smallest victims. Pregnant women infected with AIDS may transmit the disease to their fetuses; most cases of pediatric AIDS (children who have AIDS) result from maternal drug use. About 2,000 babies are born with HIV each year, and the majority will die before age ten.[58] Infants born to mothers who abuse drugs or alcohol while pregnant—and 11 to 15 percent do—may themselves be addicted or suffer birth defects.[59] Cocaine, for example, can constrict blood vessels leading to the womb, cutting the fetus's supply of oxygen and nutrients and causing mental retardation. Cocaine babies run a much higher risk of sudden infant death syndrome (SIDS), a disorder in which a baby stops breathing and dies. They are likely to be irritable and display impaired mental and physical responses. Heroin, marijuana, amphetamines, tobacco, and many other drugs are also prenatal threats. Maternal drinking can cause fetal alcohol syndrome (FAS). Children with FAS may have short attention spans, defective memory, learning disabilities, lowered IQs, and poor school achievement.[60]

Proper care for children affected by substance abuse, therefore, will probably entail special teaching techniques and smaller classes. Estimates of the extra educational cost for each substance-affected child range from $40,000 to $90,000 for the prekindergarten years alone.[61] How many substance-affected children are there? Again, experts disagree. The National Association for Perinatal Addiction Research in Education (NAPARE) says there are about 375,000,[62] but other experts believe 30,000 to 50,000 is more accurate.[63] Even the lowest number represents a staggering economic cost, but the personal toll is much higher.

Drug Abuse and the Fabric of Society

"For the first time since we've been in the business, we don't know where the mothers are. She walks in the front door, she walks out the back door, and we don't see her again," commented Dr. Lorraine Hale, executive director of Hale House, a refuge for addicted babies in Harlem, New York.[64] Dr. Hale was discussing crack-addicted mothers, a group that challenges all previous assumptions about parent-child relationships.

Society has long been accustomed to one-parent families resulting from drug addiction, but social workers now talk of the no-parent family. In the past, most drug abusers were men, but the number of female addicts is rising. Some experts believe this is because crack cocaine is especially attractive to women (whether this attraction is physiological or psychological is uncertain). As difficult as it is for a child to lose a father to drugs, it is even more difficult when a single mother or both parents are lost to addiction.

Strung out on drugs, mothers often leave their children in the hospital. The children become known as *boarder babies*. Patrick Murphy, public guardian of Cook County, Illinois, described boarder babies as "languishing, unparented, in hospitals while the most important days of their lives, those days in which they learn the most basic communication and social skills—are passing them by."[65] Hospital charges for boarder babies are astronomical—about $18,000 per month in some areas.[66] Child welfare agencies strive to place these children in foster homes, but particularly in areas with many drug abusers, foster parents are in short supply.

For about three million American children, grandparents take up the slack.[67] Others are not so lucky. The *New York Times* reported recently on nine-year-old Dameel, whose crack-addicted mother beat him with a plastic baseball bat and whose father is unknown. Dameel stayed briefly with a grandmother and then in a group home. Mostly, he raised himself. After several incidents of stealing, Dameel was placed in a residential treatment center for emotionally handicapped boys.[68] Social welfare agencies around the nation report steep rises in cases of child abuse and neglect. In California, for example, substance abusers accounted for an 84 percent jump in the number of children needing protective custody in the last three years.[69]

Even in families with functioning parents, drug abuse takes a toll. Such families tend to be closed off from the rest of society. Studies show that substance-abusing parents practice inconsistent discipline, being overly harsh when they are sober, lax when they are not. Children in these circumstances become confused and lose self-esteem. Some children reverse roles, hiding the parents' incompetence from the world, managing the household, and otherwise taking on adult responsibilities and characteristics. Others withdraw or act out their troubles in misbehavior.

A growing number of children are themselves involved in the drug business, particularly in the inner cities where despair reigns and legitimate outlets for energy and ambition are scarce. Since the law punishes minors less severely, drug dealers often employ young children as lookouts and couriers. It is hard for a parent to discipline a child who is earning hundreds of dollars a week, especially when the parent is unemployed or earning minimum wage. The traditional family structure is devastated.

So is the neighborhood. Washington Heights, a section of New York City, used to be the home of hardworking immigrants, people putting in long hours for low wages to give their children a chance at a better life. Hardworking immigrants still live there, but in the early 1980s, drug dealers discovered that Washington Heights was a convenient spot to sell drugs to suburbanites driving into the city from New Jersey and northern New York State. Within a few years, the area had become an open-air market for illicit drugs, and it had the highest murder rate in New York City. Residents who could move out did so; those who remained felt besieged by the dealers, and in some cases, by the police.

One incident illustrates a particularly vicious effect of drugs on the neighborhood. In the summer of 1992, police officer Michael O'Keefe shot and killed Jose Garcia, whom O'Keefe said was threatening him with a loaded gun. The Washington Heights neighborhood erupted in riots. Some residents claimed that the dead man was innocent, a victim of police brutality. The area rang with bitter complaints that the police did nothing about the drug plague and at the same time treated every resident as a criminal. The police countered with tales of their own anguish: As foot soldiers in the war on drugs, they faced death daily with little support. Officer O'Keefe was eventually cleared of all charges, but the incident illustrates how the polarization of police and citizens is tragically sharpened in drug-infested areas.[70]

Drugs and Homelessness

"Drinking is responsible for keeping many men on the road," commented one writer in 1923, illustrating the traditional link between drugs and homelessness.[71] Throughout this century, writers have often described skid row alcoholics who slept in flophouses or single-room occupancy hotels (SROs). Now the nation is facing the new homeless, as some experts call them. The new homeless live in public shelters or on the street, the SROs having disappeared in the last two decades. They are poorer than the so-called old homeless, more likely to be mentally ill, and more likely to abuse illicit drugs and alcohol. Studies show that between 25 and 40 percent of homeless men drink heavily.[72] Almost 60 percent of homeless male alcoholics said their condition resulted from their drug use; others said they began drinking after they lost their homes.[73] From 10 to 30 percent of homeless people abuse drugs other than alcohol, and up to one-third use both drugs and alcohol.[74] A small percentage of people become homeless because of the crimes of family members; in 29 states the family of a drug dealer can be evicted from public housing, and houses in which drugs are found are subject to forfeiture.

Sadly, treatment programs for homeless addicts are scarce, and many shelters refuse people who are under the influence of a psychoactive drug. Since many shelters coordinate welfare, food stamps, Medicaid, and other aid programs for their clients, the homeless substance abuser loses more than a night's sleep.

Drugs in the Workplace

Can you make a reservation on American Airlines? Recently the answer to that question was no, you cannot. An employee who had been smoking marijuana at work forgot to load a crucial computer tape into the airline's central reservation system, erasing important information and causing the entire system to crash for eight hours. Cost to the airline: $19 million.[75]

Chances are that someone at American Airlines suspected the computer operator's activities but decided to mind his own business and say nothing. In the United States today, however, minding one's own business means ignoring employees or co-workers who abuse drugs, and the odds are that they will. About two-thirds of all drug addicts are employed, as are an even larger percentage of occasional drug users. NIDA and the National Institute on Alcohol Abuse and Alcoholism estimate that at least 10 percent of the U.S. work force suffers from alcoholism or other addictions.[76] In a recent Gallup poll, 22 percent of employees said that illegal drug use was widespread in their workplace, and 32 percent claimed that drugs were sold there.[77]

What does this mean for business? Decreased productivity—about one-third less, according to some studies.[78] More sick days: Illicit drug users are 2.5 times more likely to be absent more than eight days a year.[79] Frequent on-the-job accidents: Drug abusers are 3.6 times more likely to injure themselves or another at work.[80] Lower profits: Drug-addicted employees can cost a company between 5 and 10 percent of its payroll.[81] Estimates of the total cost of drug abuse to American industry range from $25 billion to $149 billion a year.[82]

Losing money is distressing; losing life is tragic. In January 1987, several passengers were killed when an Amtrak train whose engineer and brakeman were high on marijuana crashed. In the ten-year period between 1975 and 1984, alcohol or other drugs were implicated in 48 train accidents resulting in 37 deaths and 80 nonfatal injuries.[83]

These incidents make it clear that drug use impairs reflexes and compromises public safety. Experimental data bear this out. A study at Stanford University showed that pilots tested on flight simulators crashed frequently after smoking relatively weak marijuana cigarettes. Even more frightening is the fact that 24 hours later, when the pilots were aware of no residual effects of the drug, they still crashed during simulations.[84] Tests on pilots 14 hours after they drank alcohol showed a decrease in precision and accuracy even though no alcohol was detectable in their blood.[85]

Drug Testing

"Quality workmanship, safe operation, and a good mental outlook of the employees toward the company"[86]—that is what one construction contractor believes his employee drug program accomplishes. His program includes education and counseling for all workers and drug testing. This last element is a controversial but increasingly popular tactic in the war against drugs in the workplace. The momentum came from the White House; in 1986, President Reagan issued executive order 12564, which required the federal government to "show the way in achieving drug-free workplaces."[87] It called for federal agencies to identify illegal drug users through testing. The federal government has also required drug testing in many industries such as rail, trucking, airline, and nuclear power. Private industry has followed suit. The number of

Fortune 200 companies that test for drugs jumped from 3 percent in 1983 to 98 percent in 1991.[88]

Most employers use a two-step process, and they usually test only for the most common psychoactive drugs: cocaine, heroin, and marijuana. (Alcohol tests are less frequent and are handled in a different way.) First the employee's urine sample is collected, coded for confidentiality, and divided into two vials. One sample is subjected to immunoassay or thin-layer chromatography, two relatively simple laboratory tests. If the result is positive, the second sample is tested by gas chromatography or mass spectrometry, a more elaborate procedure. If both halves of the employee's specimen test positive, the lab reports a *hit* to the employer.[89]

Which employees are tested? Company policies vary; the most common subjects are job applicants and current employees whose behavior appears suspicious. More and more businesses, especially those with safety-sensitive jobs, also run random drug tests. An employee might be told, "Come in tomorrow for a drug test." Since tracers (substances that provide evidence of drug use) for marijuana remain in urine from two to five days, and cocaine tracers about three days, a drug user cannot get rid of this evidence with a one-day warning. (A collection of beliefs has arisen about methods that supposedly beat the drug tests, but the tests are quite sophisticated. Examiners even test the temperature of the urine to be sure it matches body temperature. Successful cheating is probably rare.)

Although the majority of American workers favor some sort of drug-testing program, many object to random drug testing, citing the right to privacy. An employee who is doing a good job, critics charge, should not be forced to undergo such an intimate test. Opponents of drug testing also worry that it can be used to harass a disliked employee or that inaccurate test results can unfairly penalize an innocent person. Critics also cite the cost of random testing. Negative results far outnumber the positive ones; one study of federal agencies concluded that for each hit, $77,000 worth of negative tests were conducted.[90]

Supporters believe that the cost of testing, both economic and personal, is small compared with the benefits it brings. The U.S. Supreme Court shares this view. It has ruled in several cases that the loss of individual privacy is offset by the public's right to safety. Furthermore, proponents of testing believe that the low number of hits may be due to the deterrent effect. A Wells Fargo Guard Service executive commented, "The most effective part of the program is the sign that says, 'We drug test.' When job applicants see it, they then decide they have to go out and put money in the meter or something, and we end up with a half-filled job application."[91] Strict regulations about the frequency and conditions of testing are often negotiated with employees' unions. These safeguards calm some fears about misuse of the procedure.

International Drug Traffic

A culprit often cited for U.S. economic woes is the trade deficit, the amount by which the value of U.S. imports exceeds its exports. The huge numbers reported on the evening news, however, are far too low. Drugs, one of this country's costliest imports, add millions of dollars to the flow of cash out of the United States.

International sources supply the three illicit drugs most commonly consumed in the United States: heroin, marijuana, and cocaine. Most heroin is grown in Southeast and Southwest Asia (the Golden Triangle and the Golden Crescent), but Mexico supplies a substantial amount and Colombia is entering the market.[92] The bulk of the marijuana consumed in the United States is also grown in Mexico; another portion comes from Colombia and Jamaica, and most of the rest is domestic (grown in this country). The major source for cocaine is South America, specifically Bolivia, Colombia, and Peru.

Cartels, organized much like multinational corporations, control illegal drug trafficking around the world. Cartels often exhibit the same behavior as local gangs, but in magnified form. A gang takes over a neighborhood; a cartel tries to seize an entire country. In Southeast Asia, for example, drug lord Khun Sa operates an army of 15,000 heroin traffickers. While this area is nominally part of Burma, in practice Khun Sa functions as its ruler and is more powerful than the government. Those who disobey him may be buried alive, drawn and quartered, or hanged. In Peru drug trafficking is mixed with politics. A Maoist rebel group named Shining Path (Sendero Luminoso) has waged a guerrilla war on the government for years, financing its activities with cocaine production.

Another power in the drug world is the so-called Coca Nostra of Colombia, four cartels named for their home areas of Medellin, Cali, Bogota, and North Coast. With more cash and better weapons than the average army, these cartels have brought about a reign of terror in Colombia. Farmers who refuse to grow the raw materials, police who arrest drug traffickers, judges who try them, and diplomats who oppose them all face what the cartels call *plata o plomo* — silver (bribes) or lead (bullets); that is, they must accept a bribe from the cartel and do its bidding or be shot. In the last few years, drug traffickers have assassinated 187 government officials, 50 judges, and 150 court employees. The cartels murdered a leading anti-drug political candidate, Luis Carlos Galan, as he spoke at a rally. They are also responsible for at least 250 bombings.[93] The cartels will even blow up an airplane in order to silence opponents. In November 1989, five informers were on a flight from Bogota to Cali. The plane exploded, killing the five plus 102 completely uninvolved passengers. Cartel violence is not confined to the home country; in 1992, for example, Miguel de Diaz Unanue, an anti-drug investigative journalist for a Spanish-language newspaper, was gunned down as he dined in a restaurant in Queens, New York.

Governments around the world have fought this lawlessness in a variety of ways. Since the days of the League of Nations in the 1920s and even before, a number of treaties have attempted to regulate dangerous drugs. The modern basis of control is the United Nations Single Convention on Narcotic Drugs, a 1961 treaty that requires all governments to strive for national and international control of psychoactive drugs (whether medically classified as narcotics or not).[94] The convention calls for the regulation of crops and of the manufacturing, shipment, and sale of dangerous drugs. In 1988, the United Nations Convention on Drug Trafficking set some guidelines for law enforcement, particularly the seizure of drug dealers' assets.[95] Many nations have also entered into less comprehensive treaties designed to limit drug trafficking between two or three countries.

U.S. treaties aim to cut supply by destroying coca (the plant from which cocaine is made) and other drug crops while they are still growing (crop eradication) or by giving farmers an incentive to grow something else (crop substitution). In collaboration with local governments, crops are sprayed with defoliants (plant-killing chemicals that alarm environmentalists) or uprooted manually, an effort requiring huge amounts of labor.

Of course, the entire anti-drug effort is a massive labor. Coca, for example, can be grown almost anywhere in the world between the Tropic of Cancer and the Tropic of Capricorn. The plants live for 30 to 40 years and produce a harvest every other month. Marijuana is literally a weed that can spread naturally without cultivation. Drug farmers, faced with pressure from their governments, often plant these adaptable crops in remote areas. There is certainly enough incentive; coca farmers in the Huallaga Valley of Peru earn about eight times more than other Peruvian farmers. This amount does not represent luxury but rather the difference between starvation and survival for many growers and their families.

The governments of the United States and many other countries also try to disrupt the drug-manufacturing process by regulating chemicals such as ether that are used in cocaine production or by destroying drug laboratories. Operation Blast Furnace, for example, raided laboratories in Bolivia using American helicopters and Bolivian troops.

Another target is the smuggling routes from manufacturing sites through the borders of the United States. The Coast Guard, U.S. Customs, and the Drug Enforcement Agency all work in this phase of the drug war, which is called interdiction. This is another daunting task. The United States has 12,000 miles of seacoast and 7,000 miles of land border, largely unguarded. Each year more than half a million planes, a hundred million cars, and a hundred thousand ships cross into U.S. territory. A single automobile tire can hold $1 million worth of cocaine or $10 million worth of heroin. We would like our borders to be walls against drugs; instead they are porous filters.

Foreign Policy

The drug war strains our foreign policy because the United States continually pressures other governments to do more to combat the growth and manufacture of psychoactive substances and uses foreign aid to keep the pressure on. According to the 1986 Anti–Drug Abuse Act, each year the president must certify that a foreign government is cooperating in anti-drug efforts;[96] if it is not, the amount of foreign aid and loans to that nation can be cut by up to 50 percent. This stick is paired with a carrot: Countries that are helpful receive U.S. funds for equipment, crop subsidy, and other uses.

Even with external incentives, the drug war can be tough to sell in some countries. Bolivia earns about $600 million a year from cocaine; that is one-third more than the total worth of all of

Bolivia's legal exports. At least 61,000 Bolivian families make their living from the drug trade.[97] Drug lords sometimes play Robin Hood to their communities, donating public facilities and earning the devotion of their neighbors. Furthermore, to many Latin Americans cocaine is essentially a U.S. problem. One Bolivian soldier refused to attack drug manufacturers, explaining that Bolivians should not shoot other Bolivians just because the United States has too many drugs. This attitude is not entirely accurate. Drug-producing nations have found that it is not possible to hold the tail of a tiger without being bitten: Addiction rates in drug-producing countries are extremely high. In Pakistan, for example, there are more than two million heroin addicts.

Supply-side control is complicated by the fact that the United States has at times violated its own policies against drug trafficking. A committee headed by Senator John F. Kerry, D-Mass., reported in 1989 on instances in which the United States had turned a blind eye toward drug dealing in order to carry out a political agenda. When the leftist Sandinistas were in power in Nicaragua, the United States supported many groups who helped the opposition (the contras). Funds were given to companies willing to pass them on to the contras, including some companies owned by drug traffickers.

Similarly, because of Panama's strategic canal and its aid to the contras, for several years the United States ignored the fact that the country's leader, Manuel Noriega, was involved in drug trafficking. Indicted in 1989, Noriega refused to leave Panama to stand trial in the United States. President Bush sent the U.S. army in after him, invading Panama and toppling its government. Noriega stood trial in Miami and was found guilty in 1992 on eight counts of drug trafficking.[98] Although many Latin Americans, including many Panamanians, were happy to see Noriega go, the United States was widely criticized. Some questioned why citizens of other countries should put their lives on the line to fight drugs when U.S. efforts were less than wholehearted.

In the Noriega affair many viewed the United States as acting solely in its own interests, heedless of the rights of other nations. In 1992, the case of a drug trafficker who had tortured and killed an American DEA officer, Enrique Camarena, reinforced this impression. American agents kidnapped the accused murderer in Mexico and brought him to trial in the United States. The U.S. Supreme Court ruled that this capture was acceptable, even though kidnapping by the police would be illegal within the

United States. Once again, Latin Americans felt that their rights were regarded as unimportant when they conflicted with U.S. concerns. Small wonder that a U.S. Senate report on "Drugs, Law Enforcement, and Foreign Policy" stated, "There are few issues which have caused greater strain on our relations with other nations, particularly with our Latin American neighbors, than that of drug trafficking."[99]

Drug Prevention and Treatment

The alternative to a supply-side drug war focuses on demand— the prevention and treatment of drug addiction. According to critics, this aspect of the drug war was sorely underfunded in the 1980s and early 1990s, when the major portion of the federal drug budget went to law enforcement, interdiction, and foreign aid. Treatment programs have received so little funding that addicts who apply for entrance have actually been put on waiting lists for months. Critics of recent federal drug policies would like to see more emphasis placed on demand reduction. They cite the Weed and Seed program, created in response to the 1992 Los Angeles riots, as an example of misplaced focus. Only 20 percent of the first year's funding is for social programs; the rest is for law enforcement. In some of the 20 test sites, no money at all was allocated to social services. Federal authorities, however, have been reluctant to pour money into such programs because none guarantee sobriety and few have had high success rates. Of course, crime is urgent and affects all Americans. It is hard to wait, perhaps for years, for job training, drug prevention, and drug treatment programs to reduce the magnitude of U.S. inner-city problems.[100]

Waiting has never been the strong point of most Americans. Our whole culture is oriented to instant gratification; just about every television commercial promises instant relief from something, and those expectations may fuel the desire for drugs. The media also bombard us with messages that drugs are a part of life. One study concluded that the average child has seen 75,000 drinking scenes on television by age 18.[101]

Many Americans, however, are fighting back. Who has not seen the eye-catching commercials by the Partnership for a Drug-Free America? ("This is your brain. This is your brain on drugs.")

Every school curriculum now includes information on the biological effects of illicit drugs, alcohol, and tobacco. Research has shown, however, that information alone is not enough to stop a child from experimenting with psychoactive substances. Children also need to learn how to face problems in a drug-free way. Consequently, many drug-prevention programs include exercises in communication, assertiveness training, and resistance to peer pressure. Former First Lady Nancy Reagan told kids to just say no. Unfortunately many children fear losing friends if they say no, so drug counselors role-play and let children practice refusals, such as, "No thanks, my mom would ground me forever." In many communities young people have also formed clubs such as Students Against Driving Drunk (SADD) to fight the drug problem. SADD chapters hold alcohol-free parties and distribute contracts for life, in which students promise to call home if there is no sober driver. Prevention efforts also involve parents by teaching them to recognize the signs of drug use and by helping them to form support networks. When children say that everyone else is allowed to try drugs, adults can counter with united, anti-drug force. Prevention groups also work to ensure that alternative, healthful activities are available in the community.

When all this fails, drug hotlines are often the first to know. Hotlines, or helplines, take calls anonymously from users or from those concerned about someone using drugs. Hotlines intervene in emergencies, and helplines provide information and advice, as well as referrals to treatment centers. Probably the most famous helpline is (800) COCAINE, which has taken more than three million calls since it was founded in 1983.[102]

Those who answer (800) COCAINE might suggest an in-patient treatment program to the most seriously addicted patients. These individuals need round-the-clock care, both to ensure their health as their bodies go through detoxification—adjustment to nondrugged functioning—and to avoid relapses. The terms *relapse* and *patient* are both words used for medical conditions, and they reflect the current view that addiction is a disease. This is a relatively new idea; addiction was once seen as a moral problem and addicts as weak-willed individuals who could not resist temptation.

The current theory holds that addicts have an incurable illness which, like diabetes or high blood pressure, requires lifelong care. Former addicts speak of themselves as *recovering* and *staying straight* (or sober) *one day at a time*. These terms were coined by

Alcoholics Anonymous (AA), an outpatient self-help program whose members attend frequent meetings and help each other to avoid alcohol. AA's method is called the 12-step approach; in it an addict admits that he or she is powerless over alcohol and must recover one day at a time. AA has been the model for Narcotics Anonymous, Pills Anonymous, Cocaine Anonymous, and other groups.

Therapeutic communities like Phoenix House and Daytop also emphasize group support. In these programs (some residential and some outpatient) counselors who are themselves recovering addicts take patients through a rigorous, supervised regimen of work, study, and self-examination. Counselors generally cannot be fooled by the addicts' excuses; they once used the same escape routes themselves. Groups or individual counseling are also offered by many school and churches. Recently, businesses have gotten involved by setting up employee assistance programs (EAPs). Employees who fail drug tests or whose behavior suggests a problem may be referred to the company's EAP.

Other treatments for addiction provide substitute drugs that are less harmful to the body and that allow the addict to function in society. Methadone, given to narcotics addicts, is the most common. Some therapies employ drug antagonists, chemicals that block the effects of the addictive substance or that cause ill effects if the addict gives in to the urge to take the drug. A dose of Antabuse, for example, followed by even a small amount of alcohol, makes an alcoholic feel deathly ill. Millions of dollars have been spent in recent years to find a cocaine substitute or antagonist. Some antidepressants look promising, but so far no miracle drug has been found.

That is probably the primary lesson of the war on drugs. There are no miracles, only sustained, painful, inch-by-inch progress. The amount of drugs available will probably increase as more impoverished or greedy suppliers (Americans included) fight for a piece of the market. As this book goes to press, the price of a hit of crack was as low as 75 cents in New York City because the market was flooded with the drug.[103] If foreign intervention and interdiction slow the tide of drugs from abroad, designer drugs will probably be produced in greater quantities within the United States. This is already beginning: The American West has been hit with a wave of ice, a synthetic amphetamine. American entrepreneurs will claim an increasing share of the drug market. Domestic marijuana is already one of the country's most lucrative cash crops.

If prevention efforts prevail and if current trends continue, drug use will decline very gradually as we enter the twenty-first century. A helpful factor is the aging of the huge baby boom generation. Drug use is higher among the young, and as the country's average age rises, demand for psychoactive chemicals may fall at a faster rate.

On the other hand, if the historical model of the drug cycle proves true, the country will remain in an anti-drug mood for a few decades. Then drugs will bounce back into popularity if we allow ourselves and future generations to forget the terrible effects of drugs on our society.

Notes

1. Daniel K. Benjamin and Roger L. Miller, *Undoing Drugs: Beyond Legalization* (New York: Basic Books, 1991), 3.

2. U.S. Department of Justice, Bureau of Justice Statistics Fact Sheet, *Fact Sheet on Drug Use Trends* (Washington, DC: U.S. Department of Justice, May 1992), 3.

3. Americans for Nonsmokers' Rights, Fact Sheet.

4. Pierre Andre, *Drug Addiction: Learn about It before Your Kids Do!* (Pompano Beach, FL: Heath Communications, 1987), 3.

5. "The Streets Are Filled with Coke," *U.S. News and World Report*, 5 March 1990, page 24.

6. U.S. Department of Justice, 2.

7. U.S. Department of Justice, 2.

8. U.S. Department of Justice, 4.

9. National Council on Alcoholism and Drug Dependence (NCADD), *Fact Sheet on Alcoholism and Alcohol Related Problems* (New York: November 1990).

10. "Guess Who's Winning the War against Smoking," *The Bottom Line on Alcohol in Society* (Lansing, MI: Alcohol Research Information Service, Spring 1992), 61.

11. U.S. Department of Justice, 4.

12. NCADD, *Alcoholism and Alcohol Related Problems*.

13. Joseph B. Treaster, "Hospital Data Show Increase in Drug Abuse," *New York Times*, 9 July 1992, B1.

14. Benjamin and Miller, 63.

15. Mark S. Gold, *800 COCAINE* (New York: Bantam, 1990), 7.

16. "Drug Abuse Not Confined to Cities," *Drug Abuse Update* (Atlanta, GA: National Families in Action, Spring 1992), 5.

17. David R. Buchanon, "A Social History of American Drug Use," *Journal of Drug Issues* (Winter 1992): 31.

18. Ibid.

19. Tom Stewart, "Update on the Drug Enforcement Administration," *Drug Abuse Update* (Atlanta, GA: National Families in Action, Spring 1992), 10.

20. NCADD, *Fact Sheet on Youth and Alcohol,* (New York: June 1990).

21. Charles P. Cozic and Karen Swisher, *Chemical Dependency* (San Diego: Greenhaven, 1991), 99.

22. Ibid.

23. NCADD, *Youth and Alcohol.*

24. L. Greenbaum, "Youth and Drug Abuse—Breaking the Chain," *USA Today,* November 1989, 45.

25. "Early Initiation of Smoking Associated with Higher Consumption in Adulthood," *New England Journal of Medicine* (September 1991): 968.

26. "Stopping Alcohol and Other Drug Use before It Starts: The Future of Prevention," OSAP Prevention Monograph (Washington, DC: U.S. Department of Health and Human Services Public Health Service, Office of Substance Abuse Prevention, 1989), 3–12.

27. Ira Berkow, "Troubled Times beyond the Lines," *New York Times,* 20 July 1992, C1.

28. Ishmael Reed, "Living at Ground Zero," *Utne Reader,* May-June 1991, page 60.

29. NCADD, *Alcoholism and Alcohol Related Problems.*

30. Gold, 25.

31. Alex Kotlowitz, *There Are No Children Here* (New York: Anchor Books, 1991), x.

32. George Bush, "National Drug Control Strategy," *Vital Speeches of the Day* (1 October 1989), 738.

33. Arnold H. Lubasch, "Jury Is Shown Rigged Briefcase with Gun Meant for Prosecutor," *New York Times,* 14 July 1992, B3.

34. Barbara Flicker, "The Drug War," *American Bar Association Journal* (February 1990): 64.

35. "A DEA Hero Is Busted," *Newsweek,* 28 August 1988, page 32.

36. Television news report, NBC News, 1 July 1992.

37. Dennis Cauchon, "The Government Doesn't Have To Prove Guilt," *USA Today,* 18 May 1992, 1.

38. Fox Butterfield, "Are American Jails Becoming Shelters from the Storm?" *New York Times,* 19 July 1992, Week in Review, 4.

39. "Mother Gets Six Years for Drugs in Breast Milk," *New York Times,* 28 October 1992, B9.

40. Arnold S. Trebach and Kevin B. Zeese, "Judge Gray Joins Other Jurists in Ruling against the Drug War," *Orange County Register,* 19 April 1992.

41. Glen Elsasser, "A Just Cause? Washington Group Wages War on the War on Drugs," *Chicago Tribune*, 24 May 1990.

42. Ibid.

43. Neal Bernards, *War on Drugs* (San Diego: Greenhaven, 1990), 73.

44. "Barricades and Passes for Drug Neighborhoods," *New York Times*, 22 December 1992, B8.

45. Diana Reynolds, "The Golden Lie," *The Humanist*, September-October 1990, 10.

46. Robert E. Peterson, "Stop Legalization of Illegal Drugs," *Drug Prevention Newsletter* (Danvers, MA: Committees of Correspondence, June 1990), 3.

47. Erik Eckholm, "AIDS, Fatally Steady in the U.S., Accelerates Worldwide," *New York Times*, 28 June 1992, Week in Review.

48. Charles B. Rangel, "Providing Needles Is a Dangerous Idea," *Drug Watch International* (Danvers, MA: Committees of Correspondence, March 1992), 4.

49. "Most IV Users Do Not Practice Safe Sex," *Drug Abuse Update* (Atlanta, GA: National Families in Action, Spring 1992), 5.

50. Benjamin and Miller, 122.

51. "Crack May Play a Role in Development of TB," *Morbidity and Mortality Weekly Report* 40, no. 29 (1991): 485–488.

52. "Ban Urged on Secondhand Smoke in Public Places," *New York Times*, 11 June 1992, A20.

53. "OSAP Mobilizes To Combat a National Crisis," *OSAP The Fact Is* (Washington, DC: Office for Substance Abuse Prevention, Spring 1991): 1.

54. NCADD, *Alcoholism and Alcohol Related Problems*.

55. *New York Times*, "Ban Urged."

56. Mark A. DeBernardo, *What Every Employee Should Know about Drug Abuse* (Washington, DC: Institute for a Drug-Free Workplace, 1992), 7.

57. "Employees Respond to High Costs of Substance Abuse," *Boston Herald*, 15 July 1991.

58. Eckholm, 5.

59. NCADD, *Alcoholism and Alcohol Related Problems*.

60. Susan Jenks, "Drug Babies," *Medical World News* 12 (February 1990): 43.

61. Benjamin and Miller, 126.

62. Jenks, 43.

63. Douglas J. Besharov, "The Children of Crack: Will We Protect Them?" *Public Welfare* (Fall 1989): 6.

64. Ibid.

65. "State Sued over Handling of Cocaine Baby Cases," *Chicago Tribune*, 27 September 1991. Reprinted in *Drug Abuse Update* (Atlanta, GA: National Families in Action, Summer 1992), 17.

66. Ibid.

67. "To Grandma's House We Go," *Time,* 5 November 1990, page 86.

68. Linda Richardson, "Imaginary Town Is Real Life for Troubled Children," *New York Times,* 12 July 1992, 30.

69. "Working with Substance Abuse Families and Drug Exposed Children, the Child Welfare Response," *Public Welfare* (Fall 1991): 37.

70. David Gonzalez and Jane Fritsch, "A Collision of Differences in Washington Heights," *New York Times,* 12 July 1992, 1.

71. Lisa Orr, *The Homeless* (San Diego: Greenhaven, 1990), 76.

72. Committee on Health Care for Homeless People, *Homelessness, Health, and Human Needs* (Washington, DC: National Academy Press, 1988), 62.

73. Ibid.

74. Ibid., 65.

75. DeBernardo, 10.

76. Gary F. Kohut and Virginia T. Geurin, "Attitudes of Personnel Managers toward Substance Abuse Policies," *Journal of Drug Issues* (Summer 1991): 493.

77. "Drug Abuse in the Workplace," *Employee Drug Education Bulletin* (Summer 1992): 1.

78. DeBernardo, 6.

79. DeBernardo, 7.

80. Ibid.

81. Ibid.

82. Ibid.

83.. NCADD, *Alcoholism and Alcohol Related Problems.*

84. DeBernardo, 10.

85. "How High Is Your Airline Pilot?" *ICPA Dispatch International,* order no. W:2,89.

86. "Quotes," *The Drug-Free Workplace Report* (Washington, DC: Institute for a Drug-Free Workplace, Summer 1991).

87. Frank J. Thompson, Norma M. Riccucci, and Carolyn Ban, "Drug Testing in the Federal Workplace: An Instrumental and Symbolic Assessment," *Public Administration Review* (November-December 1991): 515.

88. DeBernardo, 5.

89. Ibid.

90. Thompson, Riccucci, and Ban, 520.

91. "Quotes," 3.

92. Joseph B. Treaster, "Bush Sees Progress, but U.S. Report Shows Surge in Drug Production," *New York Times,* 1 March 1992, 12.

93. Rensselaer W. Lee III, "South American Cocaine: Why the U.S. Can't Stop It," *Current* (June 1989): 22.

94. Herbert S. Okun, letter to the *New York Times,* 29 June 1992, A14.

95. "The War on Drugs," *The Bottom Line on Alcohol in Society* (Lansing, MI: Alcohol Research Information, Spring 1992), 61.

96. Mary H. Cooper, "Does the War on Drugs Need a New Strategy?" *Congressional Quarterly* (27 January 1990), 243.

97. Lee, 22.

98. Larry Rohter, "Noriega Sentenced to 40 Years in Jail on Drug Charges," *New York Times,* 11 July 1992, 1.

99. Subcommittee on Terrorism, Narcotics, and International Operations for the Senate Foreign Relations Committee, *Drug Law Enforcement and Foreign Policy* (Washington, DC, 1988).

100. Michael deCourcy Hinds, "Experts Are Critical of Bush Anti-Drug Program," *New York Times,* 20 July 1992, A12.

101. NCADD, *Youth and Alcohol.*

102. Gold, 7.

103. Treaster, "Hospital Data."

2

Chronology

MANY PEOPLE THINK OF DRUG USE as a modern phenomenon, perhaps arriving in our national life in the 1960s and becoming an area of public concern as late as the 1980s. In fact, psychoactive drugs were used at least 5,000 years ago in the Middle East, and they have been consumed by almost every society, in every part of the world, since that time. Similarly, communities have always viewed the use of psychoactive drugs as a potential or an actual problem. The following chronology describes the discovery of, attitudes toward, regulations on, and court disputes concerning psychoactive drugs in the United States. To provide a historical context, some information on the precolonial and colonial eras in the Western Hemisphere is also included.

The Precolonial Era

The ancient inhabitants of both North and South America, like the members of all human societies, consume an extensive array of psychoactive drugs. South Americans chew coca leaves as a mild stimulant and appetite suppressant, and shamans in Peru use coca to facilitate divination (telling the future). Organic hallucinogens such as peyote and psilocybin mushrooms are prized for the visions they bring, and they form part of the religious rites on both continents. Tobacco is cultivated in North America. The burning leaves are used in ceremonies and may be smoked for pleasure.

Colonial America

When they reach the New World, Europeans discover many plants new to them and transport some samples back to their home countries. Drugs derived from these plants are often touted as cure-alls, although more prudent observers warn of their effects. Old World rulers sometimes embrace the new substances and at other times discourage their use by taxation, fines, and punishment. In the colonies, native drugs face the same mixed response. The substances may be suspect, especially if they are part of non-Christian religious ceremonies. On other occasions they may be embraced as wonder drugs. Alcohol, which the colonists bring from the Old World, is established quickly as a fundamental part of life for both colonists and Native Americans. In the late seventeenth century, distillation is perfected, and alcoholic drinks become more potent. Cannabis (marijuana), native to Asia, is brought to Chile, and its cultivation spreads throughout North and South America, primarily to supply hemp fiber.

1551	Missionaries in South America denounce the use of coca at the first Ecclesiastical Council, held in Lima, Peru.
1561	Jean Nicot, French ambassador to the Portuguese court, takes tobacco plants to France as a present for Catherine de Medici. Tobacco soon becomes *herba panacea* (cure-all plant) and is used for wounds, headaches, carbuncles, chilblains, worms, and venereal disease.
1567	Coca is again denounced by missionaries in Peru as "strengthening the wicked in their delusions . . . [causing] the death of innumerable Indians . . . [and ruining] the health of the few who survive."
1602	*Work for Chimney Sweepers* is published in England, denouncing smoking as a "pestiferous vice."
1604	King James I of England publishes the *Counterblast to Tobacco*, in which he attacks the medicinal value of the plant, sarcastically saying that it will "not deign to cure here any other than cleanly and gentlemanly diseases." In

1604
cont.

the same year, James taxes tobacco, hoping the increased cost will discourage users. This is the first attempt to control drugs by making them more expensive. By the end of the century tobacco is heavily taxed throughout Europe.

1611

The cultivation of marijuana is introduced in Virginia, and by 1629 the plant is also grown in New England.

1620

In accordance with a document issued by the Inquisition, missionaries formally condemn peyote as a substance whose "fantasies suggest intervention of the devil."

1642

The pope, leader of the Roman Catholic Church, issues an encyclical (an official letter to his followers) condemning tobacco smoking. He repeats the condemnation in a 1650 encyclical.

1730

German doctor Friedrich Hoffman markets liquid ether as a remedy for many diseases. Ether becomes popular as a psychoactive inhalant drug.

1776

Joseph Priestley discovers nitrous oxide (laughing gas).

1784

In *An Inquiry into the Effects of Ardent Spirits upon the Human Body and Mind,* Dr. Benjamin Rush, a signer of the Declaration of Independence, argues that consumption of beer and wine should be encouraged in order to forestall the drinking of hard liquor.

1794

Corn and rye farmers of the new United States, who find it profitable to convert their crops into whiskey, rebel against a federal tax. The Whiskey Rebellion is eventually quashed by federal troops sent by President George Washington.

1798

Dr. Rush takes on tobacco in his essay, "Observations upon the Influence of the Habitual Use of Tobacco upon Health, Morals, and Property." Rush believes that tobacco adversely affects all three and leads to excessive drinking because it brings on a thirst that cannot be satisfied with water.

The Nineteenth Century

Chemistry becomes much more sophisticated in the nineteenth century; a number of drugs are extracted from their organic base, increasing potency, danger to the body, and potential for abuse. During the second half of the century, the patent medicine business booms. Preparations containing morphine, cocaine, cannabis, and alcohol are widespread. Many Civil War veterans (400,000 by some estimates), originally dosed with morphine to treat their painful wounds, are addicted. (Narcotics addiction, or morphinism, is known as the soldier's disease.) Another large group of addicts forms in the civilian population, perhaps because the medical profession, which has few cures at its disposal, often prescribes opiates (drugs from opium) to relieve the tension and pain illness brings. Upper-middle-class women form the largest group of medically created addicts. Also in the post–Civil War years, smoking increases rapidly, largely because of Northern soldiers who have picked up the habit while stationed in the South's prime tobacco-growing country. In the last two decades of the century, cocaine is celebrated as an ideal medicine and is sold in tonics and patent medicines. As the nation moves westward into Native American lands, previously isolated tribes are introduced to alcohol. Alcoholism soon devastates many tribes.

Conversely, fear of drugs grows in the last two decades of the century. Articles appear in the national press linking the habit of smoking opium with Chinese immigrants and claiming that the drug leads to intermarriage between Chinese men and white women. As the century closes, the movement to prohibit alcoholic beverages gains force. So does the antismoking movement; tobacco reformers succeed in banning cigarettes in many cities. The tide of public opinion begins to turn against narcotics and cocaine as the nation confronts a rate of addiction twice that of current times.

1805   Morphine is extracted from opium poppies. The substance is named for Morpheus, the Greek god of sleep and dreams.

1822   Thomas de Quincey publishes *Confessions of an English Opium Eater,* praising opium as "the secret of happiness" and the bearer of "portable ecstasies." De Quincey coins the term *tranquilizer* in this work.

1827   Merck & Company, a German pharmaceutical firm, begins commercial manufacture of morphine.

1828   Codeine is synthesized.

1831   Chloroform is synthesized and used as an anesthetic and as a psychoactive inhalant. Throughout the nineteenth century, as more drugs are discovered, inhalant parties grow in popularity. Guests inhale the vapors to the point of intoxication.

1839   The first Opium War breaks out as China tries to ban the importation of Indian opium by British merchants. Britain forces China to end trade restrictions, and the opium trade flourishes. A second Opium War follows in 1856; China is forced to open still more ports to British trade.

1840   A Swede, Magnus Hess, becomes the first to use the term *alcoholism*.

1851   A bill to prohibit alcoholic beverages (excluding hard cider) is passed in Maine, although citizens may import alcohol for their own use. Twelve other states soon follow Maine's lead.

1853   The hypodermic needle is invented. Morphine is injected for the first time. Many scientists believe (falsely) that intravenous morphine is nonaddictive because it does not pass through the digestive system.

1857   Amyl nitrate, a psychoactive inhalant, is discovered. It is used medically to treat angina pectoris, a constriction of blood vessels.

1860   A German chemist, Albert Niemann, isolates the active ingredient of coca, cocaine.

1863   A mixture of wine and cocaine named Vin Mariani, advertised as a beverage that "refreshes . . . aids digestion . . . [and] strengthens the system," is marketed. It is one of a group of hugely successful cocaine-laced so-called health tonics on sale without prescription.

1864   The first barbiturates are synthesized.

1868	Cigarettes are manufactured in the United States for the first time. Previously, smokers had to roll their own.
1869	*Beeton's Book of Household Management* warns that patent medicines given to children to make them sleep often prove fatal. Despite the warning, many patent medicines containing narcotics, such as Mother Bailey's Quieting Syrup and Infant's Friend, sell well.
1869	Chemist Oscar Liebreich synthesizes chloral hydrate, a sedative.
1869	Opposition to alcohol grows. The National Prohibition party is formed and wins some seats in state legislatures. In 1890, the party wins a seat in Washington, D.C.
1870	Dr. Clifford Allbutt, a physician, becomes the first writer in English to warn of narcotic addiction. His work is published in Great Britain and the United States. Allbutt also speculates on a debate still raging today: Is addiction caused by the substance, or by a particular person's reaction to it?
1870	The Comanches, a Native American tribe, begin to use peyote in their religious rites. In the twentieth century, the practice, now common to many tribes, is outlawed.
1874	The English researcher C. E. Wright synthesizes heroin, but after observing adverse effects on dogs, he abandons his research.
1875	San Francisco, experiencing a wave of immigration from China, becomes the first municipality to ban opium smoking and close opium dens. Several other cities follow. By 1914, 27 cities and states have similar bans.
1882	Under the name of Barbital, barbiturates are marketed and used in medicine.
1884	Sigmund Freud publishes an article titled "On Coca" in which he praises the drug and suggests various therapeutic uses for it. Carl Koller, a scientist, tests Freud's idea that the drug might be used as a local anesthetic by dripping it into a frog's eye. Soon the drug is widely used in eye surgery.

1885	Dr. Albrecht Erlenmeyer warns against the use of cocaine to treat morphine addiction.
1887	Amphetamines are synthesized.
1896	Mescaline, the active ingredient in peyote, is isolated.
1898	Heroin is synthesized by the Bayer Company (of aspirin fame) and marketed. Around this time, many local antinarcotics laws are passed. Ironically, heroin is promoted as a cure for morphine and opium addiction.

The Early Twentieth Century (1900–1920)

During the first few years of this century the country wrestles with the problem of control over narcotics and cocaine. Political factors include the interests of pharmacists, who profit from drug sales, and of doctors, who generally oppose government interference in their power to prescribe drugs. While the force of public opinion is firmly against drugs, no one knows how to deal with the country's quarter of a million addicts. What happens to them if their legal supply is withdrawn? Cocaine, once immensely popular, begins to lose its healthful reputation. In the South, rumors spread that cocaine makes African Americans impervious to bullets, and many southern police departments switch to a higher-caliber bullet to overcome the drug's effects. Several local laws against cocaine are passed.

1903	In reaction to the growing fear of cocaine, a soft drink manufacturer removes the drug from its product. Coca-Cola, originally formulated with both cocaine and caffeine, now contains only caffeine.
	The American Pharmaceutical Association recommends strong penalties for illegal drug sales and a ban on imported opium. The association also urges that heroin be available only by nonrenewable prescriptions.
1904	The Opium Exclusion Act is passed, and the importation of what is known as smoking opium into the United States is banned.

1906   The Pure Food and Drug Act is passed. This landmark legislation requires accurate labeling of patent medicines. Heroin, cocaine, and other drugs must be listed on the label. The act bans interstate shipment of cocaine and places a limit on the import of coca leaves.

1909   The United States convenes the Shanghai Conference, the first international meeting to consider the opium traffic. Turkey, a major producer, does not attend. Persia, another producing nation, has only a local merchant to represent its interests. Britain maintains that the Chinese trade issue should be settled by Britain and China only. India is reluctant to give up its profitable opium trade. In spite of these obstacles, the conference writes several resolutions, none of which are binding: that each government take measures to suppress the use of opium gradually, that each nation examine its own laws on opium use, and that no nation export opium unless the importing nation agrees.

1911   An International Conference on Opium convenes at the Hague, the Netherlands. Again, Turkey is absent. An accord is reached to control narcotics (understood to mean opium, morphine, heroin, and cocaine), to limit the nonmedical use of opium, and to establish a quota on narcotic exports. The conference agrees to regulate Indian hemp (marijuana) if, after study, "the necessity of such a course makes itself felt." Conferences in 1913 and 1914 follow up on the resolutions, and more countries— ultimately 44—sign the treaty, but less than half of those nations ratify it in their home legislatures, and only 7 put it into effect. Efforts begin in the United States to regulate narcotics, but marijuana is exempt.

1913   Despite a presidential veto, the Webb-Kenyon Bill is passed, prohibiting the import of alcoholic beverages from wet states, in which liquor is legal, to dry states, in which it is not.

1914   The Harrison Narcotics Act is passed. A landmark bill, this is the first anti-drug law with clout. The Harrison Act limits the amount of opium and morphine that can be sold in over-the-counter drugs. (Cannabis is not regulated.) The act requires that anyone who produces, transports, prescribes, or sells narcotics be registered and

1914
cont.

possess a special tax stamp. The tax itself is small; the true intent is to ensure that anyone who buys black-market drugs will be in violation of the law. Doctors and dentists who prescribe the drug must record transactions with the Internal Revenue Service (IRS). The same is true for pharmacies and manufacturers.

The act states that a doctor may prescribe narcotics "in the course of his professional practice only." This vague phrase is subject to debate in the first few years after the act takes effect. The government holds that maintenance of a patient's drug habit is not professional practice and that mere possession of the drug by an addict is illegal. At first the Supreme Court, in *United States v. Jin Fuey Moi,* disagrees. The court rules that Congress did not intend "to make the probably very large proportion of citizens who have some preparation of opium in their possession criminal." By 1919, however, condemnation of narcotics is so universal that the court reverses itself. In two cases, *United States v. Doremus* and *Webb v. United States,* the court holds that maintaining an addict's narcotics habit is not medical practice. Prescriptions must show a steadily diminishing amount as proof that the addict is being weaned by the doctor.

1919

Methamphetamine (a stimulant) is synthesized.

The 1920s and 1930s

The 1920s roar in, along with Prohibition, as the Eighteenth Amendment is ratified. Prohibition represents a major economic loss for the U.S. government because alcohol taxes are the largest source of federal revenue. While the law against alcohol is widely broken in the Roaring Twenties, the amount of alcohol abuse does plummet. (Interestingly, purchase of alcohol is not a crime under Prohibition; selling, distributing, and production are illegal.) Prohibition gives rise to bootleggers (i.e., gangsters) and the accompanying violence is a national preoccupation. Repeal is celebrated in 1933.

Narcotics addicts, their legal supply withdrawn, are treated at clinics with a variety of drugs, therapies, and attempts to cure addiction. The success rate is extremely low, and many seek the drug on the black market. During the Great Depression, the popular press attributes horrible crimes, supposedly committed under the influence of marijuana, to Mexican farm workers. Marijuana has long been prescribed medically in the United States, but the Mexicans use the drug for recreation. Anticannabis sentiment grows.

1920   Prohibition begins as the Volstead Act takes effect. This act, also known as the National Prohibition Act, enforces the Eighteenth Amendment, which bans intoxicating beverages.

The League of Nations is established. At the first meeting, an advisory committee on opium and other drugs is set up to collect information on drug traffic and to see that members adhere to drug treaties.

1922   The Supreme Court, in *Behran v. United States,* outlaws any prescription of narcotics to addicts.

The Jones Miller Act, also known as the Narcotic Drug Import and Export Act, establishes the Federal Narcotic Control Board and provides for fines up to $5,000 and ten years in prison for narcotics traffickers (sellers and importers). Exports of narcotics are permitted to those nations agreeing to monitor the use and distribution of the drugs.

1923   A study of homeless men concludes that "drinking is responsible for keeping many men on the road."

1924–1925   A second international conference on opium is held, this time in Geneva, Switzerland. The U.S. delegates aim to suppress the production and export of narcotic drugs, the first of many efforts—continuing today—to control drug abuse in the United States by limiting the supply from abroad. The conference resolves that international trade in cannabis be limited to medicinal and scientific consumption. Frustrated by the weakness of other proposed measures, the U.S. delegation walks out.

1925   In *Linder v. United States,* the Supreme Court allows physicians to prescribe small doses of narcotics to ease withdrawal symptoms. This is a change from the 1922 Behran ruling.

1929   A *New York Times* article titled "Waging the War upon Narcotics" is an early expression of the concept of a war against drugs. In 1948 *Collier's* magazine continues the metaphor with an article titled "War against Dope Runners," discussing how Mexican and American border agents fight the importation of narcotics. Two years later *Reader's Digest* follows with "Our Global War on Narcotics."

1930   The Federal Bureau of Narcotics separates from the agencies controlling alcohol; Harry Anslinger is its first head. The Federal Narcotics Commission reports that "opium dens could be found in almost any American city."

1931   Another Geneva Conference on the Limitation of the Manufacture of Narcotic Drugs is held. Delegates from the opium-manufacturing countries sign an agreement: Export of heroin is to stop except at the request of the importing nation, illicit heroin seized is to be destroyed or rendered harmless, and all important cases of trafficking are to be reported to the League of Nations. This conference regulates all aspects of the drug trade, from raw material to factory to hospital, lab, or pharmacy. A conference five years later improves methods for the detection of treaty violators.

1932   Benzedrine, an amphetamine, is introduced commercially in inhalers. Throughout the next few decades, amphetamine pills are widely prescribed for depression and obesity. (Amphetamines are no longer approved for these conditions.)

The Uniform Narcotic Act requires standardized federal, state, and local records of drug prescription and sales.

1933   Prohibition is repealed by the Twenty-First Amendment to the Constitution.

1935   A federal facility, called a farm, for the treatment of addicts is established in Lexington, Kentucky. Later another is built in Texas.

Alcoholics Anonymous, a therapeutic self-help group that will soon become the model for many other substance-abuse recovery programs, is founded.

1937   Amphetamines are first used to treat hyperactive children. Paradoxically, the stimulant calms overactive children.

Using the same method as the Harrison Narcotics Act, the government attempts to regulate the use of marijuana through the Marijuana Tax Act. Marijuana producers, distributors, and others in the business must be registered and pay a special tax. Anyone using marijuana who does not possess a tax stamp is subject to arrest. The new law effectively outlaws marijuana for recreational purposes.

1938   The hallucinogen LSD (d-lysergic acid diethylamide) is synthesized by Albert Hoffman, a Swiss chemist.

Professor Raymond Pearl of Johns Hopkins University reports to the New York Academy of Medicine that a major study has shown a link between impaired longevity and smoking. This is the earliest of more than 50,000 studies showing that smoking is harmful.

Demerol, a synthetic opiate, is introduced.

The 1940s and 1950s

During World War II, the nation pulls together to fight fascism. Use of illegal drugs is very low, and cocaine is almost unheard of. Cigarettes are distributed free to GIs, and after the war the number of smokers increases rapidly. Amphetamines are given to soldiers to increase alertness. In the 1950s severe laws are passed setting penalties up to and including the death penalty for drug offenses. The Beats (called beatniks by a disparaging media) are a prominent rebellious group that experiments with marijuana and hallucinogens. LSD is used in mental hospitals on chronically ill patients who are withdrawn and unresponsive. The long-term results lead most psychiatrists to discontinue the practice. Experts predict that the use of illicit drugs in the United States is in its death throes. The baby boomers begin to arrive, however, paving the way for the drug explosion of the late 1960s.

1940s   Methadone, a long-acting substitute for narcotics, is invented in Germany by Nazi scientists who fear that the nation's supply of medicinal opium will be cut off by the Allies.

Several studies show that barbiturates are addictive and that withdrawal symptoms occur. Shortly thereafter a media campaign is launched to combat the abuse of these sedatives.

1942   The Opium Poppy Control Act is passed to regulate the legal cultivation of opium poppies.

1943   LSD is first used on humans.

1945   With the founding of the United Nations (U.N.), a Commission on Narcotic Drugs is established. Three years later the task of narcotics control is given to the World Health Organization.

1949   Manufacture of benzedrine (an amphetamine) in inhalers is halted because of widespread abuse and the potential for overdose.

1950s   Barbiturates become a major drug of abuse.

1950   U.S. soldiers fighting the Korean War mix amphetamines with heroin to create speedballs.

A report linking smoking and cancer is published in the *Journal of the American Medical Association* by Evarts A. Graham. Thousands of subsequent studies reaffirm that smoking increases the risk of cancer.

Meprobamate, a minor tranquilizer, is synthesized. A related group of drugs, benzodiazepines, follows. Minor tranquilizers are widely prescribed and continue to be among the most prescribed medicines today.

1951   The Boggs Act imposes heavy mandatory (required) penalties for narcotics offenses. Four years later a similar law provides for sentences up to and including the death penalty for drug trafficking.

1953   The United Nations gives only seven countries a license to produce opium. Compliance is to be supervised by a permanent central opium board of the United Nations.

1958   Synanon, the first therapeutic community for the treatment of drug addiction, is founded in California by Charles Dederich. It is followed in the next few years by Odyssey House, Daytop, Phoenix House, and others.

                The American Medical Association (AMA) and the American Bar Association Joint Commission on Narcotic Drugs recommends less severe penalties for narcotics violations, as well as the outpatient treatment of addiction.

1959   PCP (phencyclidine) is developed as an anesthetic. After adverse effects are reported in humans, the drug is used only for veterinary medicine. Because it becomes a drug of abuse and because better compounds are developed, PCP is withdrawn from animal medicine in the 1970s.

Late 1950s   Glue sniffing grows in popularity among teens.

The 1960s

President John F. Kennedy opens the decade with a strong commitment to mental health treatment, and the government sees addiction as more of a health problem than a law enforcement issue. This attitude is tested by the Psychedelic Sixties, which really begin in the latter half of the decade, although the avant garde (i.e., groups such as the Merry Pranksters) has publicly promoted the use of illegal drugs for several years. Drugs are so widespread among rebellious youth that one observer later writes, "If you remember the Sixties, you weren't there." Marijuana is the drug of choice, smoked publicly at rock music concerts and be-ins, and psychedelics (hallucinogens) are touted by Timothy Leary and others. In Southeast Asia, U.S. troops use marijuana and heroin, but many give up the practice upon their return home. By the early 1970s, the dark side of drugs is evident. Counterculture heroes Lenny Bruce, Janis Joplin, Jim Morrison, Brian Jones, and Jimi Hendrix all die from the effects of drug use.

1960   Articles begin to appear in the media describing the dangers of inhalants as glue sniffing becomes popular.

The Federal Trade Commission bans claims by cigarette companies that a cigarette filter is efficient to make cigarettes less dangerous and aids health.

1961   The United Nations adopts the Single Convention on Narcotic Drugs, which places coca under the same limits as opiates.

1962   In *Robinson v. United States,* the Supreme Court rules that only addicts who refuse commitment to drug treatment facilities should be jailed.

1963   The President's Commission on Narcotics and Drug Abuse recommends fewer jail sentences for drug offenses and more emphasis on treatment and prevention.

1964   Two insurance companies begin to provide insurance for alcoholism treatment, and in the next decade, many other companies follow. By the mid-1970s, outpatient treatment for alcoholism is also covered in many health plans. (Treatment for the abuse of other types of drugs is covered less frequently, and not at all until the 1980s.)

Surgeon General Luther Terry issues a landmark report on smoking, linking that habit with serious health problems including cancer.

Two Rockefeller University scientists, Dr. Vincent Dole and Dr. Marie Nyswander, develop the methadone maintenance treatment of heroin addiction. Addicts take a long-acting methadone dose to block the physical withdrawal symptoms of heroin.

1965   The Drug Abuse Control Amendment formulates stricter rules on amphetamines, limiting the approved medical uses of the drugs.

A law is passed requiring warning labels on cigarette packs. After intense lobbying by the tobacco industry, the label informs smokers only that smoking "may be hazardous" to their health.

1966   The Narcotic Addict Rehabilitation Act allows civil commitment to treatment facilities for some of those convicted of drug offenses. The law also drops the mandatory minimum sentence for heroin traffic adopted during the 1950s.

In *Schmerber v. California,* the Supreme Court rules that a blood test taken from a suspected drunken driver is constitutional, even without a warrant. The court holds that the need to test right away overrides the requirement for a warrant, since the evidence (blood alcohol concentration) would disappear before a warrant could be obtained. The court further states, however, that a blood test is search and seizure as defined under the Fourth Amendment, and without "a clear indication that in fact evidence will be found" the search violates the defendant's rights.

1967   *Time* magazine names the younger generation as its Man of the Year.

1969   Operation Cooperation begins. This agreement calls for joint action against drugs by the United States and Mexico.

1969–1971   These years mark the peak of the heroin epidemic.

The 1970s

The rock festival Woodstock, in which drugs are consumed openly, begins the decade, and psychoactive drugs are rife. As the Vietnam War becomes increasingly unpopular, student protests spread. The sense that the nation is out of control grows. The use and abuse of legal tranquilizers increase, as does the number of bad trips and deaths from illegal drugs. Methadone maintenance increases in popularity as a treatment for heroin addiction, and halfway houses (reentry communities for recovering addicts who have been released from the hospital) become popular. A number of laws (both federal and local) are passed to stem the tide of drug use. At the end of the decade, cocaine begins its comeback to popularity, and drug abuse is increasingly defined as an illness and covered by private medical insurance.

1970   The Controlled Substances Act is passed, uniting previ-
              ous drug laws and creating a federal standard for drug
              control. Drugs with potential for abuse are divided into
              schedules. Schedule 1 lists the most dangerous drugs with
              no approved medical use: for example, heroin, LSD, and
              marijuana. Schedule 2 drugs may be used in medicine
              with strict controls: cocaine, PCP, amphetamines, and
              others. Schedule 3 drugs are considered less dangerous
              and have wider medical use: sedatives and stimulants.
              Schedules 4 and 5 include minor tranquilizers like Val-
              ium and Librium, mild stimulants, and cough medicines.
              (Some categories of drugs such as barbiturates may be in
              more than one schedule, depending on the characteris-
              tics of the particular formulation. See Drugs and the Law
              in Chapter 4 for more information.)

              The label on tobacco products is changed to read that
              smoking "is dangerous" to health, upgrading the previ-
              ous warning that it "may be hazardous."

              Broadcast advertisements for cigarettes and other to-
              bacco products are regulated. A new law calls for tobacco
              companies to finance antismoking commercials in pro-
              portion to the number of cigarette ads. Afraid of the
              negative publicity, the companies pull their television and
              radio ads entirely, and cigarette ads effectively disappear
              from the airwaves.

1971   International control is extended to hallucinogens, stim-
              ulants, and barbiturates by the U.N. Psychotropic Con-
              vention. The convention, written in 1971, is not ratified
              by the U.S. Congress until 1980.

              President Richard Nixon declares war on drugs and
              warns Turkey to curb production of opium poppies.
              Nixon devotes $3 billion to his anti-drug efforts; most of
              the money is spent on prevention and treatment.

              The National Commission on Marijuana and Drug Abuse,
              appointed by President Nixon, concludes that possession
              of small amounts of marijuana should be decriminalized.
              Nixon rejects this recommendation and declares drug
              abuse the country's "public enemy number one."

1972   Fentanyl is developed for use as an anesthetic in surgery.

The National Institute on Drug Abuse (NIDA) is established to create comprehensive health, education, and research programs for the prevention and treatment of drug abuse.

Turkey agrees to measures to end the cultivation of opium poppies.

1973   Nixon declares victory in the war on drugs. Production of Turkish opium is very low. Southeast Asia enters the market.

The Drug Enforcement Administration (DEA) is created.

Opiate receptor sites are first identified in the brain. This important discovery is a key to the puzzle of how psychoactive drugs achieve their effects. By understanding this process, scientists may be able to block the effects of psychoactive drugs and stem the craving that comes with addiction.

The French Connection case breaks a heroin ring that smuggles the drug from the Middle East through France to the United States. A very successful movie is later made about this investigation.

Fetal alcohol syndrome is identified.

1973–1979   Eleven states decriminalize possession of small amounts of marijuana, limiting penalties to small fines, but many later reverse their decisions. Alaska goes further, ruling that it is legal to grow and use small amounts of marijuana. This ruling is reversed in 1990.

1977   President Jimmy Carter endorses the decriminalization of marijuana, saying that "penalties against the possession of a drug should not be more damaging than the drug itself." Under Carter's proposal, marijuana would not be legal, but penalties for possession of small amounts of the drug would be limited to fines. (Dr. Peter Bourne, Carter's special assistant for health issues, supports decriminalization. Bourne is later involved in a scandal when he writes a prescription for methaqualone, a sleep-

1977
cont.
ing pill, with a false name for an employee. Bourne is also accused of snorting cocaine at a party given by the National Organization for the Reform of Marijuana Laws [NORML]. Bourne resigns, and efforts to decriminalize marijuana fall into disrepute.)

1978
Anti-drug funds and materials, such as helicopters to spray paraquat and drug-detecting equipment, are given to Mexico by the United States in hopes of curbing new crops of Mexican heroin. Mexico concentrates its efforts on marijuana and begins to spray its marijuana fields with paraquat, a toxic herbicide. Marijuana smokers fear lung damage from the paraquat-laced drug. In response to this fear, domestic cultivation of marijuana increases. By the end of the decade, illegal marijuana is the largest cash crop in California, Hawaii, and Oregon. The plant is often grown in remote areas of national parks.

1979
Cocaine reaches a new height of popularity.

The 1980s

This decade embodies two contradictory trends. On the one hand, cocaine use surges, particularly in the middle class, as yuppies (young, upwardly mobile professionals) embrace the feeling of success it brings. By mid-decade, however, drug use in the middle class declines, and the drug becomes associated with crime and addiction. Crack cocaine (a smokeable form of cocaine) hits the streets in 1986, and a new wave of destruction ensues. Use of crack rises in the inner cities. As AIDS (Acquired Immune Deficiency Syndrome) spreads, the use of intravenous (IV) drugs becomes even more dangerous. Presidents Ronald Reagan and George Bush both declare war on drugs (Reagan's is called a crusade) and increase law enforcement and interdiction budgets dramatically. Very little funding is provided for treatment, and though private insurance covers some employed addicts, low-income people often find that publicly funded drug treatment programs are filled to overflowing. Many grass-roots anti-drug efforts begin as parents see the dangers faced by their children.

1980
First Lady Nancy Reagan launches her anti-drug campaign, Just Say No.

1981   Crack cocaine first appears.

AIDS cases begin to be recognized; AIDS and IV drug use are linked.

The Model Drug Paraphernalia Act is passed, banning the sale of hashish pipes and other devices used with illicit drugs.

In *Zamora v. Pomeroy*, a federal court upholds locker searches in a school after a trained dog has sniffed marijuana inside a locker. The court says that in a school in which the authorities maintain master keys and clearly exercise control over the lockers, a search warrant is not required.

1983   In *United States v. Villamonte-Marquez et al.*, the Supreme Court holds that U.S. Customs Services officers may board a boat without a search warrant and without "reasonable suspicion of a law violation" because boats have never been subject to the same standards as land vehicles. The court cites a 1790 law as precedent for the practice. The case involves Customs Services officers who saw a sailboat rocking violently. When they boarded the vessel to check the safety of the sailors, the officers found bales of marijuana in the open hatch. In his dissent, Justice William J. Brennan says, "Today, for the first time ... the court approves a completely random seizure and detention of persons and an entry onto private, noncommercial premises by police officers, without any limitations whatever on the officers' discretion or any safeguards against abuse."

In *United States v. Knotts*, the Supreme Court upholds the use of a beeper to track a drug violator. Suspecting that recently purchased chloroform was to be used to manufacture illicit drugs, Minnesota law enforcement officers placed a tracking device in one container of the chemical. Officers followed the car by monitoring the beeper signal. They then obtained a warrant and searched a secluded cabin, discovering materials for the production of amphetamines.

1984   The Omnibus Drug Bill provides increased penalties for major drug offenses and gives federal prosecutors new

1984
cont.

authority to seize assets of drug dealers (forfeiture). Forfeiture is later challenged because, with all of their assets seized, many accused drug traffickers cannot hire private attorneys and must rely on court-appointed attorneys. The Supreme Court rules in 1989 that attorneys' fees are not exempt from forfeiture. Justice Byron White notes that the new law supports the old proverb, "Crime does not pay." He adds that the court has no intention of creating a new proverb, "Crime does not pay except for attorneys' fees."

The Pizza Connection case is tried, and a major Mafia distribution network for heroin is dismantled.

Colombia extradites Carlos Lehder Rivas, a drug trafficker, and cartel members storm the Colombian Supreme Court, killing half the members of the court and more than 100 others.

In *Oliver v. United States,* the Supreme Court rules that, without search warrants, police are allowed to search for drugs on private property, even if it is surrounded by locked gates and fences and marked with no-trespassing signs. The case involves marijuana plants growing in secluded fields.

In *United States v. Montoya de Hernandez,* the Supreme Court rules that routine searches of people and their effects at border crossings may be performed, even without reasonable suspicion of a crime. In the majority opinion, the court refers to the U.S. drug problem as "a veritable national crisis." The court also upholds a lower court decision (*Storms v. Coughlin*) that permits large-scale searches of prisoners, stating that such searches are not an invasion of privacy because the need for prison security overrides individual rights.

The Colombian government launches Operation Primavera (Spring) on cocaine-processing labs. The ten-day campaign is the most successful in Colombian history.

1985

In *New Jersey v. T.L.O.,* the Supreme Court rules that unreasonable searches of students are not allowed. If there is suspicion that the student has violated school rules or the law, however, school officials may search without a warrant. The case involves a student caught smoking in a restroom. When the student denied the charge, the school official checked the student's handbag and found rolling papers and other evidence of illegal drug use.

MDMA (also called Adam or Ecstasy), a so-called designer drug, is officially banned. Within days, a slightly different drug, Eve, is created to take its place. A new law is passed to allow authorities to schedule (ban) a new drug within days of its appearance. This closes the loophole that underground chemists often exploited as they created new, perfectly legal—and deadly—compounds.

Marinal, a synthetic compound of marijuana's active ingredient (THC), is approved for the treatment of nausea.

Enrique Camarena, a DEA agent, is tortured and killed in Mexico by drug traffickers. In 1992, the Supreme Court rules that the kidnapping of Camarena's murderer outside of the United States in order to bring him to trial in the United States is permissible.

To strengthen the warning on tobacco products, a law is passed requiring four rotating labels on the packages and advertisements, each mentioning a specific disease linked to smoking.

The AMA calls for a complete ban on tobacco advertising and promotion, to no avail.

In *McDonell v. Hunter*, a U.S. District Court judge rules that urinalysis, in this case required of a prison guard, is a search within the definition of the Fourth Amendment, and that the test can be carried out only if individual reasonable suspicion exists. On appeal, the court rules that random drug testing of prison guards is permissible as long as it is systematic and not arbitrarily given to only one employee.

San Francisco becomes the first jurisdiction in the country to pass a law regulating drug tests. The law allows drug testing only if the employer has reasonable grounds for suspecting a worker to be impaired, the worker's impairment is "a clear and present danger" to self or others, and the results of the urinalysis can be contested by the employee.

1986   Crack use becomes widespread.

John Lawn, director of the DEA, thanks the ruler of Panama, Manuel Noriega, for his "vigorous, anti–drug trafficking policy."

Len Bias, a basketball star, dies after using cocaine.

In *California v. Ciraolo*, the Supreme Court rules that searches by low-flying planes are permissible without a search warrant. Dante Ciraolo, whose yard was enclosed by a high fence, was found to have 75 marijuana plants after his property was searched from the air.

Declaring war on drugs, President Reagan calls on Americans to "mobilize for a national crusade against drugs . . . to help us create an outspoken intolerance for drug use." He issues executive order 12564, directing the federal government to "show the way in achieving drug-free workplaces." He requires federal agencies to identify illegal drug users through testing and to take appropriate action in response.

The Anti–Drug Abuse Act almost doubles spending to combat drug availability and use. The law allows U.S. military assistance to friendly governments for the purpose of controlling illicit narcotic production and trafficking. The law also requires the president of the United States to certify that a foreign nation has cooperated in anti-drug efforts. Nations that do not cooperate may lose up to half of their allotted foreign aid. An amendment to the Controlled Substances Act provides special penalties for trafficking within 1,000 feet of a school.

Another law is passed to combat designer drugs. The Controlled Substances Analogue Reinforcement Act places analogues (synthetic forms) of controlled drugs in schedule 1. Any drug created to produce stimulation, depression, or hallucination in the nervous system may also be considered illegal. Individuals may be prosecuted for drugs they claim to be psychoactive, even if the drugs do not produce such an effect.

The surgeon general issues a report indicating that secondhand smoke causes lung cancer.

1986
cont.

In the case of *Capua v. City of Plainfield, New Jersey*, in which fire fighters were forced to submit to an unannounced drug test, a federal district court rules that the tests are unconstitutional because "in order to win the war against drugs, we must not sacrifice the life of the Constitution in the battle."

1987

The DEA, along with 12 countries of Latin America, creates a unified plan for fighting drugs in each of the member countries.

In *United States v. Dunn*, the Supreme Court rules that police who searched a barn for drugs did not violate the owner's rights. A barn that is adjacent to a residence may be checked without a search warrant.

Chinese gangs become prominent in the heroin trade in New York.

Drug testing, previously unregulated, is the subject of new restrictive laws in seven states—Vermont, Connecticut, Rhode Island, Montana, Minnesota, Oregon, and Iowa. The laws limit employers' ability to order random tests and also safeguard employees' rights. Utah passes a pro-testing law, granting an employer legal immunity from employee lawsuits if certain standards of testing are met.

Douglas Ginsburg, a nominee to the Supreme Court, is rejected when it is revealed that he had used marijuana. The inquiry into Ginsburg's drug use becomes a pattern as the media race to investigate possible past drug use, particularly during the 1960s, by court nominees or political candidates.

1988

Louisiana becomes the first of several states to deny unemployment benefits to workers who were fired because of drug abuse. The following year, Louisiana also passes a law denying workers' compensation to employees injured on the job while intoxicated by drugs or alcohol.

The U.N. Convention on Drug Trafficking, designed to combat money laundering, is signed by 43 nations. The convention calls upon the nations to develop guidelines for freezing the bank accounts and assets of drug traffickers. During the same year, a multinational bank,

1988
cont.

Bank of Credit and Commerce International, is indicted for money laundering of drug funds.

The Anti–Drug Abuse Act of 1988 again increases anti-drug spending sharply. The act gives judges authority to impose the death penalty in drug-related murders and imposes stiffer penalties against occasional drug use. The act also reverses a 1975 prohibition against training police forces in repressive regimes and suspends civil liberties in drug cases. The act creates the office of drug czar, a national coordinator of anti-drug efforts; the official title is director of the Office of National Drug Control Policy. The Chemical Diversion and Trafficking Act, part of the Anti–Drug Abuse Act, regulates 20 chemicals used to manufacture drugs frequently abused. Chemical manufacturers must report large orders to the DEA and keep accurate records of the sale of these substances. (For more details on the law, see Drugs and Law in Chapter 4.) Under threat of losing federal highway funds, all states adopt a minimum drinking age of 21. (In 1980, half of the states had a younger minimum age for drinking.)

An International Drug Enforcement Conference is held in Guatemala. Representatives from 30 countries attend and resolve to face drug trafficking with united action.

1989

President Bush declares war on drugs.

In *Florida v. Riley,* the Supreme Court rules that police may spy for marijuana plants from craft such as helicopters flying as low as 400 feet. A Florida sheriff had observed marijuana plants in a greenhouse. Justice Brennan, in his dissent, quotes from George Orwell's novel of totalitarianism, *1984.*

In *United States v. Sokolow,* the Supreme Court rules that reasonable suspicion of drug activity is required for drug enforcement agents to stop and question airline passengers traveling within the country. The case involves a passenger, Sokolow, traveling between Hawaii and Miami who was carrying a lot of cash and seemed nervous. The passenger, who refused to check his luggage, stayed in Miami for only a short time and was searched upon his return to Hawaii. DEA agents found that Sokolow was

1989
cont.

transporting more than 1,000 grams of cocaine. Sokolow challenged the search, saying that a preconceived profile of a drug smuggler was not sufficient basis for a search.

The Supreme Court ruling in *Skinner v. Railway Labor Executives* upholds drug tests for employees whose jobs may endanger public safety. Justice Anthony Kennedy writes that the tests are reasonable searches because of the risk to passengers and other workers. In his dissent, Justice Thurgood Marshall writes that "acceptance of dragnet . . . testing ensures that the first, and worst, casualty of the war on drugs will be the precious liberties of our citizens." In a similar case involving Customs Services officers in New Orleans (*National Treasury Employees Union v. Von Raab*), the Fifth Circuit Court of Appeals rules that "because of the strong governmental interest in employing individuals for key positions in drug enforcement who themselves are not drug users . . . [the search] is reasonable and, therefore, is not unconstitutional." The Supreme Court later upholds the lower court decision.

U.S. troops invade Panama to arrest Manuel Noriega, under indictment for drug trafficking. Noriega is seized and brought to the United States for trial. He is eventually convicted on eight counts of drug trafficking and sentenced to 40 years in prison.

The Drug-Free Workplace Act, part of the Omnibus Drug Initiative Act, is passed. For federal contracts of $425,000 or more, the law requires that employers adopt, among other measures, a formal drug-abuse policy and notify employees of its provisions, establish a drug-free awareness program, notify contracting agencies within ten days of an employee's violation, and penalize or terminate convicted employees.

In a landmark pregnancy prosecution, Jennifer C. Johnson is convicted of giving drugs to her children through the umbilical cord in the 60 to 90 seconds after their birth and before the cord was detached. In 1992, the conviction is reversed by the Florida Supreme Court.

Luis Carlos Galan, an anticartel candidate for president of Colombia, is killed at a political rally.

The 1990s

In the 1990s, the war on drugs is funded at record levels—up to $12 billion from the federal government by fiscal 1992. Slightly more money is given to drug prevention and treatment, but law enforcement and interdiction still capture the largest share. Cocaine use among the middle class, which dropped in the 1980s, appears to level off, and crack remains entrenched. Ice, an amphetamine, spreads across the country after it is introduced on the West Coast.

1990   Mandrake, an African-American man using a pseud-onym, splashes white paint on a billboard advertising cigarettes on Chicago's South Side. Thus begins a grass-roots movement to protest the targeting of minority populations by alcohol and cigarette companies. Soon activists, often members of the clergy, are obliterating alcohol and tobacco billboard ads across the country.

Saint Sabrina, a Catholic elementary school in Chicago, becomes the first elementary school in the United States to do random drug tests.

In *Oregon v. Smith,* the Supreme Court upholds the right of the state to dismiss two employees of a drug rehabilitation program because they used peyote during religious rites. Alfred Smith and Galen Black, members of the Native American Church, had argued that the drug was part of a long-standing religious tradition. Oregon's Supreme Court had previously ruled that ceremonial use of peyote is permissible under state law, and 23 states allow the religious use of peyote in Native American ceremonies.

Alaska votes to reinstate criminal penalties for possession of small amounts of marijuana, overturning the state's 1975 ruling that legalized the cultivation and use of small amounts of the drug. The vote is immediately challenged in court; the case is still pending.

The IRS, the DEA, the Federal Bureau of Investigation, and the Customs Services join together for Operation

1990
cont.
Polar Cap, the largest drug money–laundering investigation in the nation's history.

In Operation Green Sweep, the army, National Guard, and federal agents eradicate marijuana plants in California.

A law is passed requiring warning labels on beer, wine, wine coolers, and spirits. The warning states that "women should not drink alcoholic beverages during pregnancy because of the risk of birth defects" and that alcoholic beverages "impair your ability to drive a car or operate machinery and may cause other health problems."

Representatives of Peru, Bolivia, Colombia, and the United States hold a drug summit in Cartagena to plan a common anti-drug strategy.

Frightened by the link between intravenous drugs and AIDS, many addicts avoid needles and begin to snort or smoke heroin.

1991
In *International Brotherhood of Teamsters v. Department of Transportation,* an appeals court allows random and post-accident testing of employees in the ground transportation industry.

The city of Oakland, California, establishes the first federally funded training program for grandparents who must care for the offspring of their drug-addicted sons and daughters.

The United States constructs and staffs new radar stations at airfields in the Amazon region of Peru in order to interrupt shipments of coca base, an intermediate stage in the manufacture of cocaine. In the first three months of 1991, nine planes are intercepted—out of a estimated total of six planes flying per day.

1992
A needle-exchange program to combat the spread of AIDS among IV drug users is planned in New York City. In other areas, legal and illegal needle swaps already exist.

Federal authorities rescind approval for the experimental treatment with marijuana of glaucoma and the nausea that accompanies chemotherapy on the grounds that better, safer medicines are available.

The Federal Court of Appeals rules that the eviction of suspected drug users from public housing is unconstitutional without due process of law.

Peruvian President Alberto Fujimori, facing insurrection from the Maoist revolutionary group Shining Path, which is heavily involved in cocaine traffic, suspe ɟ the constitution of Peru in order to regain control of the country. Shining Path retaliates with a series of vicious bombings. A few months later, the leader of Shining Path, Abimael Guzman Reynoso, and many influential members are captured.

Pablo Escobar, the imprisoned leader of a Colombian drug cartel, escapes. Soon it is revealed that his prison was really a luxurious mansion, built at government expense and staffed by guards chosen by Escobar. Escobar's flight was probably a response to a threat of being sent to a real jail.

In Bolivia, every candidate for the presidential election runs on a campaign of greater independence from the United States and more Bolivian control over the anti-drug efforts within the country. This reflects the tension in Bolivian–United States relations created by an extensive DEA presence in the country.

New York City approves a bill to require tobacco companies to fund one antismoking ad for every four cigarette ads displayed on city property or on property that receives a license from the city (e.g., a stadium). This is one of the toughest antismoking advertising laws in the country.

Zurich, Switzerland, closes its experimental needle park, in which drug use was tolerated, because of an increase in crime, including vandalism, and medical emergencies.

A Weed and Seed program is created in response to riots in Los Angeles. Drug use, among other problems, is to be addressed in the inner cities by increased law enforcement (weed) and prevention and treatment (seed). Critics

1992
cont.

charge that the program is heavily tilted toward the weed aspect.

Maine passes a law legalizing the use of marijuana for medical treatment, becoming the thirty-third state to do so. The federal law, which bans such use, overrules the state law. The state law is merely a statement of belief and a guarantee that state residents using marijuana for medical reasons will be prosecuted only under federal laws. This is rare because state and local prosecutions far outnumber federal prosecutions. In a recent year, there were almost 400,000 state and local prosecutions for marijuana offenses, and only 4,890 for federal marijuana offenses.

Ecstasy, a mixed amphetamine/hallucinogen, gains popularity on the East Coast after a few years of growing popularity on the West Coast. The drug is taken at raves, all-night dancing and drinking parties that are held in random locations and that purport to serve vitamin-laced beverages marketed under the name of *smart drinks*. The smart drinks are accompanied by doses of Ecstasy.

The Supreme Court rules in *Cipollone v. Liddell Group, Inc.* that, despite the warning labels on cigarette packaging and advertisements, tobacco companies may still be sued for damages resulting from use of their products. The suits will be difficult to win because the plaintiffs will have to prove that health information was withheld by the tobacco manufacturers. A few months later, the Cipollone family drops the suit, but other, similar cases remain in litigation.

Mexico, angry at the U.S. Supreme Court ruling allowing kidnapping of a drug trafficker within its boundaries, announces that it will no longer accept funds (and by implication, control) from the United States for its anti-drug efforts. The Mexican government pledges to continue its own campaign against drugs, without U.S. interference.

More than 165 people on three continents are arrested for drug trafficking and money laundering in what authorities call one of the largest drug busts ever. Those arrested are members of the Sicilian Mafia and the

1992
cont.

Colombian Cali drug cartel. According to the DEA, the Mafia has been distributing cocaine from South America throughout Europe. The Cali cartel is also responsible for two-thirds of the cocaine sold in the United States.

A California woman is sentenced to prison for passing drugs to her baby by means of breast milk. The baby, Hannah Gillespie, died from the effects of methamphetamine taken by her mother, Alicia.

1993

President Bill Clinton drastically cuts the number of employees in the Office of National Drug Control Policy, but he proposes raising the position of "drug czar" to cabinet level. Clinton also announces that he will cut foreign aid and emphasize treatment and prevention of drug abuse.

3

Biographical Sketches

THE WAR ON DRUGS, AN ABSTRACT CONCEPT around which many laws and government programs have been formed, has always been fought by real individuals who in unique ways have sought to enforce drug laws, comfort the victims of drug abuse, educate the public, and reclaim lives. In this chapter many heroic figures of the nineteenth and twentieth centuries are profiled, as are some ordinary individuals who made a difference in the nation's anti-drug efforts. To round out the picture, biographies of a few proponents of drug use are included.

Harry J. Anslinger

President Franklin Delano Roosevelt sent a message to Harry Anslinger: If Anslinger ever submitted a clemency request for a drug pusher, Anslinger should staple his resignation to the letter. FDR's harsh view of narcotics dealers matched that of the average American in 1930, the year that Harry Anslinger became the first commissioner of narcotics for the federal government.

Anslinger, born in 1892 in Altoona, Pennsylvania, was the son of a Pennsylvania Railroad employee. Anslinger worked for the railroad also, investigating suspicious incidents for the captain of the railroad police force. Later the captain moved to the fire department, and Anslinger went with him, tracking down arsonists. After World War I ended, Anslinger joined the State Department. Stationed in Hamburg, Germany, Anslinger discovered that heroin dealers were bribing American sailors to smuggle their products into the United States. Soon he was in Venezuela, checking on rumrunners violating Prohibition. Anslinger's successes led him to the post of chief of the Foreign Control Section of the Treasury Department's Prohibition unit.

By 1930, support for Prohibition was waning, just as public distaste for narcotics was growing. When a new division devoted exclusively to control of these drugs was formed, Anslinger was named commissioner. In one of his first speeches, Anslinger told his agents to ignore the "corner drugstore and the family doctor and get after the smugglers and racketeers." A dedicated anti-drug crusader, Anslinger headed the department for more than 30 years. He retired just before the drug craze of the 1960s hit, believing that narcotics use was almost extinct in the United States, in part because of his efforts.

William Bennett

Bennett has "the teacher's gift and the scholar's temperament," according to an observer who saw him in action as a tutor in a social science program at Harvard. Tutoring was only one step in Bennett's long career in education; Bennett has also served as director of the National Endowment for the Humanities, a professor of religion and philosophy, and an administrator at various universities. In many ways, his appointment in 1988 as the nation's first drug czar—director of the Office of National Drug Control Policy—was also an educational post. Bennett's job was to teach the government agencies fighting drugs how to work together and also to teach the nation the severity of the problem.

Bennett, born in 1943 in Brooklyn, New York, says he was a streetwise youth. His family was not affluent; he paid for college with a combination of scholarships, loans, and jobs. Bennett has always held strong conservative beliefs, espousing traditional views of the United States and "patriotism, self-discipline, thrift, honesty . . . respect for elders."

As drug czar, Bennett presided over a massive increase in federal anti-drug funding. He paid little attention to drug treatment, successfully lobbying for an emphasis on interdiction and foreign efforts as well as law enforcement in the United States. This approach, together with his flamboyant manner, earned him much criticism, but it also publicized the issue of drugs and provoked much discussion of the best way to curtail illicit drug use.

Bennett resigned in 1990 to become head of the Republican National Committee, but he later declined that post in order to concentrate on speeches and writing.

Calvin Butts

One day Calvin Butts, the pastor of New York City's Abyssinian Baptist Church, was walking on Lenox Avenue in Harlem. A young man spotted him and threw his cigarette away, saying, "Reverend Butts, I'm with you." If the young man had never bought the cigarettes in the first place, he would have been more firmly *with* the Rev. Butts, one of the nation's most fervent crusaders against the use of alcohol and tobacco in the African-American community.

Butts spent his childhood in a housing project in New York City. He recalls that "the projects were great, a truly integrated community." After graduating from Atlanta's Morehouse College, Butts enrolled at Union Theological Seminary and then joined the staff of Abyssinian, an important spiritual and social force in Harlem. Since the beginning of his career, he has been outspoken about issues that affect his flock, particularly the targeting of minorities by cigarette and alcohol companies.

Butts's ideas are expressed concretely during his Saturday morning patrols in central Harlem. He dons a painter's cap and overalls and splashes black paint over cigarette and alcohol billboards. He has also picketed Philip Morris's headquarters. Butts's point is simple: African Americans already have a lower life expectancy than other ethnic groups. To Butts the use—and the marketing   of life-shortening substances is nothing short of evil. He believes that his crusade conforms to "a higher moral law" and he tells children firmly, "Don't smoke and don't drink—don't even think about it! Clean up your own community. You have something that you can do."

Charles Dederich

A native of Toledo, Ohio, Charles (Chuck) Dederich saw too much tragedy in his childhood. Before he reached the age of 12, his father, an alcoholic, had died in a car crash, a brother had also died, and his mother had been remarried—to a man her son hated. Dederich, whose sharp intelligence got him into Notre Dame University, dropped out after only 18 months. He drifted from one menial job to another, drinking heavily, until he came to

Ocean Park, California. There Dederich joined Alcoholics Anonymous (AA). In the famous self-help group, Charles Dederich dried out.

A passionate supporter of AA, Dederich began to experiment with its traditional methods, applying them to a desperate drug addict named Rex, who showed up one day in 1958. At that time no real system for treating substance abuse had been developed, and many so-called experts simply dismissed addicts as hopeless. Rex stayed with Dederich and his group, and he stayed clean. Soon four more drug addicts arrived, and Dederich realized that "we are stumbling onto something."

The something was Synanon. (The name came from an addict's mispronunciation of *seminar.*) Operating first from a storefront and later growing into a national organization, Synanon departed from the traditional AA format, adding lectures and intense encounter groups in which addicts challenged one another's behavior in an effort to achieve self-examination and change. Dederich himself was amazed at what evolved. He called Synanon a six-and-a-half-sided peg with no slots to fit it. The Synanon philosophy was widely publicized, and groups such as Daytop and Phoenix House were influenced by its methods.

Synanon itself has undergone some difficult moments. It was challenged repeatedly by the Internal Revenue Service (IRS) and beset by legal troubles (including an accusation that Dederich and others attempted to murder an attorney by putting a rattlesnake in the man's mailbox). Synanon eventually became the Synanon Church and is currently headed by Charles Dederich's daughter, Jady Dederich, who succeeded her late father.

Judianne Densen-Gerber

While she was a resident in psychiatry at New York's Metropolitan Hospital in 1965, Judianne Densen-Gerber was pregnant with her third child. She asked for maternity leave, but the chairperson of the psychiatric department made a counteroffer: He would give her an easy assignment in the drug treatment unit. At that time it was widely believed that narcotics addicts were beyond help. Since Dr. Densen-Gerber could do nothing to help these patients, the job should have required little effort.

That is not the way it worked out. Densen-Gerber is not the type of person to accept defeat without a fight. She worked with a group of 17 addicts who did not want to take a narcotics substitute and helped them to do without drugs entirely. When the addicts were discharged from the official treatment program, they came to see Dr. Densen-Gerber. They had $3.82 among them. Could Dr. Densen-Gerber accept that contribution and continue her work with them?

From that small sum of money and a large fund of determination, Odyssey House was born. The drug-free treatment organization has since expanded to many cities in the United States and abroad. Densen-Gerber, who says she is from "the third generation of liberated females in my family," is a true pioneer. She treated children addicted to drugs when the state refused to acknowledge that such problems existed. After resigning from Odyssey House in 1974, she created Odyssey Institute, a non-profit agency to provide health care for the disadvantaged. She has also been extremely active in the fight against child abuse, particularly sexual abuse. Densen-Gerber, who describes herself as "abrasive, difficult, demanding, perfectionist, [and] short-tempered," has received criticism throughout her career, including charges of financial irregularities in her foundation.

Pablo Escobar

"I can't imagine life without Pablo Escobar," a young Colombian woman said recently. "I can't imagine life without fear." To equate Pablo Escobar with fear is perfectly reasonable: Escobar is the leader of the Medellin drug cartel, the major supplier of cocaine on the world market.

Escobar was born in 1949 in the wooded mountains that surround Medellin. Escobar's first criminal enterprise was stealing gravestones from a local cemetery. Later he graduated to car theft. In the late 1970s, he got involved in the biggest Colombian growth industry—cocaine. In 1982, he used drug profits to finance a successful campaign for the Colombian congress. When his ties to the drug trade were disclosed, Escobar lost his position. He immediately ordered the assassination of the politician who had revealed Escobar's criminal career, only one of the murders carried out under Escobar's orders; at one point he offered a bounty of $4,000 for every police officer killed in Medellin. Despite Escobar's violence, many poor Colombians think of him as a modern-day Robin Hood. He has lavished new apartment buildings, swimming pools, and other amenities on Medellin.

A combined United States–Colombian effort pressured Escobar into a negotiated surrender to the Colombian authorities in 1991. He demanded—and received—a luxurious mountaintop prison, complete with wide-screen television, fax machine, and cellular telephones, from which he continued to run the drug trade. In 1992, fearful that he would be transferred to a real prison or even extradited to the United States, Escobar escaped, probably by walking past his hand-picked and well-bribed guards.

Clara Hale

"I'm not an American hero," Clara Hale told an interviewer shortly after President Ronald Reagan named her as such in his 1985 State of the Union address. Most people would disagree with her. Clara Hale, whom everyone called Mother Hale, did more for drug-addicted infants than any other person in the United States.

Mother Hale, who died in 1992, was the founder of Hale House, an institution caring for newborns through four-year-olds in New York City's neighborhood of Harlem. At Hale House, a mother can be sure that her baby is in good hands as she goes through drug treatment. If the mother does not enter treatment, she can leave her baby at Hale House anyway. The Hale House staff does not pass judgment on anyone. They follow Mother Hale's tradition: Accept the baby and give it what it needs most—love.

Hale House did not start out as an institution. It started out as Clara Hale's cramped, walk-up apartment. In 1968, Mother Hale, who raised her children alone after her husband died of cancer, had just retired from her role as foster mother to 40 children over a period of 27 years. The kids had stayed with her, 7 or 8 at a time, and had grown up to become "doctors, lawyers, everything," explained Mother Hale, adding, "Almost all of them stay in touch."

Mother Hale's retirement was brief. Her daughter, Dr. Lorraine Hale, saw a woman nodding on a park bench, too drugged to notice that her two-month-old baby was sliding off her lap. Lorraine Hale told the woman that she knew a place where she and her child could get some help. The next day the woman brought the baby to Mother Hale. Only two months later, Mother Hale was caring for 22 addicted infants. Her apartment contained wall-to-wall cribs.

Hale House moved to larger quarters twice, and it now employs houseparents, social workers, aides, and health workers. Mother Hale, even during her 80s, still had the energy to rock the infants, especially as they went through the painful withdrawal from heroin or crack. Never one to boast, Mother Hale described herself only as "a person that loves children."

Ken Kesey

Ken Kesey's espousal of drugs as a creative force won him the admiration of many a rebellious youth during the 1960s, and his home in Oregon became almost a pilgrimage site for hippies who saw Kesey as the center of their quest for a different way of life. Kesey himself never really welcomed this role.

Born in Colorado in 1935, Kesey is descended from a long line of farmers and ranchers. After college, Kesey volunteered for a government experiment at the Menlo Park Veterans' Hospital in California, where he worked as a psychiatric aide. He was given a variety of psychedelic drugs and asked to report their effects. (At the time, some psychiatrists believed that hallucinogens might be valuable in psychiatric treatment.) Mainstream medicine eventually abandoned the use of hallucinogens, but Kesey was enthralled. He felt that the drugs had opened a door to creativity.

In the early 1960s, profits from Kesey's best-selling novel, *One Flew over the Cuckoo's Nest,* helped to finance a cross-country trip in an old bus, whose destination sign read "Further" and whose rear advised motorists "Caution: Weird Load." Kesey and his fellow travelers held public acid tests, in which visitors were urged to try LSD and other drugs.

In the mid-1960s, Kesey was arrested twice for possession of marijuana. He fled to Mexico and then returned to the United States and served a few months of jail time. By 1970, Kesey said that he was an abstainer and that he had gone through the doorway of drugs and did not need to pass through it again and again.

Khun Sa

To the villagers who live in northeastern Myanmar (Burma), Khun Sa is Prince Prosperous, but to the U.S. Drug Enforcement Administration (DEA), he is the Prince of Death. Khun Sa, a ruthless drug trafficker, maintains a private army of 15,000 men. Khun Sa controls an estimated 40 percent of the heroin traffic into the United States. This enterprise brings him fabulous wealth.

Khun Sa was born in a village in eastern Burma. While he was a boy, Nationalist Chinese soldiers invaded his village and stole his family's livestock. Later, Khun Sa allied himself with these same soldiers to establish himself in Burma's lucrative opium trade. After he broke away and started his own drug ring, he was arrested. Khun Sa says that the money he earns from drug trafficking is used to finance a revolution against the central government so he can "liberate" the Shan state, his native region. Claiming that "power does not accompany us forever," he says his reign as the prince of Asian drug trafficking will pass. The United States would like to make this prediction come true. Khun Sa is under indictment for crimes that could bring him ten life sentences, but the United States has not been able to extradite him from his mountain stronghold.

Timothy Leary

"Turn on, tune in, and drop out," said Timothy Leary in the 1960s, and thousands followed his advice. A former Harvard University psychology professor and a respected author of books about psychology, Leary clashed with the university when he performed psychological experiments on his students using the hallucinogen LSD. Dismissed from his job, Leary formed a commune in upstate New York and gathered around him a group of searchers, who sampled a wide variety of psychedelic substances.

In 1970, Leary was arrested for drug possession. He escaped from prison and fled to Algeria, where he was involved with expatriate Black Panthers, a radical U.S. political group. When the Panthers rejected his ideas on drug use, Leary fled to Switzerland, where he asked for political asylum on the grounds that he had been arrested because of his opposition to the Vietnam War, not because of his drug use. His request was denied, and Leary next turned up in Afghanistan. Upon his extradition to the United States, Leary served a year in prison. Regarding drugs, he says, "Adult Americans are supposed to make their own decisions about personal matters." He acknowledges, however, that "people who abuse drugs or booze or money or guns should be prevented from acting irresponsibly."

Candy Lightner

When Candy Lightner said good-bye to her 13-year-old daughter Cari one day in 1980, she had just scolded her for some childish misdeed. She ended the conversation with, "Cari, you know that I love you, don't you?" Cari, who did know, told her mother not to be so mushy. Lightner never saw her daughter alive again. A drunken driver hit the little girl so hard that her body was thrown 125 feet.

Lightner collapsed when she heard the news. Then she got up and went to work—not as a real estate agent, her job at the time of the accident—but as an advocate for drunken-driving victims. The trooper investigating the accident told her that the driver would probably never even go to jail. "That's the way the system works," he said. Lightner was not willing to accept that answer. She turned her grief into energy and founded Mothers Against Drunk Driving (MADD). She worked all day, every day, on this terrible problem, earning national recognition for her work and the satisfaction of changing public attitudes toward drunken driving.

In 1985, Lightner stepped down from her position as chairman of the board of MADD to take time to grieve for Cari. After a time, she turned to writing, trying to help others with her book, *Giving Sorrow Words: How To Cope with Grief and Get on with Your Life.*

Bob Martinez

The grandson of Spanish immigrants, Bob Martinez has an authentic American dream story, the kind that continues to draw people to our shores. From humble beginnings he rose to his post in the early 1990s as federal drug czar. Only the second person ever to hold that position, Martinez was in charge of coordinating all of the anti-drug efforts of the U.S. government.

On the road to Washington, Martinez was a semiprofessional baseball player, a high school civics teacher, head of a teachers' union, and mayor of Tampa, Florida. Then he became governor of the state. Finding that drug-related crime was a major concern in Florida, a gateway for drugs shipped from South America, Martinez devoted a great deal of attention to drug problems. He also became the spokesman on the issue for the National Association of Governors.

After he lost a bid for a second term as governor, Martinez was nominated to succeed William Bennett, who resigned as drug czar in 1990. Martinez won confirmation but was severely criticized during Senate hearings by those who felt that his record as governor of Florida showed too great a reliance on law enforcement and imprisonment and too little attention to prevention and treatment. (These same criticisms were also leveled at Bennett.) Martinez says that he recognizes the importance of prevention, but adds, "It's pretty hard to get the message to a youngster in a school house, despite whatever prevention and education programs exist, if when the school bell rings he sees a pusher standing on the corner . . . [indicating] that society must not think it's all that bad."

Martinez describes himself as an implementer, a person who likes to "execute and to monitor what is to be done." Friend and foe alike see him as less flamboyant than Bennett, with a low-key style.

Otto Moulton

The original Committees of Correspondence were formed by Samuel Adams in 1772. Adams perceived a crisis that could only be overcome by concerted effort from the American people, and the committees' role was to exchange information and build a unified approach to the problem. Otto Moulton did the same thing in 1977; this time the enemy was not the British, but drugs.

Moulton's indignation about the problem had been aroused one day when he stopped to buy a newspaper. On impulse, he bought a copy of *High Times,* a magazine promoting the use of drugs, particularly marijuana. Moulton could not believe his eyes. He immediately bought every copy of the magazine he could find and destroyed them. Moulton was also distressed to learn that a few members of his Little League baseball and hockey teams were using drugs.

Moulton called a town meeting for concerned parents and began to organize. The Committees of Correspondence was born. Today it is one of the country's most influential grass-roots movements opposing the use of illicit drugs.

The owner of a successful business and the father of five children, Moulton has financed the committees largely from his own resources. Together with his wife, Connie, he maintains an extensive library of pamphlets, videotapes, and books, which he makes available upon request. His goal is to be sure that correct information appears in the media, at legislative hearings, and in schools. Former Senator Paula Hawkins, R-Fla., calls Moulton "America's number one warrior against drugs."

Carry Nation

When it was time for what she called a "hatchetation of joints," Carry Nation would grab her famous hatchet (and later a more efficient iron rod) and head for the nearest bar. Then she would invade it like a one-woman army, breaking liquor bottles, fixtures, windows, and whatever else was handy. Soon Nation would be arrested, and her name would be in all the papers. This did not dismay her. Nation knew, as most effective activists do, that the real battle to change ideas is fought in public opinion.

Carry Amelia Moore was born in Kentucky in 1846. Her first husband, Dr. Charles Gloyd, was an alcoholic, and Nation's fierce hatred of alcohol can be traced to that period in her life. She left Gloyd, and shortly afterward he died. Her second husband, David Nation, divorced her in 1901 when she performed her first hatchetation on a saloon in Wichita, Kansas. Nation's 30 arrests were punctuated by speaking engagements about the advantages of Prohibition. Lecture fees and the proceeds from the sale of souvenir hatchets financed a home for the wives of alcoholics in Kansas City, Kansas.

Although Nation was also a suffragette who fought for the right of women to vote, she was not supported by the network of women's organizations that was active in the early twentieth century, possibly because of her fiery and eccentric ways. Some biographers believe that Nation was subject to hallucinations. Whether this is true or not, she did help to muster national distaste for the legal sale of alcohol. Nation died in 1911, nine years before the passage of the Volstead Act, which ushered in Prohibition.

Eliot Ness

Portrayed by Robert Stack in a long-running television show and by Kevin Costner in a movie, Eliot Ness cannot help being a larger-than-life figure. In his case, however, real life matches the legend. As a courageous crime fighter in Chicago during the age of gangsters, Ness's mission was "to get Capone."

Ness was a recent graduate of the University of Chicago when he was hired in 1929 as a special agent by the U.S. Department of

Justice. He was made head of the Prohibition bureau in Chicago, where gangster Al Capone was the prime bootlegger. Ness assembled a team of dedicated law officers who refused to be corrupted; hence their title—the Untouchables. For four years Ness and his team raided warehouses, distilleries, and speakeasies (illegal bars). The newspapers gave prime coverage to his work, and Ness became a folk hero. Evidence that the Untouchables seized was eventually used to convict Capone for income tax evasion, a charge that was easier to prove than the many murders Capone had ordered.

After the repeal of Prohibition, Eliot Ness went on to run the alcohol tax unit of the U.S. Department of the Treasury. During World War II he did other government work and then went into private industry. He died in 1957.

Manuel Antonio Noriega

Born in 1938 in Panama City, Manuel Noriega attended a military academy and joined Panama's National Guard. After a 1968 coup, General Omar Torrijos, commander of the National Guard, came to power; Noriega, his protégé, became commander of Panama's military intelligence agency in 1970 and formed ties with the U.S. Central Intelligence Agency. By 1983, Noriega had promoted himself to general and taken charge of the nation.

Throughout his career, rumors of Noriega's involvement with drug traffickers spread. As late as 1986, however, John Lawn, the director of the U.S. DEA, thanked Noriega for his "vigorous, anti–drug trafficking policy." Noriega was also valuable during the 1980s for his help with the contras, a Nicaraguan anticommunist group. Partly for this reason the U.S. government was reluctant to interfere with Noriega's drug dealings.

In 1988, however, Noriega was indicted on charges of drug trafficking. In the meantime, opposition was growing in Panama to his autocratic rule. In 1989, Operation Just Cause was launched and U.S. soldiers invaded Panama. Noriega went on trial in Miami; in 1992, he was convicted of eight counts of drug trafficking.

William O'Brien

"I'd like to say I've saved 55,000 lives in Daytop," says Monsignor William O'Brien. He adds, "I haven't. I've been an instrument to push them in the right direction of getting in touch with all these healing tools." O'Brien is being modest. His personality and beliefs have helped to shape Daytop, a successful treatment program that he helped to found and that has, in spite of what he says, saved countless addicts from a literal death or a living death.

In the 1950s, O'Brien was a parish priest in New York. He was dismayed by the drugs and violence he saw daily. Then in 1957, three violent gangs met in a park for what they called a peace talk, in which two teens were killed. The mother of one of the gang members begged Msgr. O'Brien to help. O'Brien tried to work with gang members, many of whom were drug addicts, for several years. His early efforts were fruitless. (He calls himself the biggest disaster in New York during that period.) He recalls that addicts would listen to his sermons and then go into the rectory bathroom to shoot up.

Finally, O'Brien investigated the methods of Synanon, a treatment group started by a recovering alcoholic, Charles Dederich. With the help of former members of Synanon, O'Brien adapted the techniques and established a center on Staten Island, a borough of New York City. "I thought I was the Father Flanagan of drug abuse," O'Brien now says, referring to the founder of Boys' Town. He believes that the key element in drug treatment and prevention, the cornerstone of a healthy society, is the family. If the family learns to pull together, O'Brien feels, violence, crime, and drug use will disappear.

Cathy Palmer

After a former DEA informer tried to kill her by sending her a briefcase with a rigged shotgun inside, Cathy Palmer received a message. Khun Sa, leader of the Southeast Asian heroin trade, wanted her to know that he was not responsible for the booby trap. Although Palmer had succeeded in indicting him after agents seized a ton of heroin in Bangkok, Khun Sa did not hold a grudge.

That message indicates something of the impression Palmer has made in her seven years in the DEA task force on Asian drug smuggling. At only 36, she was recently described by her boss in the U.S. Attorney's Office as "without a doubt the premier federal prosecutor in the country in the area of Southeast Asian heroin smuggling."

Born and raised in Massachusetts (and a fervent fan of the Boston Red Sox), Palmer graduated from Boston University and received a law degree from Catholic University. She practiced law for a few years with a private firm, but felt the need to contribute through government service. Today she spends long hours checking and rechecking stories from informants—"telephone records, shipping records, that kind of stuff"—to make airtight cases against drug processors, smugglers, and dealers. According to the DEA, more than 30 extraditions from Hong Kong alone in the last five years have put a real dent in the Southeast Asian heroin trade. Everyone who works with her praises her efforts, but Palmer downplays her role, preferring to praise the field agents. "I'm not on the front lines," she comments.

Charles Rangel

Never one to mince words, Congressman Charles B. Rangel, head of the House Select Committee on Narcotics Abuse and Control, called President George Bush's anti-drug funding "1,000 points of light without batteries." A crusader for his home district in New York's Harlem, Rangel was fighting drugs before they became a national issue. In his view, the drug crisis has a critical impact on his African-American constituency.

Rangel was born in Harlem in 1930. A high school dropout, he served in the U.S. army during the Korean War and won a Bronze Star for bringing 40 men out from behind enemy lines. After leaving the service, Rangel earned a high school diploma and a degree from New York University. He was graduated from St. John's University Law School in 1960 and soon began a career in politics, being elected to the New York State Assembly in 1966 and to the U.S. Congress in 1970.

Almost immediately Rangel demonstrated his interest in fighting drugs—and his lack of fear of the powers that be. He criticized President Richard Nixon in 1971 for not dealing more firmly with Turkey, a major supplier of opium poppies, and with France, a conduit for the drugs entering the United States. Through his efforts, a bill to authorize the president to reduce foreign aid to countries that do not cooperate in fighting the war on drugs was passed in the House. In his 20 years of service, Rangel has remained an opponent of efforts to legalize drugs or to soften the laws against them. He has consistently supported treatment and prevention programs. Rangel has been described as "*the* voice on Capitol Hill sounding the alarm" against drugs.

Sue Rusche

In a record shop in a suburb of Atlanta, Georgia, Sue Rusche saw an interesting display. One object seemed to be a toy space gun and another looked like a soft drink can. These objects were not so innocent. The space gun was a power hitter, a smoking device that increases the amount of marijuana a smoker can inhale in each puff. The soda can had a secret compartment in which to hide one's stash—marijuana, pills, cocaine, or some such substance. Rusche was horrified. She visited several stores and bought examples of drug paraphernalia (accessories) in each, including some items complete with tags explaining how to get high and a comic book promoting cocaine.

Then she got to work. Rusche enlisted members of her Parent Teachers Association to urge store owners to remove the drug paraphernalia. From this nucleus, National Families in Action, a grass-roots anti-drug organization, was formed. By 1978, Rusche had succeeded in getting three bills through the Georgia legislature banning the sale of drug-related objects (such as coke spoons, water pipes, and other objects with more than one purpose but related to drug use) or literature to minors and the sale of drug devices to anyone.

Rusche, a graphic artist, put her career on hold and crusaded for anti–drug paraphernalia laws in other states as well. Today she serves as executive director of National Families in Action. Through her organization, Rusche provides the latest information about drugs and their effects to people across the nation. The group's hotline averages 500 calls a month from drug users and those who are concerned about drug problems. Not satisfied with this achievement, Rusche is lobbying for a National Drug Prevention Corps, similar to the Peace Corps.

Bill W.

Bill W. was a modest man. When people thanked him for saving their lives (and many did), he would shrug and say simply, "Pass it on." That is what Bill W. did when he, along with a few friends, founded Alcoholics Anonymous in 1935. They passed on a method they had discovered for regaining control of their lives and staying sober. (True to the traditions of AA, during his lifetime Bill W. was always known only by his first name and last initial.)

Bill W. was born in East Dorset, Vermont, in 1895. His youth was marred by his parents' continual arguments, and when Bill was ten, they divorced. Bill was raised by his grandparents, and he did not have a single taste of alcohol until he was 22. During World

War I, Bill served in the army. Alcohol seemed to help the shy young man mix at parties, but Bill had no control over it. Almost immediately after taking a drink, he lost control and became, in his words, a drunk. Although he went on to law school, marriage, and a business career, Bill's life was dominated by alcohol. In 1934, he entered a hospital that specialized in the treatment of alcoholism. Shortly after he returned home, however, his wife found him hanging over a fence, intoxicated.

Just when hope was almost gone, a boyhood friend of Bill's came to visit. He began to talk of an organization in England, the Oxford Group, in which people met to talk about their problems. Bill's friend, formerly a heavy drinker, told Bill that he had been sober for six months by following the group's advice. Bill still was not ready. He continued to drink until he hit the "very bottom" and called out to God that he was "ready to do anything."

That was the turning point. Bill never took another drink. He spent his time searching bars for others who needed help, bringing them to Oxford Group meetings or to the hospital. Bill's mission did not work, however, until he stopped preaching *at* alcoholics and started talking *with* them. He passed on his own experience, support, and care. In this way, Alcoholics Anonymous was born. Bill remained active in the organization until his death in 1971. Only then was his full name revealed: William Griffith Wilson.

Hamilton Wright

Hamilton Wright, known as the Father of American Narcotics Control, was a physician who worked in a tropical-disease research station in the Far East, where he mistakenly declared that he had discovered the cause of beriberi and achieved brief fame. In 1909, he was chosen by President Theodore Roosevelt as one of the members of the U.S. delegation to the first worldwide narcotics convention, held in Shanghai. To prepare for the meeting, Wright gathered data on the extent of opium use in the United States, writing to prisoners, police, boards of health, pharmacies, morphine manufacturers, and others.

Wright was an impassioned foe of narcotics abuse. His belief in the dangers of narcotic drugs was so strong that he was willing to use almost any tactic to gain his point, and his campaigns made him many enemies. Wright believed that the solution to the U.S. drug problem lay not only in domestic laws, but also in international control, and he pressed vigorously for treaties that would limit production and import of narcotics.

Wright's view that the United States could be made drug-free if other nations limited their production and export of drugs is still a mainstay in the war on drugs. He also thought that it would be morally wrong to press other countries to control drugs without making a strong domestic effort. He lobbied extensively for strict anti-drug laws, and his efforts led to the passage of the first comprehensive prohibition of narcotics, the Harrison Narcotics Act of 1914.

4

Facts, Statistics, and Documents

THIS CHAPTER PAINTS A STATISTICAL AND FACTUAL portrait of drug abuse in American society, beginning with information on who uses psychoactive drugs today and who has used them in the past. Factors that seem to increase or decrease the risk of drug addiction are listed next. Society's response, including major league sports organizations' drug policies and information on the criminal justice system and anti-drug laws, follows. The effects of drugs on health and the health care system, including prenatal and neonatal drugs (those used by a mother that affect a baby before and just after it is born), and the link between intravenous (IV) drugs and AIDS (Acquired Immune Deficiency Syndrome), are covered next. Other social consequences of drug use, including homelessness, violence, and accidents, are discussed, as well as drug testing. The chapter closes with a discussion of the economics of drug trafficking and government anti-drug efforts, some information on treatment, and several key documents. These include declarations of a war on drugs by former presidents Nixon, Reagan, and Bush and an argument for the legalization of drugs by David Boaz, vice-president of the Cato Institute and a leading proponent of the idea.

TABLE 1 PERCENTAGE OF AMERICANS WHO REPORT USING ILLICIT DRUGS						
	Year Surveyed					
Age	1979	1982	1985	1988	1990	1991
12–17 Ever Used Drugs	34.3%	27.6%	29.5%	24.7%	22.7%	20.1%
12–17 Used Drugs in the Past Year	26.0%	22.0%	23.7%	16.8%	15.9%	14.8%
12–17 Used Drugs in the Past Month	17.6%	12.7%	14.9%	9.2%	8.1%	6.8%
18–25 Ever Used Drugs	69.9%	65.3%	64.3%	58.9%	55.8%	54.7%
18–25 Used Drugs in the Past Year	49.4%	43.4%	42.6%	32.0%	28.7%	29.2%
18–25 Used Drugs in the Past Month	37.1%	30.4%	25.7%	17.8%	14.9%	15.4%
26+ Ever Used Drugs	23.0%	24.7%	31.5%	33.7%	35.3%	36.1%
26+ Used Drugs in the Past Year	10.0%	11.8%	13.3%	10.2%	10.0%	9.6%
26+ Used Drugs in the Past Month	6.5%	7.5%	8.5%	4.9%	4.6%	4.5%

Source: National Institute on Drug Abuse, National Household Survey.

Who Uses Drugs?

How many Americans use illicit drugs? In 1991, more than 26 million, according to the National Household Survey, conducted by the National Institute on Drug Abuse (NIDA). Table 1 shows the percentage of each age group who reported taking an illegal drug in the past month, the past year, or ever in their lives. The

TABLE 2
PERCENTAGE OF HIGH SCHOOL SENIORS REPORTING USE OF SPECIFIC DRUGS

Drug	Lifetime	Past Year	Past Month
Marijuana	40.7%	27.0%	14.0%
Cocaine	9.4%	5.3%	1.9%
Stimulants	17.5%	9.1%	3.7%
LSD	8.7%	5.4%	1.9%
PCP	2.8%	1.2%	0.4%
Heroin	1.3%	0.5%	0.2%

Source: National Institute on Drug Abuse, High School Senior Survey, 1991.

FIGURE 1
PERCENTAGE OF STUDENTS REPORTING USE OF ILLICIT DRUGS

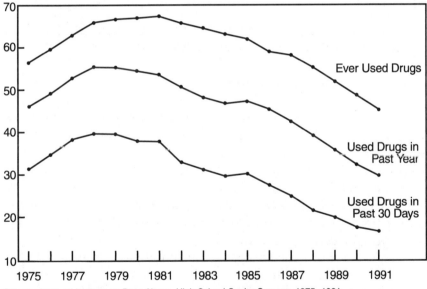

Source: National Institute on Drug Abuse, High School Senior Surveys, 1975–1991.

homeless, college students, and the armed forces are represented only in the 1991 numbers.

Because drug use by young people has greater physiological and social consequences than for adults, NIDA questions high school seniors about their drug use each year. Table 2 indicates the percentage of students reporting usage of each illicit drug. Dropouts are not included.

FIGURE 2
PERCENTAGE OF STUDENTS REPORTING USE OF
MARIJUANA, COCAINE, AND HEROIN DURING THE PAST YEAR

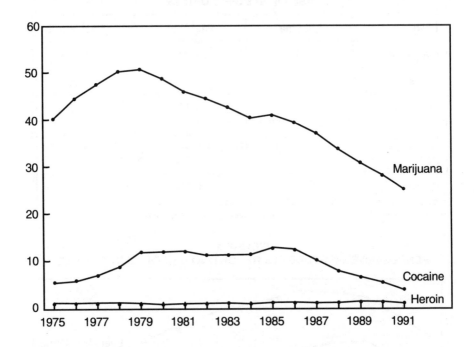

Source: National Institute on Drug Abuse, High School Senior Surveys, 1975–1991.

Figure 1 (page 87) shows trends in drug use over time and the percentage of seniors reporting illicit drug use at some time in their lives, in the past year, and in the past 30 days. The time span begins in 1975, when the high school senior survey was first taken, and ends in 1991. Figure 1 includes all of the drugs in table 2 as well as nonprescribed barbiturates and tranquilizers, inhalants, and other opiates. This figure shows clearly that drug use by students is declining.

Figure 2 shows the percentage of seniors who reported use in the past year of three drugs: marijuana, cocaine, and heroin. The percentage is shown for each year from 1975 to 1991.

In the 1980s, cocaine became a particular concern, especially after the advent of crack (a smokeable form of cocaine) in mid-decade. Figure 3 shows the percentage of adult Americans reporting use of the drug at some time in their lives.

Marijuana use peaked in 1979, but as figure 4 shows, it is still a common drug among young adults.

FIGURE 3
PERCENTAGE OF AMERICANS REPORTING USE OF COCAINE
DURING THEIR LIVES

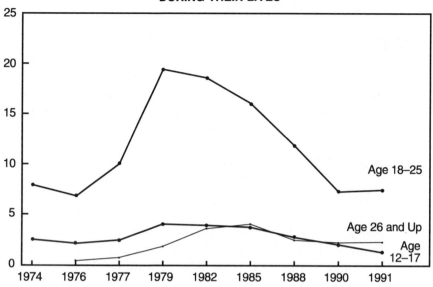

Source: National Institute on Drug Abuse, National Household Surveys, 1974–1991.

FIGURE 4
PERCENTAGE OF AMERICANS REPORTING USE OF
MARIJUANA DURING THEIR LIVES

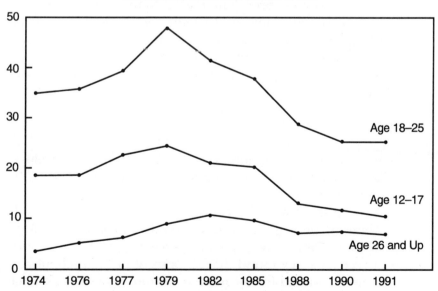

Source: National Institute on Drug Abuse, National Household Surveys, 1974–1991.

Information about Other Drugs

Inhalants

- Between 1974 and 1991, on average, about 2 percent of high school seniors had used an inhalant drug within the past month. (Source: National Institute on Drug Abuse, High School Senior Survey.)

Barbiturates and Tranquilizers

- Since 1975, the use of nonprescribed barbiturates has dropped steadily from 5.4 percent to 1.6 percent in 1991. Nonprescribed tranquilizers show a similar decrease, from 4.1 percent in 1975 to 1.3 percent in 1991. (Source: National Institute on Drug Abuse, National Household Survey.)

Tobacco

- Cigarette smoking is at its lowest level in 37 years. About a quarter of adult Americans smoked in 1990.
- Smoking is most prevalent among Native Americans, high school dropouts, and people aged 25–44.
- Smoking is least prevalent among the elderly (6.5 percent) and college graduates (13.5 percent).
- African-American teens smoke at a lower rate than white teens. (Source: Centers for Disease Control.)

Alcohol

- Per capita consumption of alcohol declined in the 1980s, but about 10.5 million Americans show signs of alcoholism.
- Two-thirds of Americans drink.
- About 55 percent of adult women drink moderately, 5 percent drink heavily, and 40 percent abstain.
- A recent survey found that 35 percent of high school seniors had had five or more drinks in a row at least once during the two weeks prior to the survey.

- According to a 1984 study, drinking levels were lower among African Americans than among whites.
- Asian Americans are less likely to drink than members of other ethnic groups.
- Alcohol is illegal for anyone younger than 21; it is the most widely used illicit drug among young people. Among college students alcohol is used twice as frequently as marijuana and nine times as frequently as cocaine. Nearly 90 percent of college students report drinking at least once during the preceding year.
- More than 90 percent of alcoholics are also heavy smokers. (Source: National Council on Alcoholism and Drug Dependence.)

Risk Factors for Drug Use

There is no foolproof way to predict drug abuse. Even people who seem to have the most difficult backgrounds may triumph over the odds and live chemical-free, productive lives, while others who appear to possess every advantage may become addicted to drugs. Nevertheless, numerous studies have identified risk factors that seem to predict a higher than usual rate of drug abuse. In the same way, protective factors have been found that appear to prevent an individual from drug abuse. A summary of identified risk and protective factors appears in table 3 (page 92).

Drug Policies of the Major Sports Leagues

The field of professional sports is by no means the only one facing the problem of drug abuse, but it is probably the most visible. The league authorities and players' unions of the major sports have negotiated drug policies, which are summarized here.

Basketball

- Any National Basketball Association (NBA) player who is convicted of or pleads guilty to a crime involving heroin or cocaine, or is found to have used these drugs, shall be immediately and permanently dismissed from the NBA.

TABLE 3
RISK AND PROTECTIVE FACTORS IN KEY SYSTEMS

Risk Factors	Protective Factors

Family
Family Management Problems:
   Unclear expectations for behavior
   Lack of monitoring
   Inconsistent or harsh discipline
   Lack of bonding and caring
   Marital conflict
   Condoning teen use of alcohol and
     other drugs
   Parental misuse of tobacco, alcohol,
     and other drugs
   Low expectations of children's success
   Family history of alcoholism and drug
     problems

School
Negative school climate
School policy not defined or enforced
Availability of tobacco, alcohol, and other
   drugs
Transition between schools
Academic failure
Lack of student involvement
Labeling and identifying students as
   high-risk
Truancy and suspension

Peers
Early antisocial behavior
Alienation and rebelliousness
Favorable attitudes toward drug use
Early first use
Greater influence by and reliance on
   peers than parents
Friends who use tobacco, alcohol, and
   other drugs

Community
Economic and social deprivation
Low neighborhood attachment and
   community disorganization
Lack of employment opportunities and
   youth involvement
Easy availability of tobacco, alcohol, and
   other drugs
Community norms and laws favorable to
   misuse

Protective Factors:

Family
Seeks prenatal care
Develops close bonding with child
Values and encourages education
Manages stress well
Spends quality time with children
Uses a high warmth/low criticism parenting
   style (rather than authoritarian or
   permissive)
Is nurturing and protective
Has clear expectations
Encourages supportive relationships with
   caring adults beyond the immediate
   family
Shares family responsibilities

School
Expresses high expectations
Encourages goal setting and mastery
Staff members view themselves as
   nurturing caretakers
Encourages prosocial development
   (altruism, cooperation)
Provides leadership and decision-making
   opportunities
Fosters active involvement of students
Trains teachers in social development and
   cooperative learning
Involves parents
Provides alcohol/drug-free alternative
   activities

Peers
Involved in drug-free activities
Respect authority
Bonded to conventional groups
Appreciate the unique talent that each
   person brings to the group

Community
Norms and public policies support nonuse
   among youth
Provides access to resources (housing,
   health care, child care, job training,
   employment, and recreation)
Provides supportive networks and social
   bonds
Involves youth in community service

Source: *Together We Can Reduce the Risks of Alcohol and Drug Use among Youth,* Gibbs and Bennett Interactive Learning Systems, 1990. Reprinted with permission.

- Any player who voluntarily seeks help will be given treatment at the expense of the club for which he plays. The player will continue to receive his salary and will not be subject to punishment. If a player comes forward a second time for help, he will be suspended without pay during treatment, but he will not be subject to further punishment. A third instance of use, possession, or distribution of drugs, even if voluntarily admitted, will result in permanent dismissal from the NBA.
- Upon suspicion of drug use, the NBA's expert on drug matters may authorize testing. Tests may be given up to four times in six weeks at times determined by the league.
- Banned players may apply for reinstatement after two years.
- New players (rookies) are subject to preemployment testing for drugs once during the regular training camp. No prior notice will be given. If the test is positive, the rookie's contract will be terminated and the player will be suspended for at least a year.
- Rookies are also subject to three random drug tests during their first year. A positive test will result in termination of the player's contract and suspension from the league for the current season. The league will provide treatment.
- The NBA also sponsors mandatory drug-prevention seminars twice per season. (Source: National Basketball Association.)

Football

- The National Football League (NFL) tests players for anabolic steroids, or drugs that increase muscle mass, as well as for illegal psychoactive drugs.
- All players are tested during the pre-season.
- Weekly tests for steroids will be given to players selected randomly by computer during the season and the off-season.
- Upon suspicion of drug use, players will be tested.
- Players seeking treatment voluntarily will be helped without disciplinary action. Confidentiality will be maintained, and the player will receive his salary.
- Positive tests will result in these disciplinary actions:

First positive steroid test—suspension for four regular-season games

First positive psychoactive drug test—medical evaluation and treatment

Second positive test for steroids or psychoactive drugs—suspension for six games

Third positive test for steroids or psychoactive drugs—suspension for at least one year

- Players convicted of drug-related crimes are subject to suspension, even if it is their first offense.
- Refusal to take a drug test may be treated as a positive test.
- Alcohol abuse that results in violation of the law will subject the player to penalty. (Source: National Football League.)

Baseball

- Players who have admitted using drugs or been detected using drugs are subject to mandatory testing.
- From those who have been detected in a single or infrequent use, samples of urine may be taken no more than four times a season. In cases where prior drug dependency has been detected, players may be tested more often, including during the off-season.
- Players who commit a first offense or request help will not be disciplined. Players will be offered the opportunity to enter an employee assistance program with no loss of salary.
- Second offenses or convictions for drug crimes will result in immediate discipline.
- Refusal to take a test or failure to appear for a test will subject a player to discipline. (Source: Major League Baseball Commissioner's Office.)

Drugs and Crime

Law enforcement professionals, as well as most nonprofessionals, know that drugs and crime are linked. But to what extent? A

TABLE 4

DRUG USE BY ARRESTEES IN SELECTED CITIES
(The First Figure is the Percentage of Males Testing
Positive; the Second Refers to Females.)

City	2 or more	Cocaine	Marijuana	Amphet-amines	Opiates	PCP
New York	29%,31%	64%,65%	24%,11%	0%,0%	16%,18%	2%,2%
San Diego	42%,36%	45%,33%	42%,23%	19%,25%	15%,19%	<1%,3%
Philadelphia	33%,23%	65%,62%	19%,18%	<1%,<1%	13%,8%	4%,<1%
Los Angeles	21%,31%	40%,62%	23%,14%	7%,9%	7%,18%	4%,2%
Houston	17%,22%	54%,49%	19%,11%	0%,<1%	4%,8%	0%,0%
Cleveland	12%,15%	42%,76%	18%,7%	0%,0%	2%,4%	<1%,4%
Ft. Lauder-dale	14%,14%	40%,48%	28%,18%	0%,0%	1%,2%	0%,0%
Washington, D.C.	19%,20%	54%,73%	13%,5%	<1%,0%	10%,10%	4%,1%

Source: U.S. Department of Justice, Bureau of Justice Statistics, 1991.

recent U.S. Department of Justice survey of inmates in local jails reported that 77.7 percent of inmates had used an illicit drug at some time in their lives. More than half said they had been under the influence of drugs or alcohol at the time of their offense.

Drug Use among Arrestees

Table 4 indicates the percentage of those arrested who tested positive for each drug in 1991. (The figures for two or more drugs exclude marijuana.) The numbers support the public perception that women are becoming more involved in drugs than ever before.

Convicted Criminals and Drugs

- More than half of the men and 45 percent of the women arrested in the United States in 1991 tested positive for some type of drug. (Source: Federal Bureau of Investigation [FBI].)
- Urinalysis of jail inmates in 20 major U.S. cities in 1991 revealed that 50 percent were positive for cocaine and 15 percent were positive for heroin. In a similar check in 1987, 53 percent to 79 percent were positive for some

type of drug. (Source: Stephen Magura, Andrew Rosenblum, and Herman Joseph, "AIDS Risk among Intravenous Drug-Using Offenders," *Crime and Delinquency* (January 1991): 87.)

- Prison may be a breeding ground for drug use. Half of the inmates in state prisons across the country say they had not used drugs until after their first arrest and incarceration. (Source: Daniel K. Benjamin and Roger L. Miller, *Undoing Drugs: Beyond Legalization* [New York: Basic Books, 1991], 105.)
- The substances most often abused by criminal defendants are cocaine, marijuana, and alcohol. As many as one-third test positive for more than one drug. (Source: John S. Goldkamp, Michael R. Gottfredson, and Doris Weiland, "Pretrial Drug Testing," *Journal of Criminal Law and Criminology* (Fall 1990): 607.)

Drug Use among Convicted Criminals

Table 5 shows the percentage of convicted criminals who reported that they had used each type of drug at some time in their lives

TABLE 5
PERCENTAGE OF CONVICTED CRIMINALS REPORTING DRUG USE AT SOME TIME IN THEIR LIVES: A COMPARISON BETWEEN 1983 AND 1989

Type of Drug	1983	1989
Any Drug	46.1%	43.9%
Cocaine/Crack	11.8%	23.6%
Heroin	7.9%	7.0%
LSD	3.0%	1.6%
PCP	3.0%	1.7%
Methadone	0.8%	0.6%
Marijuana	38.6%	28.1%
Amphetamines	9.4%	5.4%
Barbiturates	5.9%	3.3%
Other	3.0%	2.4%

Source: U.S. Department of Justice, Bureau of Justice Statistics.

when they were surveyed in 1983 and in 1989. While the trend is downward, the number of cocaine and crack abusers has risen dramatically in the jail and prison population.

Drug Use as the Motivation for Crime

Drug users need large amounts of cash to support their habits, and about one-third of drug addicts have no jobs. The rate of drug-related crimes in an area increases in direct proportion to the amount of drug activity in that area.

- The average offender commits 100 to 300 crimes against property or persons each year to support his or her drug habit. The frequency of crimes increases with the intensity of drug use. (Source: Magura, et al., 87.)
- The U.S. Department of Justice estimates that heroin addicts alone commit 100,000 robberies, burglaries, and car thefts every day. (Source: Bureau of Justice Statistics.)
- Many studies have shown a direct relationship between narcotics addiction and property crime. The crime rate of crack users appears to be the same as or greater than that of narcotics users. (Source: Magura, et al., 87.)
- Drug-related crime costs the public an average of more than $15,000 a year per addict. Each addict in treatment saves the public 20 percent of that amount in the year following treatment. (Source: E. P. Deschenes, M. D. Anglin, and G. Speckart, "Narcotics Addiction: Related Criminal Careers, Social and Economic Costs," *Journal of Drug Issues* [Spring 1991]: 388.)
- Drug users who are arrested and freed on bail commit twice as many crimes as others on bail who do not use drugs. (Source: Bureau of Justice Statistics.)

Drug Use and Violence

It is a popular belief that using drugs, particularly alcohol and PCP, makes people more likely to commit acts of violence. Some studies support this view.

- Alcohol is the real culprit in 40 percent of court cases involving members of the same family. Alcohol accounts for up to half of all violence between spouses and is involved in one-third of reported child molestations. (Source: U.S. Department of Health.)

- The U.S. Department of Justice estimates that nearly one-third of state prison inmates drank heavily before committing rapes, burglaries, assaults, and other violent crimes. (Source: Bureau of Justice Statistics.)
- Many studies have shown that PCP is likely to cause violent behavior. (Source: Timothy W. Kinlock, "Does PCP Use Increase Violent Crime?" *Journal of Drug Issues* [Fall 1991]: 795.)
- Crack users have higher rates of violent crime than users of narcotics. (Source: Magura, et al., 87.)
- According to the U.S. Department of Justice, more than half of all (federal and local) inmates convicted of violent crimes (rape, manslaughter, other assaults, and murder) had used alcohol shortly before the offense. (Source: Bureau of Justice Statistics.)

Crimes Committed by Adult and Juvenile Prisoners While under the Influence of Drugs or Alcohol

Tables 6 and 7 indicate drug use, as reported by criminals, during or immediately preceding their crimes.

Additional Information on Violence and Drug Trafficking

- In only one month (August 1991), Chicago police attributed 120 murders to crack. Every 16 hours,

TABLE 6
PERCENTAGE OF ADULT PRISONERS WHO REPORT THAT THEIR CRIMES WERE COMMITTED UNDER THE INFLUENCE OF ALCOHOL OR DRUGS

Offense	Drugs Only	Alcohol Only	Drugs and Alcohol
All Offenses	15.4%	29.2%	12.1%
Violent Crime	8.8%	30.7%	16.1%
Property Crime	18.2%	17.9%	12.8%
Drug Crime	28.6%	7.3%	12.3%
Public-Order Crime	6.4%	54.1%	9.6%

Source: U.S. Department of Justice, Bureau of Justice Statistics, 1989.

TABLE 7
PERCENTAGE OF JUVENILE PRISONERS WHO REPORTED THAT THEIR CRIMES WERE COMMITTED UNDER THE INFLUENCE OF ALCOHOL OR DRUGS

Offense	Drugs Only	Drugs and Alcohol
All Offenses	15.7%	23.4%
Violent Crime	12.1%	24.2%
Property Crime	16.8%	23.1%
Drug Crime	34.4%	24.9%
Public-Order Crime	15.9%	20.6%
Juvenile Status Crime	15.3%	17.6%

Source: U.S. Department of Justice, Bureau of Justice Statistics, 1987.

someone is killed in Washington, D.C., in drug-related violence. (Source: "Arrival of Crack in Chicago Tied to Increase in Violence," *New York Times*, 24 September 1991.)
- Posses (Jamaican crack gangs) have been responsible for at least 1,000 murders in the United States since 1985, according to the U.S. Department of Alcohol, Tobacco, and Firearms. (Source: Benjamin and Miller, 71.)
- In New York City, 32 innocent bystanders were killed in drug shoot-outs in a recent year. Across the United States, 200 to 300 other bystanders are murdered each year. (Source: Benjamin and Miller, 71.)
- African-American children run a particularly high risk of becoming casualties of drug violence. Nationwide, African-American teens are killed at seven times the rate of white children. (Source: Benjamin and Miller, 71.)

The Criminal Justice System

The 1980s saw a renewed assault on drug crimes as part of the Reagan and Bush wars on drugs. Nationwide about 1.2 million people are arrested on drug charges per year, almost double the number arrested for drugs in 1983. About 90 percent of those arrested plea-bargain (plead guilty to a less serious crime to avoid going to trial for a more serious crime) and serve little jail time.

About 25 percent of all drug arrests are for trafficking (sale); 75 percent are for possession or use.

Analysis of drug abusers in the criminal justice system also indicates that

- In the federal court system, drug prosecutions have increased 280 percent in the last ten years. (Source: "Drug Cases Clog the Courts," *ABA Journal* [April 1990]: 34.)
- More than one-third of current federal prison inmates and more than one-tenth of state prisoners were convicted on drug charges. (Source: Benjamin and Miller, 77.)
- The growth rate of the U.S. prison population is the highest ever. At the current rate, the prison population will double in five years. (Source: Benjamin and Miller, 76.)
- In 1990, about 43 percent of the states were served with court orders to solve their prison overcrowding problems. The prison populations of 80 percent of the states have reached an all-time high. (Source: "Drug Cases," 34.)
- The annual cost of imprisonment is $35 billion. In 1990 alone, $11 billion was spent on building new jail cells. (Source: Benjamin and Miller, 77.)

Table 8 indicates the number of state and local arrests for drug offenses, as estimated by the FBI.

Seizures of Illicit Drugs

The law enforcement response to the increase in drug-related crime is not limited to arrests. Illicit drugs are also seized and destroyed by the Drug Enforcement Administration (DEA), the FBI, the U.S. Customs Services, and the U.S. Coast Guard, as indicated in table 9.

Forfeiture

Under provisions of the 1986 anti-drug bill, property of suspected drug offenders or property on which drugs are stored or transported is subject to forfeiture. The proceeds from these seizures must be used for law enforcement. In 1990, forfeitures resulted in a substantial amount of money, as shown in table 10 (page 102).

TABLE 8
STATE AND LOCAL ARRESTS FOR DRUG OFFENSES, 1981 TO 1990

Year	Total Arrests for Drug Offenses	Sale/ Manufacturing	Possession
1981	559,900	111,420	448,480
1982	676,000	137,904	538,096
1983	661,400	146,169	515,231
1984	708,400	155,848	552,552
1985	811,400	192,302	619,098
1986	824,100	206,849	671,251
1987	937,400	241,849	695,551
1988	1,155,200	316,525	838,675
1989	1,361,700	441,191	920,509
1990	1,089,500	344,282	745,218

Source: Federal Bureau of Investigation.

TABLE 9
DRUG SEIZURES IN FISCAL YEAR 1990

Drug	Pounds Seized
Heroin	2,214
Cocaine	233,094
Cannabis (Marijuana)	482,948

Source: U.S. Department of Justice, Bureau of Justice Statistics.

TABLE 10
NONDRUG ASSETS SEIZED FOR DRUG OFFENSES
IN FISCAL YEAR 1990

Type of Asset	Number of Seizures	Value
Total	18,293	$1,068,268,486
Currency	7,622	$363,717,740
Vehicles	5,674	$60,579,075
Property	1,599	$345,617,695
Other Financial Instruments	444	$49,879,454
Vessels	187	$16,522,303
Airplanes	51	$25,586,000
Other	2,716	$206,376,219

Source: U.S. Department of Justice, Bureau of Justice Statistics.

FIGURE 5
FORFEITURE INCOME (IN MILLIONS)

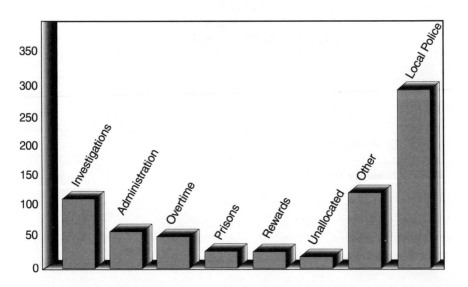

Source: U.S. Department of Justice, Bureau of Justice Statistics.

Forfeiture Income: How It Is Spent

According to the forfeiture law, assets seized from drug traffickers may be sold. The profits are returned to law enforcement. Figure 5 (page 102) shows the distribution of forfeiture income— $692.2 million seized from drug traffickers—for fiscal year 1991.

Drugs and the Law

Federal narcotics legislation is based on the Controlled Substances Act (CSA), passed in 1970 and amended several times afterward. The CSA consolidates and supersedes all previous federal laws regulating narcotics.

The CSA divides drugs into five schedules based on these eight criteria:

1. Potential for abuse
2. Pharmacological effect
3. Current state of scientific knowledge about the drug
4. History of the drug and current patterns of abuse
5. Scope, duration, and significance of abuse
6. Risk to public health
7. Possibility of dependence
8. Whether the substance is an immediate precursor (a form of a drug that precedes its final usable form) of a substance already controlled under the CSA

Controlled Substances Act: Federal Trafficking Penalties

Drugs on schedules 1 and 2 have a high potential for abuse. Schedule 1 drugs have no currently accepted uses in medical treatment in the United States. Schedule 2 drugs have currently accepted medical uses with severe restrictions. Schedule 1 drugs are considered unsafe, even under medical supervision. Schedule 2 drugs, when abused, may lead to severe psychological or physical dependence.

Schedule 3 drugs have less potential for abuse than drugs in schedules 1 and 2. Schedule 3 drugs have currently accepted medical treatment uses in the United States and may lead to low or moderate physical dependence or high psychological dependence.

TABLE 11
FEDERAL PENALTIES FOR DRUG TRAFFICKING

CSA	PENALTY (2nd Offense)	PENALTY (1st Offense)	Quantity	DRUG	Quantity	PENALTY (1st Offense)	PENALTY (2nd Offense)
I and II	Not less than 10 years. Not more than life.	Not less than 5 years. Not more than 40 years.	10–99 gm or 100–999 gm mixture	METHAMPHETAMINE	100 gm or more or 1 kg[1] or more mixture	Not less than 10 years. Not more than life.	Not less than 20 years. Not more than life.
	If death or serious injury, not less than life.	If death or serious injury, not less than 20 years. Not more than life.	100–999 gm mixture	HEROIN	1 kg or more mixture	If death or serious injury, not less than 20 years. Not more than life.	If death or serious injury, not less than life.
			500–4,999 gm mixture	COCAINE	5 kg or more mixture		
			5–49 gm mixture	COCAINE BASE	50 gm or more mixture		
	Fine of not more than $4 million individual, $10 million other than individual.	Fine of not more than $2 million individual, $5 million other than individual.	10–99 gm or 100–999 gm mixture	PCP	100 gm or more or 1 kg or more mixture	Fine of not more than $4 million individual, $10 million other than individual.	Fine of not more than $8 million individual, $20 million other than individual.
			1–10 gm mixture	LSD	10 gm or more mixture		

Drug	Quantity		First Offense	Second Offense
Others*	Any	Fentanyl: 40–399 gm mixture / 400 gm or more mixture Fentanyl Analogue: 10–99 gm mixture / 100 gm or more mixture	Not more than 20 years. If death or serious injury, not less than 20 years, not more than life. Fine $1 million individual, $5 million not individual.	Not more than 30 years. If death or serious injury, life. Fine $2 million individual, $10 million not individual.
III	All		Not more than 5 years. Fine not more than $250,000 individual, $1 million not individual.	Not more than 10 years. Fine not more than $500,000 individual, $2 million not individual.
IV	All		Not more than 3 years. Fine not more than $250,000 individual, $1 million not individual.	Not more than 6 years. Fine not more than $500,000 individual, $2 million not individual.
V	All		Not more than 1 year. Fine not more than $100,000 individual, $250,000 not individual.	Not more than 2 years. Fine not more than $200,000 individual, $500,000 not individual.

Note: CSA is the Controlled Substances Act.
Source: U.S. Department of Justice, Drug Enforcement Administration (1988).
* Does not include marijuana, hashish, or hashish oil.
¹Law as originally enacted states 100 gm. Congress requested to make technical correction to 1 kg.

Schedule 4 drugs have low potential for abuse compared to the drugs in schedule 3. They are currently used in accepted medical practice in the United States. Abuse may lead to less severe physical or psychological dependence than that caused by the drugs in schedule 3.

Schedule 5 drugs have the lowest potential for abuse. They are currently used in accepted medical practice in the United States, and they may lead to limited physical or psychological dependence.

Table 11 (pages 104–105) lists federal penalties for trafficking in all substances in schedules 1 through 5 except marijuana, hashish, and hashish oil. Penalties for trafficking in these substances can be found in table 12.

TABLE 12
FEDERAL PENALTIES FOR TRAFFICKING IN MARIJUANA, HASHISH, AND HASHISH OIL (ALL IN SCHEDULE 1)

For 1,000 kg or more, 1,000 or more plants of marijuana, or mixture containing any detectable quantity of marijuana, hashish, or hashish oil:

> First Offense—10 years to life. If death or serious injury occurs, 20 years to life. Fines not more than $4 million individual or $10 million nonindividual.

> Second Offense—20 years to life. Mandatory life for death or serious injury. Fines not more than $8 million individual or $20 million nonindividual.

For 100 kg or more, 100–999 plants of marijuana, or mixture containing any detectable quantity of marijuana, hashish, or hashish oil:

> First Offense—5–40 years. If death or serious injury occurs, 20 years to life. Fines not more than $2 million individual or $5 million nonindividual.

> Second Offense—10 years to life. Mandatory life for death or serious injury. Fines not more than $4 million individual or $10 million nonindividual.

For 50–100 kg of marijuana, 10–100 kg of hashish, 1–100 kg of hashish oil, or 50–99 marijuana plants:

> First Offense—Not more than 20 years. If death or serious injury occurs, 20 years to life. Fines not more than $1 million individual or $5 million nonindividual.

> Second Offense—Not more than 30 years. Mandatory life for death or serious injury. Fines not more than $2 million individual or $10 million nonindividual.

For less than 50 kg of marijuana, less than 10 kg of hashish, or less than 1 kg of hashish oil:

> First Offense—Not more than 5 years. Fines not more than $250,000 individual or $1 million nonindividual.

> Second Offense—Not more than 10 years. Fines not more than $500,000 individual or $2 million nonindividual.

Source: National Association for the Reform of Marijuana Laws (NORML).

Marijuana and the Law

Marijuana is a drug of great controversy. Federal law places it in schedule 1, among the most dangerous and addictive substances. Several states, however, have viewed possession of marijuana as a less serious offense, and some have passed laws allowing doctors to prescribe marijuana for certain medical conditions, notably glaucoma and the nausea associated with chemotherapy and some AIDS-related conditions. These state laws are superseded by federal law, which bans medical use of marijuana except for an extremely small number of experimental patients (and experimental use is being phased out). The state laws serve only as statements of principle and as guarantees that residents will be prosecuted only under federal law, a rare occurrence.

The states listed in table 13 have decriminalized the possession of small amounts of marijuana. Marijuana possession is not legal in these states, but the punishment is limited to a fine, usually $100. Alaska decriminalized possession of the drug in 1975, but recriminalized it in 1990. The Alaskan recriminalization is currently under appeal.

The states listed in table 14 (page 108) have laws allowing for the prescription of marijuana for certain medical conditions.

TABLE 13
STATES THAT HAVE DECRIMINALIZED
SMALL AMOUNTS OF MARIJUANA

California	Nebraska
Colorado	New York
Maine	North Carolina
Minnesota	Ohio
Mississippi	Oregon

Source: National Association for the Reform of Marijuana Laws.

The Anti–Drug Abuse Act of 1988

A major tactic in President Reagan's war on drugs was enacting the Anti–Drug Abuse Act of 1988. It incorporates these major provisions: policy, domestic programs, regulation of drugs, international efforts, money laundering, penalties, chemical diversion, forfeiture, and drug enforcement.

TABLE 14

**STATES THAT ALLOW PRESCRIPTION OF MARIJUANA
FOR CERTAIN MEDICAL CONDITIONS**

Alabama	New Jersey
Arizona	New Mexico
Arkansas	New York
California	North Carolina
Colorado	Ohio
Connecticut	Oklahoma
Florida	Oregon
Georgia	Rhode Island
Illinois	South Carolina
Iowa	Tennessee
Louisiana	Texas
Maine	Vermont
Michigan	Virginia
Minnesota	Washington
Montana	West Virginia
Nevada	Wisconsin
New Hampshire	

Source: National Association for the Reform of Marijuana Laws.

Policy

- Coordination of national drug policy by the establishment of the drug czar (officially, the director of the Office of National Drug Control Policy, who will prepare a national drug-control budget, devise a federal anti-drug strategy, and make recommendations to the president on activities of the federal anti-drug efforts.

Domestic Programs

- Warning labels on alcoholic beverages stating the health risks to pregnant women and to drivers and operators of heavy machinery.
- Funds for drunken-driver prevention programs.
- Grants to the states for alcohol-abuse, drug-abuse, and mental health activities. Grants are based on population at risk and the fiscal capacity of the state.
- Matching grants to the states for the construction or rehabilitation of drug treatment facilities; funds can be used for drug treatment programs for IV drug users and training of counselors, but not for sterile needle-exchange programs.

- Funds for programs to prevent the spread of AIDS through IV drug use and for community health services. States are encouraged to set up a revolving loan fund for group housing for recovering alcoholics or addicts.
- Additional funds for the Office of Substance Abuse Prevention and for programs aimed at preventing substance abuse by pregnant women, mothers, young children, Native Americans, and veterans. There are also funds to aid efforts to reduce youth participation in gangs.
- Funds to help treatment centers reduce waiting lists.

Regulation of Drugs

- New penalties for distribution and possession of anabolic steroids
- Increased regulation of butyl nitrite (an inhalant)
- Establishment of a task force to clean up hazardous waste from illegal drug laboratories

International Efforts

- Creation of an international task force, through the Organization of American States, to fight international drug smuggling
- Funds for defensive arming of helicopters given to foreign governments for anti-drug efforts
- Funds to train law enforcement officers in foreign countries, waiving a 1975 law that barred U.S. aid to countries that violate human rights
- Transfer of foreign aid funds from countries that do not meet antinarcotics standards to those that do meet standards
- Extra funds to Bolivia, Colombia, and Mexico
- Tighter requirements for anti-drug efforts; if the president cannot certify each year that these requirements have been met by the foreign country, aid must be suspended and U.S. officials will not approve loans to that country
- Power and responsibility to the secretary of state to coordinate all international aid for anti-drug efforts; permission to the State Department to offer rewards for

information concerning narcotics offenses outside the United States
- Revocation or denial of passports to anyone convicted of a federal or state felony drug violation

Money Laundering

- Negotiation between the secretary of the treasury and foreign counterparts to fight money laundering
- Improved records of international currency transactions
- Tighter controls on transactions of $3,000 or more
- Increased penalties for financial institutions that violate regulations aimed at curbing money laundering

Penalties

- Eviction from public housing of tenants, their guests, and their families if anyone in those groups is engaged in criminal activity, including drug activity, in or near public housing
- Denial of federal benefits to anyone convicted of distributing illegal drugs, except to those in long-term drug treatment; the penalty period increases with each offense
- Fines and imprisonment for anyone who endangers human life while manufacturing a controlled substance
- Increased penalties for crack possession and sales
- Increased penalties for repeat felony offenses and for driving while under the influence of drugs or alcohol; revocation of probation and parole for anyone found in possession of a controlled substance
- Possibility of the death penalty for those who kill or order the death of law enforcement officers and for those engaging in a drug-related felony offense who kill

Chemical Diversion

- Regulation of chemicals used to process or manufacture illicit drugs; regulation of importation or exportation of such chemicals; penalties for noncompliance with these regulations

Forfeiture

- Funds to enable law enforcement agencies to employ the forfeiture penalty
- Faster procedures for forfeiture of conveyances, or vehicles such as cars, vans, and trucks
- Faster return of forfeited conveyances in cases of personal-use offenses (possession of a quantity of an illegal drug assumed to be enough only for personal use) if the owner of the vehicle did not know of the offense or consent to it
- A summons instead of forfeiture of a commercial fishing boat involved in personal-use drug offenses

Drug Enforcement

- Additional funds to the Immigration and Naturalization Service; the Bureau of Alcohol, Tobacco, and Firearms; the FBI; the Federal Aviation Administration; and the DEA
- Funds for the U.S. Marshals Service to be used for forfeiture activities and for protection of federal judges and court personnel in drug-related trials
- Funds for prisons, customs, and the Coast Guard
- Mandatory penalties for using a firearm in a drug-related crime or for transferring (selling, giving, or lending) firearms subsequently used in drug crimes
- Funds for U.S. Forest Service personnel who inspect public lands to curb narcotics violations

The Drug-Free Workplace Act of 1988

Perhaps the most controversial section of the 1988 anti-drug law called for a drug-free workplace, which would be achieved in part through drug testing. Since this concept has been frequently challenged, the relevant section of the law is reprinted here in its entirety.

Sec. 5151. SHORT TITLE.

This subtitle may be cited as the "Drug-Free Workplace Act of 1988".

Sec. 5152. DRUG-FREE WORKPLACE REQUIREMENTS FOR FEDERAL CONTRACTORS.

(a) DRUG-FREE WORKPLACE REQUIREMENT.—
    (1) REQUIREMENT FOR PERSONS OTHER THAN INDIVIDUALS.—No person, other than an individual, shall be considered a responsible source, under the meaning of such term as defined in section 4(8) of the Office of Federal Procurement Policy Act (41 U.S.C. 403(8)), for the purposes of being awarded a contract for the procurement of any property or services of a value of $25,000 or more from any Federal agency unless such person has certified to the contracting agency that it will provide a drug-free workplace by—
    (A) publishing a statement notifying employees that the unlawful manufacture, distribution, dispensation, possession, or use of a controlled substance is pro-hibited in the person's workplace and specifying the actions that will be taken against employees for violations of such prohibition;
    (B) establishing a drug-free awareness program to inform employees about—
      (i) the dangers of drug abuse in the workplace;
      (ii) the person's policy of maintaining a drug-free workplace;
      (iii) any available drug counseling, rehabilitation, and employee assistance programs; and
      (iv) the penalties that may be imposed upon employees for drug abuse violations;
    (C) making it a requirement that each employee to be engaged in the performance of such contract be given a copy of the statement required by sub-paragraph (A);
    (D) notifying the employee in the statement required by subparagraph (A), that as a condition of employment on such contract, the employee will—
      (i) abide by the terms of the statement; and
      (ii) notify the employer of any criminal drug statute conviction for a violation occurring in the work-place no later than 5 days after such conviction;

(E) notifying the contracting agency within 10 days after receiving notice under subparagraph (D)(ii) from an employee or otherwise receiving actual notice of such conviction;

(F) imposing a sanction on, or requiring the satisfactory participation in a drug abuse assistance or rehabilitation program by, any employee who is so convicted, as required by section 5154; and

(G) making a good faith effort to continue to maintain a drug-free workplace through implementation of subparagraphs (A), (B), (C), (D), (E), and (F).

(2) REQUIREMENT FOR INDIVIDUALS.—No Federal agency shall enter into a contract with an individual unless such contract includes a certification by the individual that the individual will not engage in the unlawful manufacture, distribution, dispensation, possession, or use of a controlled substance in the performance of the contract.

(b) SUSPENSION, TERMINATION, OR DEBARMENT OF THE CONTRACTOR.—

(1) GROUNDS FOR SUSPENSION, TERMINATION, OR DEBARMENT.—

Each contract awarded by a Federal agency shall be subject to suspension of payments under the contract or termination of the contract, or both, and the contractor thereunder or the individual who entered the contract with the Federal agency, as applicable, shall be subject to suspension or debarment in accordance with the requirements of this section if the head of the agency determines that—

(A) the contractor or individual has made a false certification under subsection (a);

(B) the contractor violates such certification by failing to carry out the requirements of subparagraph (A), (B), (C), (D), (E), or (F) of subsection (a)(1); or

(C) such a number of employees of such contractor have been convicted of violations of criminal drug statutes for violations occurring in the workplace as to indicate that the contractor has failed to make a good faith effort to provide a drug-free workplace as required by subsection (a).

(2) CONDUCT OF SUSPENSION, TERMINATION, AND DEBARMENT PROCEEDINGS.—

(A) If a contracting officer determines, in writing, that cause for suspension of payments, termination, or suspension or debarment exists, an appropriate action shall be initiated by a contracting officer of the agency, to be conducted by the agency concerned in accordance with the Federal Acquisition Regulation and applicable agency procedures.

(B) The Federal Acquisition Regulation shall be revised to include rules for conducting suspension and debarment proceedings under this subsection, including rules providing notice, opportunity to respond in writing or in person, and such other procedures as may be necessary to provide a full and fair proceeding to a contractor or individual in such proceeding.

(3) EFFECT OF DEBARMENT.—Upon issuance of any final decision under this subsection requiring debarment of a contractor or individual, such contractor or individual shall be ineligible for award of any contract by any Federal agency, and for participation in any future procurement by any Federal agency, for a period specified in the decision, not to exceed 5 years.

SEC. 5153. DRUG-FREE WORKPLACE REQUIREMENTS FOR FEDERAL GRANT RECIPIENTS.

(a) DRUG-FREE WORKPLACE REQUIREMENT.—

(1) PERSONS OTHER THAN INDIVIDUALS.—No person other than an individual, shall receive a grant from any Federal agency unless such person has certified to the granting agency that it will provide a drug-free workplace by—

(A) publishing a statement notifying employees that the unlawful manufacture, distribution, dispensation, possession, or use of a controlled substance is prohibited in the grantee's workplace and specifying the actions that will be taken against employees for violations of such prohibition;

(B) establishing a drug-free awareness program to inform employees about—

(i) the dangers of drug abuse in the workplace;

(ii) the grantee's policy of maintaining a drug-free workplace;

(iii) any available drug counseling, rehabilitation, and employee assistance programs; and

(iv) the penalties that may be imposed upon employees for drug abuse violations;

(C) making it a requirement that each employee to be engaged in the performance of such grant be given a copy of the statement required by subparagraph (A);

(D) notifying the employee in the statement required by subparagraph (A), that as a condition of employment in such grant, the employee will—

   (i) abide by the terms of the statement; and

   (ii) notify the employer of any criminal drug statute conviction for a violation occurring in the workplace no later than 5 days after such conviction;

(E) notifying the granting agency within 10 days after receiving notice of a conviction under subparagraph (D)(ii) from an employee or otherwise receiving actual notice of such conviction;

(F) imposing a sanction on, or requiring the satisfactory participation in a drug abuse assistance or rehabilitation program by, any employee who is so convicted, as required by section 5154; and

(G) making a good faith effort to continue to maintain a drug-free workplace through implementation of subparagraphs (A), (B), (C), (D), (E), and (F).

(2) INDIVIDUALS.—No Federal agency shall make a grant to any individual unless such individual certifies to the agency as a condition of such grant that the individual will not engage in the unlawful manufacture, distribution, dispensation, possession, or use of a controlled substance in conducting any activity with such grant.

(b) SUSPENSION, TERMINATION, OR DEBARMENT OF THE GRANTEE.—

(1) GROUNDS FOR SUSPENSION, TERMINATION, OR DEBARMENT.—

Each grant awarded by a Federal agency shall be subject to suspension of payments under the grant or termination of the grant, or both, and the grantee thereunder shall be subject to suspension or debarment, in accordance with the requirements of this section if the agency head of the granting agency or his official designee determines, in writing, that—

(A) the grantee has made a false certification under subsection (a);

(B) the grantee violates such certification by failing to carry out the requirements of subparagraph (A), (B), (C), (D), (E), (F), or (G) of subsection (a)(1); or

(C) such a number of employees of such grantee have been convicted of violations of criminal drug statutes for violations occurring in the workplace as to indicate that the grantee has failed to make a good faith effort to provide a drug-free workplace as required by subsection (a)(1).

(2) CONDUCT OF SUSPENSION, TERMINATION, AND DEBARMENT PROCEEDINGS.—A suspension of payments, termination, or suspension or debarment proceeding subject to this subsection shall be conducted in accordance with applicable law, including Executive Order 12549 or any superseding Executive order and any regulations promulgated to implement such law or Executive order.

(3) EFFECT OF DEBARMENT.—Upon issuance of any final decision under this subsection requiring debarment of a grantee, such grantee shall be ineligible for award of any grant from any Federal agency and for participation in any future grant from any Federal agency for a period specified in the decision, not to exceed 5 years.

SEC. 5154. EMPLOYEE SANCTIONS AND REMEDIES.

A grantee or contractor shall, within 30 days after receiving notice from an employee of a conviction pursuant to section 5152 (a)(1)(D)(ii) or 5153 (a)(1)(D)(ii)—

(1) take appropriate personnel action against such employee up to and including termination; or

(2) require such employee to satisfactorily participate in a drug abuse assistance or rehabilitation program approved for such purposes by a Federal, State, or local health, law enforcement, or other appropriate agency.

SEC. 5155. WAIVER.

(a) IN GENERAL.—A termination, suspension of payments, or suspension or debarment under this subtitle may be waived by the head of an agency with respect to a particular contract or grant if—

(1) in the case of a waiver with respect to a contract, the head of the agency determines under section 5152 (b)(1), after the issuance of a final determination under such section, that suspension of payments, or termination of the contract, or suspension or debarment of the contractor, or

refusal to permit a person to be treated as a responsible source for a contract, as the case may be, would severely disrupt the operation of such agency to the detriment of the Federal Government or the general public; or
   (2) in the case of a waiver with respect to a grant, the head of the agency determines that suspension of payments, termination of the grant, or suspension or debarment of the grantee would not be in the public interest.
 (b) EXCLUSIVE AUTHORITY.—The authority of the head of an agency under this section to waive a termination, suspension, or debarment shall not be delegated.

SEC. 5156. REGULATIONS.

Not later than 90 days after the date of enactment of this subtitle, the governmentwide regulations governing actions under this subtitle shall be issued pursuant to the Office of Federal Procurement Policy Act (41 U.S.C. 401 et seq.).

SEC. 5157. DEFINITIONS.

For purposes of this subtitle—
   (1) the term "drug-free workplace" means a site for the performance of work done in connection with a specific grant or contract described in section 5152 or 5153 of an entity at which employees of such entity are prohibited from engaging in the unlawful manufacture, distribution, dispensation, possession, or use of a controlled substance in accordance with the requirements of this Act;
   (2) the term "employee" means the employee of a grantee or contractor directly engaged in the performance of work pursuant to the provisions of the grant or contract described in section 5152 or 5153;
   (3) the term "controlled substance" means a controlled substance in schedules I through V of section 202 of the Controlled Substances Act (21 U.S.C. 812);
   (4) the term "conviction" means a finding of guilt (including a plea of nolo contendere) or imposition of sentence, or both, by any judicial body charged with the responsibility to determine violations of the Federal or State criminal drug statutes;

(5) the term "criminal drug statute" means a criminal statute involving manufacture, distribution, dispensation, use, or possession of any controlled substance;

(6) the term "grantee" means the department, division, or other unit of a person responsible for the performance under the grant;

(7) the term "contractor" means the department, division, or other unit of a person responsible for the performance under the contract; and

(8) the term "Federal agency" means an agency as that term is defined in section 552(f) of title 5, United States Code.

SEC. 5158. CONSTRUCTION OF SUBTITLE.

Nothing in this subtitle shall be construed to require law enforcement agencies, if the head of the agency determines it would be inappropriate in connection with the agency's undercover operations, to comply with the provisions of this subtitle.

SEC. 5159. REPEAL OF LIMITATION ON USE OF FUNDS.

Section 628 of Public Law 100-400 (relating to restrictions on the use of certain appropriated amounts) is amended—

(1) by striking "(a)" after "Sec. 628."; and

(2) by striking subsection (b).

SEC. 5160. EFFECTIVE DATE.

Sections 5152 and 5153 shall be effective 120 days after the date of the enactment of this subtitle.

Drugs, Health, and Health Care

People take psychoactive drugs in order to change the way they feel or the way they perceive reality. All of the drugs listed in table 15 alter mood or thought, but each drug also has many side effects—some trivial, like eye irritation, and some potentially fatal, like lung cancer.

The number of emergency-room visits because of drug abuse has risen in the last few years, a worrisome trend. In 1991, visits

TABLE 15

THE EFFECTS ON THE BODY OF VARIOUS PSYCHOACTIVE DRUGS

Drug	Description	Effects
Tobacco (cigarettes, cigars, pipe, and chewing tobacco)	Dried leaves of the tobacco plant. Principal active component is nicotine.	Chief avoidable cause of death in the United States. Increases risk of cancer, heart disase, emphysema, and bronchitis. Irritates eyes, nose, and throat.
Alcohol (beer, wine, and spirits)	Distilled from grain or fermented from grapes and other fruit.	Impairs judgment, memory, and coordination. May increase aggression as it lowers inhibitions. Very high doses depress respiration and may be fatal. Long-term consumption may damage liver and brain.
Marijuana and hashish (also called joints, pot, grass, weed, mary jane, cannabis, reefer, sinsemilla, Acapulco gold, hash)	Marijuana is dried leaves of the hemp plant (cannabis). Hashish is the resin of the hemp plant. Principal active component is Tetrahydrocannabinol (THC).	Impairs short-term memory and comprehension. Alters sense of time and coordination. Linked to "amotivational syndrome"—lack of drive and desire to achieve. May irritate lungs and precipitate paranoia or mental distress. Some studies link marijuana and hashish to impairment of the immune and reproductive systems.
Inhalants (nitrous oxide, amyle nitrite, butyl nitrite, solvents, glues, aerosol propellants, cleaning fluid, paint thinner. Also called laughing gas, poppers, and snappers)	A variety of gaseous substances, often with legitimate household uses, that are inhaled.	May cause nausea, sneezing, coughing, nosebleeds, appetite loss, and fatigue. Impairs judgment and coordination. Repeated use may result in kidney, lung, or brain damage and death.

Drug *cont'd*	Description *cont'd*	Effects *cont'd*
Cocaine (includes crack and freebase. Also called coke, snow, flake, rocks, and nose candy)	Derivative of coca leaves.	Stimulates the central nervous system. Elevates blood pressure, heart and respiration rate, and body temperature. Irritates nose. May cause insomnia, hallucinations, paranoia, seizures, fatal cardiac arrest, or respiratory failure. Intravenous use increases risk of AIDS and hepatitis.
Amphetamines (includes meth-amphetamines. Also called speed, uppers, ups, pep pills, diet pills, black beauties, crank, and crystal meth)	Pills, powders, and injections that stimulate the central nervous system.	Increases heart and respiratory rate. Dilates pupils and decreases appetite. May cause sweating, blurred vision, anxiety, insomnia, and dizziness. May precipitate irregular heartbeat and tremors. Impairs coordination. May cause stroke, fever, and heart failure. Long-term use results in paranoia, hallucinations, and psychosis. Intravenous use increases risk of AIDS and hepatitis.
Depressants (includes barbiturates, methaqualone, and tranquilizers. Also called downers, barbs, blue devils, yellow jackets, and ludes)	Tablets or capsules frequently prescribed for legitimate medical uses and often abused for their psychoactive effects.	Small amounts have a calming effect and relax muscles. Increased doses impair speech and coordination. May cause depression, respiratory failure, coma, and death. Abrupt withdrawal may result in restlessness, insomnia, convulsions, and death.
Narcotics (includes heroin, codeine, morphine, meperidine, opium, and fentanyl. Also called smack, horse, and black tar)	Derived from the opium poppy or synthesized.	May cause drowsiness, nausea, and vomiting. Large doses depress respiration and may cause convulsions, coma, and death. Im-

Drug *cont'd*	Description *cont'd*	Effects *cont'd*
Narcotics *cont.*		pairs judgment and awareness. Intravenous use increases risk of AIDS and hepatitis.
Designer drugs (includes analogues of narcotics, amphet-amines, and hallucinogens such as MPTP, MPPP, MDMA, STP, and PCE; also called China white, Ecstasy, Adam, Eve, and Essence)	Synthesized to mimic the effects of narcotics, amphetamines, and hallucinogens.	These drugs may cause the same symptoms as their organic counter-parts. Because they are stronger or may be incorrectly made, they carry increased risk of brain damage, paralysis, and mental problems.

Source: U.S. Drug Enforcement Administration.

for cocaine reactions were up 13 percent, and visits for problems caused by heroin use rose 10 percent. Of course, patients seldom volunteer the information that their chest pain or dizziness was caused by an illegal drug. Nevertheless, skillful questioning by emergency-room personnel often produces the needed information. Table 16 (page 122) shows the number of times each drug was mentioned by the patient or in the physician's report. Because each patient may name more than one drug, the number of mentions may be larger than the total number of visits to the emergency room. Totals may also include other drugs not specified in table 16. Up to four substances may be mentioned for each emergency-room visit. Therefore, the total number of drug mentions is greater than the total number of drug episodes.

AIDS

The most serious complication of intravenous drug use is the deadly disease AIDS, which is spread by contaminated needles. Worldwide, a smaller percentage of those infected with HIV (the virus that causes AIDS) get the virus from IV drug use than in the United States. Figures 6 and 7 (pages 122–123) show the causes of the disease reported during 1992.

Needle-exchange programs are designed to combat the spread of AIDS by providing addicts with clean syringes. Naturally, such programs are very controversial because of their

TABLE 16
EMERGENCY-ROOM DRUG MENTIONS, 1989–1990

Drug Type	1989	1990
Cocaine	110,013	80,355
Heroin/Morphine	41,656	33,884
Marijuana/Hashish	20,703	15,706
Methamphetamine/Speed	8,722	5,236
PCP	8,042	4,408
LSD	3,421	3,869
Methadone	3,150	2,617
Total Drug Mentions	713,392	635,460
Total Drug Abuse Episodes	425,904	371,208

Source: Drug Abuse Warning Network.

FIGURE 6
SOURCES OF HIV INFECTION, WORLD FIGURES

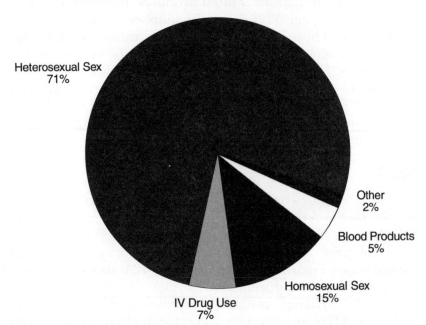

Heterosexual Sex
71%

Other
2%

Blood Products
5%

Homosexual Sex
15%

IV Drug Use
7%

Source: Harvard School of Public Health.

FIGURE 7
SOURCES OF HIV INFECTION, U.S. FIGURES

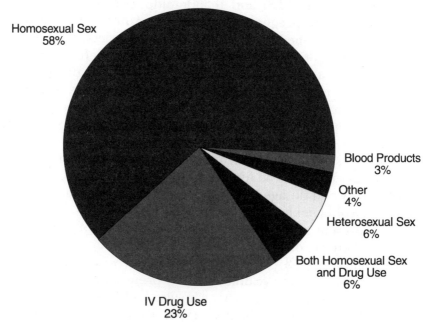

Homosexual Sex
58%

Blood Products
3%

Other
4%

Heterosexual Sex
6%

Both Homosexual Sex
and Drug Use
6%

IV Drug Use
23%

Source: U.S. Department of Health and Human Services.

implied acceptance of drug use. Table 17 lists American cities with legal needle-exchange programs as well as cities with underground programs, often run by AIDS activists in defiance of the law.

TABLE 17
AMERICAN CITIES WITH NEEDLE-EXCHANGE PROGRAMS

Underground Programs	Legal Programs
Marin County, California	Boulder, Colorado
Oakland, California	New Haven, Connecticut
Sacramento, California	Honolulu, Hawaii
San Francisco, California	Portland, Oregon
San Mateo, California	New York, New York
Santa Clara, California	Seattle, Washington
Santa Cruz, California	Spokane, Washington
Chicago, Illinois	Tacoma, Washington
Baltimore, Maryland	Vancouver, Washington
Boston, Massachusetts	
Philadelphia, Pennsylvania	

Source: Mereya Navarro, "Needle Swaps To Be Revived To Curb AIDS," *New York Times,* 14 May 1992, 1.

Drugs and Childbirth

Diethylstilbestrol (DES) and thalidomide, two drugs once prescribed legally to pregnant women in the United States and Europe, taught the medical community a valuable lesson. These two
drugs brought on a wave of children with birth defects or, in the
case of DES, a higher risk of cancer in the adult daughters of
women who had taken the drug more than 20 years earlier. To
avoid the possibility of harm to the fetus, most doctors now warn
expectant mothers to avoid all medications, including substances
as innocent as aspirin.

Needless to say, street drugs pose a particular risk because of
their ability to harm the fetus and because of the unreliability of
their purity and dosage levels. However, legal psychoactive drugs
such as alcohol, tobacco, and prescription stimulants or tranquilizers also present grave threats to the developing embryo. To determine the effects of just one drug, cocaine, a study was done in
1989 comparing 53 pregnant cocaine users with 100 pregnant
nonusers. More than five times as many premature deliveries were
necessary for the cocaine users, who also had more complications
such as hemorrhages, hepatitis, herpes, heart failure, and hyper-
tension (high blood pressure). (Source: Susan Jenks, "Drug
Babies," *Medical World News*, 12 February 1990, 43.)

Additional Facts on the Effects of Psychoactive Drugs on Health and Health Care

- Even though women consume less alcohol than men,
  women are more likely to develop liver disease and have
  a greater risk of dying once the liver is damaged. This
  may be because women have less of a stomach enzyme
  that digests alcohol than men. (Source: National Council
  on Alcoholism and Drug Dependence [NCADD].)
- In 1987, an average of 300 people died each day of
  alcohol-related causes. (Source: NCADD.)
- Passive smoking is the third leading preventable cause of
  death. (Source: Americans for Nonsmokers' Rights.)
- Cases of syphilis rose 132 percent between 1986 and
  1990, probably because of unprotected sex being given in
  exchange for or under the influence of crack. (Source:
  Benjamin and Miller, 121.)
- Crack users have a higher rate of tuberculosis than the
  population in general, perhaps because their lungs are

impaired by the drug or because of an unhealthy lifestyle. (Source: Centers for Disease Control.)

- About 90 percent of AIDS in children results from maternal drug use. (Source: Centers for Disease Control.)
- The majority of heterosexuals diagnosed with AIDS in 1990 got the disease through IV drug use. (Source: Centers for Disease Control.)
- Because cocaine users typically inject themselves up to ten times a day (in comparison with once or twice for heroin addicts), IV cocaine addicts are more likely to contract AIDS than IV heroin users. (Source: National Institute on Drug Abuse.)
- About 30,000 infants are born with fetal alcohol syndrome (FAS) each year. FAS is one of the top three causes of retardation in babies, and the only one of the three that is preventable. (Source: NCADD.)
- In 1986, the short-term cost of treating infants affected before birth by maternal smoking was estimated at $332 million. Estimates for the cost of treating newborn babies affected by their mothers' cocaine use ranged from $33 million to $1 billion. (Source: Institute for Health Policy Studies.)

Drugs and the Homeless

Public perception of increased drug use among homeless people is borne out by several studies, such as one done in Chicago in the late 1950s and one done nationwide in 1988. In the 1950s, about 25 percent of the homeless were Social Security pensioners, about 25 percent were alcoholics, and half were mentally ill. About 10 percent were called socially maladjusted by the author of the survey, and 20 percent had physical disabilities.

In the 1988 survey, one-third of the homeless people were alcoholics, more than one-third were mentally ill, and one-quarter were drug abusers. Only 10 percent were physically disabled, but more than 20 percent were victims of domestic violence. (In both surveys some people fit into more than one category, so the numbers do not add up to 100 percent.) (Source: Peter H. Rossi, "The Old Homeless and the New Homeless in Historical Perspective," *American Psychologist*, August 1990, 954–958.)

Drug-Related Accidents and Violence

Drugs and alcohol permeate our society in ways that are not immediately noticeable, except to the victims and those who love them. Figure 8 estimates the number of accidents and crimes in which drugs played a role.

Additional Information on Drugs and Accidents

- The National Highway Safety Administration defines a traffic accident as alcohol-related if either the driver or a nonoccupant (pedestrian) has a blood alcohol concentration (BAC) of 0.01 percent or more. A BAC of 0.10 percent or more is defined as intoxication.
- The U.S. Coast Guard, in a recent survey of boating accidents in four states, found that 51 percent of the

FIGURE 8
EFFECTS OF ALCOHOL AND OTHER PSYCHOACTIVE DRUGS
PERCENTAGE ASSOCIATED WITH THE USE OF PSYCHOACTIVE DRUGS

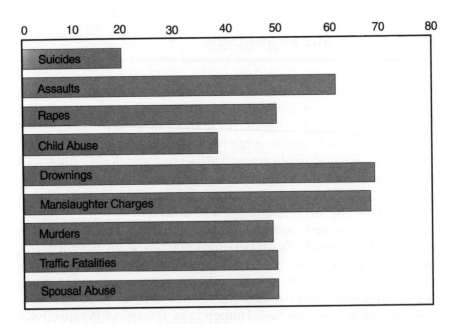

Source: U.S. Office for Substance Abuse Prevention.

fatalities involved a BAC of at least 0.04 and 31 percent involved a BAC of 0.10 or more.
- Between 1982 and 1988, there was one alcohol-related traffic fatality every 22 minutes on the nation's highways.
- In an average year, alcohol contributes to about 15,000 fatal injuries in home accidents.
- One of every three truck drivers who died in highway accidents had used drugs or alcohol.
- Between 1975 and 1984, alcohol- or drug-impaired employees were involved in 48 train accidents resulting in 37 deaths. (Source: National Council on Alcoholism and Drug Dependence.)

Drug Users on the Job

The stereotypical drug user is an unemployed, shiftless (and homeless) bum. But that image does not fit the reality, according to NIDA surveys. Only 10 percent of drug users can be categorized as unemployed. Some 70 percent work full-time; the rest are students, homemakers, and retirees. Among those who are employed, men tend to use illicit drugs more frequently than women, and the youngest workers tend to use the most illicit drugs.

Business has responded to employee drug problems in a variety of ways. More than 30 percent of companies surveyed by the Bureau of Labor Statistics had employee assistance programs, 20 percent had drug-testing programs, and more than 40 percent had formal policies for dealing with drug abuse on the job.

State Laws on Job-Related Drug Abuse

In the past five years, 19 states have passed laws denying or reducing workers' compensation for on-the-job injuries resulting from alcohol or drug abuse. These are listed in table 18 (page 128).

On-the-job accidents attributed to drug or alcohol abuse have fueled cries for drug testing, particularly for employees in safety-sensitive positions. Although drug testing has been repeatedly challenged in court, a recent Gallup poll found that most workers

TABLE 18
STATES THAT DENY OR REDUCE WORKERS' COMPENSATION FOR INJURIES RESULTING FROM ALCOHOL OR DRUG ABUSE

Alaska	New York
Connecticut	North Dakota
Florida	Ohio
Georgia	Oklahoma
Idaho	Oregon
Iowa	Rhode Island
Kansas	South Dakota
Louisiana	Virginia
Maryland	Wyoming
Missouri	

Source: Institute for a Drug-Free Workplace.

FIGURE 9
WORKERS' ATTITUDES TOWARD DRUG TESTING
PERCENTAGE OF AMERICANS IN VARIOUS OCCUPATIONS
WHO AGREED THAT DRUG TESTING IS A GOOD IDEA

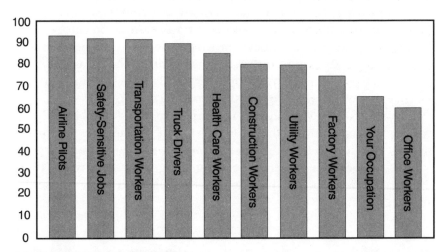

Source: Institute for a Drug-Free Workplace.

favor some sort of on-the-job testing. Figure 9 shows the percentage of people who believe that drug testing is a good idea in each of the listed occupations.

Duration of Drug Traces in Urine or Other Body Fluids

Individual metabolism, the amount and frequency of drug use, and other factors may influence the amount of time that traces of

TABLE 19
DURATION OF DRUG TRACES IN URINE

Drug	Duration
Amphetamines	2 days
Methamphetamines	2 days
Short-Acting Barbiturates (hexobarbital, pentobarbital)	1 day
Intermediate-Acting Barbiturates (amobarbital, butabarbital)	2–3 days
Long-Acting Barbiturates (phenobarbital)	7 days
Cocaine	2–3 days
Methadone	3 days
Codeine	2 days
Morphine	2 days
Cannabinoids (heavy user)	21–27 days
Cannabinoids (single use)	3 days
PCP	8 days
Methaqualone	7 days

Source: Council on Scientific Affairs, "Scientific Issues in Drug Testing," *Journal of the American Medical Association,* vol. 257, no. 22, 12 June 1987, 3112.

drugs will remain in urine and other body fluids. The numbers in Table 19 are average figures.

Federal Spending on Anti-Drug Efforts

Although it represents only about 1 percent of the federal budget, the amount of money the government spends on the war on drugs has increased dramatically since 1981. Figure 10 illustrates domestic and international expenditures and includes funds given to the Department of State, the Coast Guard, the Department of Justice, the Office of National Drug Control Policy (ONDCP), the Department of the Treasury, and other agencies. Figure 10 does not include additional money spent by state and local authorities. All years refer to fiscal years.

It is clear from figure 10 (page 130) that the government spends far more money trying to reduce the drug supply than it does in trying to reduce the demand for drugs. Perhaps to counter criticism, the 1993 budget request from the Bush administration is accompanied by this statement:

FIGURE 10
NATIONAL DRUG CONTROL BUDGET, 1981–1993

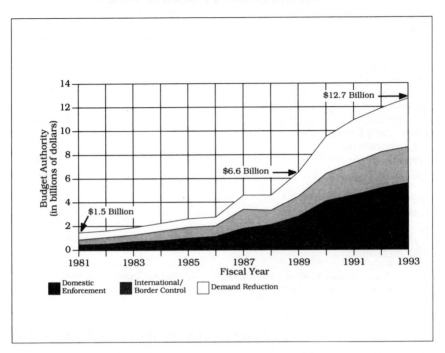

Source: Office of National Drug Control Policy (1992).

Many supply activities also have a profound effect on demand reduction, and are so intended. For example, arresting and punishing a juvenile for illegal drug use sends a message to his friends and schoolmates that will deter them from drug use. Thus, while approximately 68 percent of the 1993 Federal budget is for activities traditionally thought of as supply reduction (roughly the same percentage as Congress appropriated for 1992), a large portion of this funding will have an impact on and is aimed at reducing demand. Second, supply reduction activities are inherently expensive (patrol cars, aircraft, and prisons are all very costly), whereas many demand reduction activities rely less on capital outlays and more on community involvement and individual commitment. Getting schools to treat drug abuse seriously, for example, doesn't necessarily require a large budget. And third, many supply reduction activities are intrinsically government functions (and some, such as international operations and border control, can only be performed by the Federal government), whereas most demand reduction efforts can and should be shared by our schools, churches, and communities.

The budget summary from which the above statement is taken was prepared by the ONDCP under the direction of Drug

Czar Bob Martinez. The ONDCP coordinates the efforts of the many federal agencies that fight drug abuse. The budget summary indicates the amount of money allocated to each division, as well as an output summary—the results of the previous year's investment of time, energy, and money. In a sense, the budget summary not only tells the American public what it needs for the future, but also answers the question, What did we get last year for our anti-drug tax dollars?

Naturally, some results are impossible to measure. How can one count the number of youths who reject drugs because an education program has made them aware of the health risks these chemicals pose? How can one calculate the acres of coca not planted in other countries because of U.S. foreign aid? Still, some hard numbers are available: plants eradicated, arrests made, treatments funded, and so forth. Tables 20 to 26 present a representative sample of the output summary statements of several agencies from 1992.

TABLE 20 ALCOHOL, DRUG ABUSE, AND MENTAL HEALTH ADMINISTRATION OUTPUT SUMMARY			
	1991 Actual	**1992 Estimated**	**1993 Projected**
Treatment Equivalent Slots	636,389	633,368	669,696
Number of People Served	1,791,883	1,783,615	1,884,943
NIDA Research Grants	757	733	747
NIDA Demonstration Grants	124	113	113
Office of Substance Abuse Prevention Awards	751	772	709
Treatment Improvement Awards	201	184	243

Source: Office of National Drug Control Policy.

TABLE 21
U.S. FISH AND WILDLIFE SERVICE OUTPUT SUMMARY

	1991 Actual	1992 Estimated	1993 Projected
Marijuana Plants Destroyed	10,720	2,900	3,000
Drug-Related Arrests	44	60	60
Interdictions	59	115	115
Value of Drugs Seized	$44 million	$5 million	$10 million
Value of Marijuana Destroyed	$23 million	$6.2 million	$7 million

Source: Office of National Drug Control Policy.

TABLE 22
NATIONAL PARK SERVICE OUTPUT SUMMARY

	1991 Actual	1992 Estimated	1993 Projected
Marijuana Plants Destroyed	375,000	375,000	375,000
Drug-Related Arrests	4,300	4,300	4,300

Source: Office of National Drug Control Policy.

TABLE 23
U.S. ATTORNEYS OUTPUT SUMMARY

	1991 Actual	1992 Estimated	1993 Projected
Drug-Related Cases Filed	12,130	13,343	13,423
Drug-Related Convictions	3,065	3,376	3,400
Drug-Related Guilty Pleas	14,255	15,681	15,775

Source: Office of National Drug Control Policy.

TABLE 24
DRUG ENFORCEMENT ADMINISTRATION OUTPUT SUMMARY

	1991 Actual	1992 Estimated	1993 Projected
DEA Arrests	10,419	11,384	11,991
Other Federal Arrests	1,056	1,169	1,224
DEA Cooperative Arrests	3,651	4,040	4,232
State and Local Task Force Arrests	6,337	8,834	9,340
Foreign Cooperative Arrests	1,914	2,204	2,024
DEA/Organized Crime Force Arrests	3,805	4,138	4,315
Clandestine Labs Seized	309	324	341
Value of Assets Seized	$748 million	$876 million	$910 million
Federal Lab Exhibits Analyzed	38,300	41,000	41,000

Source: Office of National Drug Control Policy.

TABLE 25
U.S. COAST GUARD DRUG SEIZURES

	1991 Actual	1992 Estimated	1993 Projected
Cocaine (lbs.)	32,658	35,000	38,000
Marijuana (tons)	15	25	25
Vessels Seized	61	75	75
Arrests	106	150	150
Drug Cases with Coast Guard Involvement	155	175	175

Source: Office of National Drug Control Policy.

TABLE 26
U.S. CUSTOMS SERVICES OUTPUT SUMMARY
SEIZURES OF ASSETS (QUANTITY) AND DRUGS (POUNDS)

	1991 Actual	1992 Estimated	1993 Projected
Vessels	261	264	267
Aircraft	106	107	109
Vehicles	8,161	8,283	8,407
Monetary Instruments	$271 million	$275 million	$279 million
Heroin	2,960	3,000	3,050
Cocaine	169,856	172,130	174,700
Marijuana	287,520	291,830	296,200
Hashish	177,038	179,690	182,380

Source: Office of National Drug Control Policy.

Drug Spending by Users and Dealers

The economics of the drug trade are startling. Table 27 shows the costs to purchase 1 kilogram (2.2 pounds) of pure cocaine, using 1988 prices.

TABLE 27

**PRICES OF COCAINE AT VARIOUS LEVELS
OF DRUG TRAFFICKING IN 1988**

At the farm	$750
Upon export from Colombia	$2,000
Upon import to Miami	$15,000
Wholesale in Detroit, for a whole kilo	$23,000
Wholesale in Detroit, for a kilo in one-ounce units	$47,000
Retail, for a kilo in one-gram units	$135,000

Source: Mathea Falco, "Foreign Drugs, Foreign Wars," *Daedalus,* vol. 121, no. 3, Summer 1992, 8.

Advertising and Drugs

Ironically, while the United States is spending so much money and time trying to prevent the use of illicit psychoactive drugs, the manufacturers of the two legal psychoactive drugs, alcohol and tobacco, heavily advertise their products in an effort to sell more.

- The alcoholic beverage industry spends $1.2 billion per year on advertising. Three of the top 25 television advertisers are beer companies. (Source: NCADD.)
- Only about half of the fourth-graders in a 1987 study knew that beer, wine, and liquor are drugs. Almost 90 percent knew that marijuana is a drug. (Source: NCADD.)
- The tobacco industry spends $3.5 billion a year on advertising and promotion. Although tobacco ads have been banned from the nation's airwaves since 1970, tobacco company logos are prominent in sporting events the companies sponsor (e.g., the Virginia Slims Tennis Tournament). (Source: Americans for Nonsmokers' Rights.)

- Old Joe, the cartoon camel used to advertise Camel cigarettes, is as familiar to six-year-olds as Mickey Mouse. More than 90 percent of the children interviewed could link Old Joe with the product. Since Joe Camel was introduced in 1988, Camel's share of the (illegal) under-18 cigarette market has increased from 0.5 percent to 32.8 percent. (Source: Americans for Nonsmokers' Rights.)
- Commercials by Partnership for a Drug-Free America and prevention efforts by schools and parent groups have made a difference in children's perceptions of illicit drugs. In 1980, 31 percent of high school seniors believed that using cocaine was risky (mostly because of health, but also because of legal sanctions). Ten years later the figure was 59 percent. The percentage of seniors who reported that they disapproved of even infrequent use of cocaine rose from 76 percent in 1980 to 92 percent in 1990. During the same period, the percentage who disapproved of marijuana increased from 15 percent to 37 percent. (Source: NIDA.)

International Drug Trafficking

Although there were some encouraging signs during the 1980s in the war on drugs, recent statistics give officials little to cheer about on the international front. A State Department report issued in 1992 shows that production of coca and opium poppies, the raw materials of cocaine and heroin, has increased.

- The volume of coca leaf grown in 1992 is 8.2 percent higher than that of 1991, even though the number of acres devoted to coca production fell 2.6 percent. (Source: U.S. State Department.)
- The volume of opium grown in 1992 rose 6 percent, with the biggest increases occurring in Myanmar and Afghanistan. (Source: U.S. State Department.)
- In 1991, seizures of cocaine by the U.S. and Latin American governments amounted to 300 metric tons—a huge amount, but only about 1 percent of the total production. Street supplies of the drug were virtually unchanged. (Source: U.S. General Accounting Office.)

Treatment

A person with a drug-abuse problem may seek treatment as an in-patient in a hospital, an outpatient at a clinic or walk-in center, or in a long-term residential setting. Some of these institutions are devoted solely to drug and alcohol problems, while others also treat patients with nonsubstance disorders. (In that case, the people with substance-abuse cases are often housed in a separate unit.) A great many people also attend meetings of self-help groups such as Alcoholics Anonymous (AA) or Narcotics Anonymous (NA). Since these groups pride themselves on anonymity, it is difficult to estimate their total enrollment. Finally, many patients are treated by private physicians, particularly psychiatrists. Figure 11 gives the estimated daily totals for an average year.

FIGURE 11
TREATMENT FOR ALCOHOL AND DRUG ABUSE
ESTIMATED DAILY CENSUS, UNITED STATES, 1987*

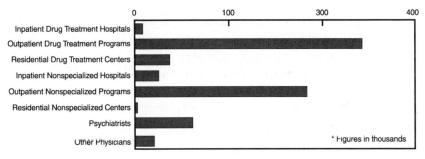

Source: Mark Schlesinger and Robert A. Dorwart, "Falling between the Cracks," *Daedalus,* vol. 121. no. 3, Summer 1992, 195.

The 12-step treatment programs all work from the basic steps written for Alcoholics Anonymous decades ago. Here are the 12 steps of AA:

1. We admitted we were powerless over alcohol—that our lives had become unmanageable.
2. Came to believe that a Power greater than ourselves could restore us to sanity.
3. Made a decision to turn our will and our lives over to the care of God as we understood Him.
4. Made a searching and fearless moral inventory of ourselves.

5. Admitted to God, to ourselves and to another human being the exact nature of our wrongs.
6. Were entirely ready to have God remove all these effects of character.
7. Humbly asked Him to remove our shortcomings.
8. Made a list of all persons we had harmed, and became willing to make amends to them all.
9. Made direct amends to such people wherever possible, except when to do so would injure them or others.
10. Continued to take personal inventory and when we were wrong promptly admitted it.
11. Sought through prayer and meditation to improve our conscious contact with God, as we understood Him, praying only for knowledge of His will for us and the power to carry that out.
12. Having had a spiritual awakening as the result of these steps, we tried to carry this message to alcoholics, and to practice these principles in all our affairs.

The Twelve Steps are reprinted with permission of Alcoholics Anonymous World Services, Inc. Permission to reprint and adapt the Twelve Steps does not mean that A.A. has reviewed or approved the contents of this publication nor that A.A. agrees with the views expressed herein. A.A. is a program of recovery from alcoholism—use of the Twelve Steps in connection with programs and activities, which are patterned after A.A., but which address other problems, does not imply otherwise.

Additional Information on Drug Treatment

- In the late 1970s and early 1980s, more private companies began to cover substance abuse in their health insurance plans. Since these plans generally reimburse hospitalization costs at a higher rate than outpatient therapy, hospitalization became a more popular treatment, even though most experts believe that short-term, inpatient treatment is less effective than other types of drug-abuse therapy. (Source: Mark Schlesinger and Robert A. Dorwart, "Falling between the Cracks," *Daedalus* [Summer 1992]: 201.)
- While private coverage soared, public funding for drug treatment declined. The poorest addicts had fewer

choices in the 1980s than in earlier decades. At many public clinics, addicts were placed on waiting lists for months. Recent increases in funding have not completely filled the gap. (Source: Schlesinger and Dorwart, 201.)

- In 1991, only 15–20 percent of all serious drug abusers received treatment. (Source: National Association of State Alcohol and Drug Abuse Directors.)
- A 1990 survey of drug-abuse treatment facilities found that more than 40 percent had more applicants for treatment than they could handle. (Source: NIDA, Drug Abuse Service Research Survey.)
- In 1992, more than 100,000 drug abusers were waiting for treatment. (Source: NIDA, Drug Abuse Service Research Survey.)
- In an effort to stem the spread of AIDS, the 1988 anti-drug law required that intravenous drug users suffering from AIDS be admitted to drug treatment programs within two weeks of applying. This rule is often broken because of overcrowded treatment centers. (Source: NIDA, National Drug and Alcohol Treatment Unit Survey.)
- Pregnant women are accepted to less than 40 percent of drug treatment programs. About a quarter of drug treat- ment programs will not accept applicants on Medicaid. (Source: NCADD.)
- Of the total number of substance abusers in treatment on an average day, about 60 percent are alcoholics and the rest are abusers of other drugs. (Source: ONDCP.)
- Each year about 500,000 admissions to community general hospitals and 100,000 admissions to veterans' hospitals are for drug or alcohol abuse. (Source: NIDA, National Drug and Alcohol Treatment Unit Survey.)

Documents

Three landmark speeches have marked major new federal initia- tives to fight drugs. The first was given by President Richard Nixon on 17 June 1971, when he launched an offensive against heroin, then the drug that most preoccupied the nation. The second, by President Ronald Reagan and his wife, Nancy Reagan, given on 14 September 1986, began the second war on drugs and focused on crack cocaine trafficking. The third was an address to the nation by President George Bush on September 5, 1989, when he told the country, "We need your help." The presidential speeches are followed by the transcript of an address by David Boaz, vice-president of the Cato Institute and a leading proponent of the legalization of drugs.

Richard Nixon: Remarks in the White House Briefing Room about an Intensified Program for Drug Abuse Prevention and Control, 17 June 1971

Ladies and Gentlemen:

I would like to summarize for you the meeting that I have just had with the bipartisan leaders which began at 8 o'clock and was completed 2 hours later.

I began the meeting by making this statement, which I think needs to be made to the Nation:

America's public enemy number one in the United States is drug abuse. In order to fight and defeat this enemy, it is necessary to wage a new, all-out offensive.

I have asked the Congress to provide the legislative authority and the funds to fuel this kind of an offensive. This will be a worldwide offensive dealing with the problems of sources of supply, as well as Americans who may be stationed abroad, wherever they are in the world. It will be governmentwide, pulling together the nine different fragmented areas within the government in which this problem is now being handled, and it will be nationwide in terms of a new educational program that we trust will result from the discussions that we have had.

With regard to this offensive, it is necessary first to have a new organization, and the new organization will be within the White House. Dr. Jaffe, who will be one of the briefers here today, will be the man directly responsible. He will report directly to me, and he will have the responsibility to take all of the Government agencies, nine, that deal with the problems of rehabilitation, in which his primary responsibilities will be research and education, and see that they work not at cross-purposes, but work together in dealing with the problem.

If we are going to have a successful offensive, we need more money. Consequently, I am asking Congress for $155 million in new funds, which will bring the total amount this year in the budget for drug abuse, both in enforcement and treatment, to over $350 million.

As far as the new money is concerned, incidentally, I have made it clear to the leaders that if this is not enough, if more can be used, if Dr. Jaffe, after studying this problem, finds that we can use more, more will be provided. In order to defeat this enemy which is causing such great concern, and correctly so, to so many American families, money will be provided to the extent that it is necessary and to the extent that it will be useful.

Finally, in order for this program to be effective, it is necessary that it be conducted on a basis in which the American people all join in it. That is why the meeting was bipartisan; bipartisan because we needed the support of the Congress, but bipartisan because we needed the leadership of the Members of the Congress in this field.

Fundamentally, it is essential for the American people to be alerted to this danger, to recognize that it is a danger that will not pass with the passing of the war in Vietnam which has brought to our attention that fact that a number of young Americans have become addicts as they serve abroad, whether in Vietnam, or Europe, or other places. Because the problem existed before we became involved in Vietnam; it will continue to exist afterwards. That is why this offensive deals with the problem there, in Europe, but will then go on to deal with the problem throughout America.

One final word with regard to Presidential responsibility in this respect. I very much hesitate always to bring some new responsibility into the White House, because there are so many here, and I believe in delegating those responsibilities to the departments. But I consider this problem so urgent—I also found that it was scattered so much throughout the Government, with so much conflict, without co-ordination—that it had to be brought into the White House.

Consequently, I have brought Dr. Jaffe into the White House, directly reporting to me, so that we have not only the responsibility but the authority to see that we wage this offensive effectively and in a coordinated way.

The briefing team will now be ready to answer any questions on the technical details of the program.

Ronald and Nancy Reagan: Address on Nationwide Television and Radio on the Campaign against Drug Abuse, 14 September 1986

The President. Good evening. Usually, I talk with you from my office in the West Wing of the White House. But tonight there's something special to talk about, and I've asked someone very special to join me. Nancy and I are here in the West Hall of the White House, and around us are the rooms in which we live. It's the home you've provided for us, of which we merely have temporary custody.

Nancy's joining me because the message this evening is not my message but ours. And we speak to you not simply as fellow citizens but as fellow parents and grandparents and as concerned neighbors. It's back-to-school time for America's children. And while drug and alcohol abuse cuts across all generations, it's especially damaging to the young people on whom our future depends. So tonight, from our family to yours, from our home to yours, thank you for joining us.

America has accomplished so much in these last few years, whether it's been rebuilding our economy or serving the cause of freedom in the world. What we've been able to achieve has been done with your help—with us working together as a nation united. Now, we need your support again. Drugs are menacing our society. They're threatening our values and undercutting our institutions. They're killing our children.

From the beginning of our administration, we've taken strong steps to do something about this horror. Tonight I can report to you that we've made much progress. Thirty-seven Federal agencies are working together in a vigorous national effort, and by next year our spending for drug law enforcement will have more than tripled from its 1981 levels. We have increased seizures of illegal drugs. Shortages of marijuana are now being reported. Last year alone over 10,000 drug criminals were convicted and nearly $250 million of their assets were seized by the DEA, the Drug Enforcement Administration.

And in the most important area, individual use, we see progress. In 4 years the number of high school seniors using marijuana on a daily basis has dropped from 1 in 14 to 1 in 20. The U.S. military has cut the use of illegal drugs among its personnel by 67 percent since 1980. These are a measure of our commitment and emerging signs that we can defeat this enemy. But we still have much to do.

Despite our best efforts, illegal cocaine is coming into our country at alarming levels, and 4 to 5 million people regularly use it. Five hundred thousand Americans are hooked on heroin. One in twelve persons smokes marijuana regularly. Regular drug use is even higher among the age group 18 to 25—most likely just entering the workforce. Today there's a new epidemic: smokable cocaine, otherwise known as crack. It is an explosively destructive and often lethal substance which is crushing its users. It is an uncontrolled fire.

And drug abuse is not a so-called victimless crime. Everyone's safety is at stake when drugs and excessive alcohol are used by people on the highways or by those transporting our citizens or operating industrial equipment. Drug abuse costs you and your fellow Americans at least $60 billion a year.

From the early days of our administration, Nancy has been intensely involved in the effort to fight drug abuse. She has since traveled over 100,000 miles to 55 cities in 28 States and 6 foreign countries to fight school-age drug and alcohol abuse. She's given dozens of speeches and scores of interviews and has participated in 24 special radio and TV tapings to create greater awareness of this crisis. Her personal observations and efforts have given her such dramatic insights that I wanted her to share them with you this evening.

Nancy.

Mrs. Reagan. Thank you. As a mother, I've always thought of September as a special month, a time when we bundled our children off to school, to the warmth of an environment in which they could fulfill the promise and hope in those restless minds. But so much has happened over these last years, so much to shake the foundations of all that we know and all that we believe in. Today there's a drug and alcohol abuse epidemic in this country, and no one is safe from it— not you, not me, and certainly not our children, because this epidemic has their names written on it. Many of you may be thinking: "Well, drugs don't concern me." But it does concern you. It concerns us all because of the way it tears at our lives and because it's aimed at destroying the brightness and life of the sons and daughters of the United States.

For 5 years I've been traveling across the country—learning and listening. And one of the most hopeful signs I've seen is the building of an essential, new awareness of how terrible and threatening drug abuse is to our society. This was one of the main purposes when I started, so of course it makes me happy that that's been accomplished. But each time I meet with someone new or receive another letter from a troubled person on drugs, I yearn to find a way to help share the message that cries out from them. As a parent, I'm especially concerned about what drugs are doing to young mothers and their newborn children. Listen to this news account from a hospital in Florida of a child born to a mother with a cocaine habit: "Nearby, a baby named Paul lies motionless in an incubator, feeding tubes riddling his tiny body. He needs a respirator to breathe and a daily spinal tap to relieve fluid buildup on his brain. Only 1 month old, he's already suffered 2 strokes."

Now you can see why drug abuse concerns every one of us—all the American family. Drugs steal away so much. They take and take, until finally every time a drug goes into a child, something else is forced out—like love and hope and trust and confidence. Drugs take away the dream from every child's heart and replace it with a nightmare, and it's time we in America stand up and replace those dreams. Each of us has to put our principles and consciences on the line, whether in social settings or in the workplace, to set forth solid standards and stick to them. There's no moral middle ground. Indifference is not an option. We want you to help us create an outspoken intolerance for drug use. For the sake of our children, I implore each of you to be unyielding and inflexible in your opposition to drugs.

Our young people are helping us lead the way. Not long ago, in Oakland, California, I was asked by a group of children what to do if they were offered drugs, and I answered, "Just say no." Soon after that, those children in Oakland formed a Just Say No club, and now there are over 10,000 such clubs all over the country. Well, their participation and their courage in saying no needs our encouragement. We can help by using every opportunity to force the issue of not using drugs to the point of making others uncomfortable, even if it means making ourselves unpopular.

Our job is never easy because drug criminals are ingenious. They work everyday to plot a new and better way to steal our children's lives, just as they've done by developing this new drug, crack. For every door that we close, they open a new door to death. They prosper on our unwillingness to act. So, we must be smarter and stronger and tougher than they are. It's up to us to change attitudes and just simply dry up their markets.

And finally, to young people watching or listening, I have a very personal message for you: There's a big, wonderful world out there for you. It belongs to you. It's exciting and stimulating and rewarding. Don't cheat yourselves out of this promise. Our country needs you, but it needs you to be clear-eyed and clear-minded. I recently read one teenager's story. She's now determined to stay clean but was once strung out on several drugs. What she remembered most clearly about her recovery was that during the time she was on drugs everything appeared to her in shades of black and gray and after her treatment she was able to see colors again.

So, to my young friends out there: Life can be great, but not when you can't see it. So, open your eyes to life: to see it in the vivid colors that God gave us as a precious gift to His children, to enjoy life to the fullest, and to make it count. Say yes to your life. And when it comes to drugs and alcohol just say no.

The President. I think you can see why Nancy has been such a positive influence on all that we're trying to do. The job ahead of us is very clear. Nancy's personal crusade, like that of so many other wonderful individuals, should become our national crusade. It must include a combination of government and private efforts which complement one another. Last month I announced six initiatives which we believe will do just that.

First, we seek a drug-free workplace at all levels of government and in the private sector. Second, we'll work toward drug-free schools. Third, we want to ensure that the public is protected and that treatment is available to substance abusers and the chemically dependent. Our fourth goal is to expand international cooperation while treating drug trafficking as a threat to our national security. In October I will be meeting with key U.S. Ambassadors to discuss what can be done to support our friends abroad. Fifth, we must move to strengthen law enforcement activities such as those initiated by Vice President Bush and Attorney General Meese. And finally, we seek to expand public awareness and prevention.

In order to further implement these six goals, I will announce tomorrow a series of new proposals for a drug-free America. Taken as a whole, these proposals will toughen our laws against drug criminals, encourage more research and treatment, and ensure that illegal drugs will not be tolerated in our schools or in our workplaces. Together with our ongoing efforts, these proposals will bring the Federal commitment to fighting drugs to $3 billion. As much financing as we commit, however, we would be fooling ourselves if we thought that massive new amounts of money alone will provide the solution. Let us not forget that in America people solve problems and no national crusade has ever succeeded without human investment. Winning the crusade against drugs will not be achieved by just throwing money at the problem.

Your government will continue to act aggressively, but nothing would be more effective than for Americans simply to quit using illegal drugs. We seek to create a massive change in national attitudes which ultimately will separate the drugs from the customer, to take the user away from the supply. I believe, quite simply, that we can help them quit, and that's where you come in.

My generation will remember how America swung into action when we were attacked in World War II. The war was not just fought by the fellows flying the planes or driving the tanks. It was fought at home by a mobilized nation—men and women alike—building planes and ships, clothing sailors and soldiers, feeding marines and airmen; and it was fought by children planting victory gardens and collecting cans. Well, now we're in another war for our freedom, and it's time for all of us to pull together again. So, for example, if your friend or neighbor or a family member has a drug or alcohol problem, don't turn the other way. Go to his help or to hers. Get others involved with you—clubs, service groups, and community organizations—and provide support and strength. And, of course, many of you've been cured through treatment and self-help. Well, you're the combat veterans, and you have a critical role to play. You can help others by telling your story and providing a willing hand to those in need. Being friends to others is the best way of being friends to ourselves. It's time, as Nancy said, for America to "just say no" to drugs.

Those of you in union halls and workplaces everywhere: Please make this challenge a part of your job every day. Help us preserve the health and dignity of all workers. To businesses large and small: We need the creativity of your enterprise applied directly to this national problem. Help us. And those of you who are educators: Your wisdom and leadership are indispensable to this cause. From the pulpits of this spiritfilled land: We would welcome your reassuring message of redemption and forgiveness and of helping one another. On the athletic fields: You men and women are among the most beloved citizens of our country. A child's eyes fill with your heroic achievements. Few of us can give youngsters something as special and strong to look up to as you. Please don't let them down.

And this camera in front of us: It's a reminder that in Nancy's and my former profession and in the newsrooms and production rooms of our media centers—you have a special opportunity with your enormous influence to send alarm signals across the Nation. To our friends in foreign countries: We know many of you are involved in this battle with us. We need your success as well as ours. When we all come together, united, striving for this cause, then those who are killing America and terrorizing it with slow but sure chemical destruction will see that they are up against the mightiest force for good that we know. Then they will have no dark alleyways to hide in.

In this crusade, let us not forget who we are. Drug abuse is a repudiation of everything America is. The destructiveness and human wreckage mock our heritage. Think for a moment how special it is to be an American. Can we doubt that only a divine providence placed this land, this island of freedom, here as a refuge for all those people on the world who yearn to breathe free?

The revolution out of which our liberty was conceived signaled an historical call to an entire world seeking hope. Each new arrival of immigrants rode the crest of that hope. They came, millions seeking a safe harbor from the oppression of cruel regimes. They came, to escape starvation and disease. They came, those surviving the Holocaust and the Soviet gulags. They came, the boat people, chancing death for even a glimmer of hope that they could have a new life. They all came to taste the air redolent and rich with the freedom that is ours. What an insult it will be to what we are and whence we came if we do not rise up together in defiance against this cancer of drugs.

And there's one more thing. The freedom that so many seek in our land has not been preserved without a price. Nancy and I shared that remembrance 2 years ago at the Normandy American Cemetery in France. In the still of that June afternoon, we walked together among the soldiers of freedom, past the hundreds of white markers which are monuments to courage and memorials to sacrifice. Too many of these and other such graves are the final resting places of teenagers who became men in the roar of battle.

Look what they gave to us who live. Never would they see another sunlit day glistening off a lake or river back home or miles of corn pushing up against the open sky of our plains. The pristine air of our mountains and the driving energy of our cities are theirs no more. Nor would they ever again be a son to their parents or a father to their own children. They did this for you, for me, for a new generation to carry our democratic experiment proudly forward. Well, that's something I think we're obliged to honor, because what they did for us means that we owe as a simple act of civic stewardship to use our freedom wisely for the common good.

As we mobilize for this national crusade, I'm mindful that drugs are a constant temptation for millions. Please remember this when your courage is tested: You are Americans. You're the product of the freest society mankind has ever known. No one, ever, has the right to destroy your dreams and shatter your life.

Right down the end of this hall is the Lincoln Bedroom. But in the Civil War that room was the one President Lincoln used as his office. Memory fills that room, and more than anything that memory drives us to see vividly what President Lincoln sought to save. Above all, it is that America must stand for something and that our heritage lets us stand with a strength of character made more steely by each layer of challenge pressed upon the Nation. We Americans have never been morally neutral against any form of tyranny. Tonight we're asking no more than that we honor what we have been and what we are by standing together.

Mrs. Reagan. Now we go on to the next stop: making a final commitment not to tolerate drugs by anyone, anytime, anyplace. So, won't you join us in this great, new national crusade?

The President. God bless you, and good night.

George Bush: Address on National Drug Control Strategy: We Need Your Help, 5 September 1989

This is the first time since taking the oath of office that I felt an issue was so important, so threatening, that it warranted talking directly with you, the American people. All of us agree that the gravest domestic threat facing our nation today is drugs.

Drugs have strained our faith in our system of justice. Our courts, our prisons, our legal system are stretched to the breaking point. The social costs of drugs are mounting. In short, drugs are sapping our strength as a nation.

Turn on the evening news, or pick up the morning paper and you'll see what some Americans know just by stepping out their front door: Our most serious problem today is cocaine, and in particular, crack.

Who's responsible?—Let me tell you straight out.

Everyone who uses drugs.

Everyone who sells drugs.

And everyone who looks the other way.

Tonight, I will tell you how many Americans are using illegal drugs. I will present to you our national strategy to deal with every aspect of this threat. And I will ask you to get involved in what promises to be a very difficult fight.

This is crack cocaine seized a few days ago by Drug Enforcement Administration agents in a park just across the street from the White House. It could easily have been heroin or PCP. It's as innocent-looking as candy, but it is turning our cities into battle zones, and it is murdering our children. Let there be no mistake, this stuff is poison.

Some used to call drugs harmless recreation. They're not. Drugs are real and a terribly dangerous threat to our neighborhoods, our friends and our families.

No one among us is out of harm's way. When 4-year-olds play in playgrounds strewn with discarded hypodermic needles and crack vials—it breaks my heart. When cocaine—one of the most deadly and addictive illegal drugs—is available to school kids—school kids—it's an outrage. And when hundreds of thousands of babies are born each year to mothers who use drugs—premature babies born desperately sick—then even the most defenseless among us are at risk.

These are the tragedies behind the statistics. But the numbers also have quite a story to tell. Let me share with you the results of the recently completed household survey of the National Institute on Drug Abuse. It compares recent drug use to three years ago. It tells us some good news and, some very bad news. First, the good.

As you can see in the chart, in 1985, the Government estimated that 23 million Americans were using drugs on a "current" basis—that is, at least once in the preceding month. Last year, that number fell by more than a third. That means almost nine million fewer Americans are casual drug users. Good news.

Because we changed our national attitude toward drugs, casual drug use has declined. We have many to thank: our brave law-enforcement officers, religious leaders, teachers, community activists, and leaders of business and labor. We should also thank the media for their exhaustive news and editorial coverage; and advertisers for running anti-drug messages.

Finally, I want to thank President and Mrs. Reagan for their leadership. All of these good people told the truth—that drug use is wrong and dangerous.

But, as much comfort as we can draw from these dramatic reductions, there is also bad news—very bad news. Roughly eight million people have used cocaine in the past year, almost one million of them used it frequently, once a week or more.

What this means is that, in spite of the fact that overall cocaine use is down, frequent use has almost doubled in the last few years. And that's why habitual cocaine users—especially crack users are the most pressing, immediate drug problem involving every family.

Earlier today, I sent this document, our first such national strategy to the Congress. It was developed with the hard work of our nation's first drug policy director, Bill Bennett. In preparing this plan, we talked with state, local and community leaders, law-enforcement officials and experts in education, drug prevention, and rehabilitation. We talked with parents and kids. We took a long hard look at all that the Federal Government has done about drugs in the past: what's worked, and—let's be honest—what hasn't. Too often, people in government acted as if their part of the problem—whether fighting drug production, or drug smuggling, or drug demand—was the only problem. But turf battles won't win this war. Teamwork will.

Tonight, I'm announcing a strategy that reflects the coordinated, cooperative commitment of all Federal agencies. In short, this plan is as comprehensive as the problem. With this strategy, we now finally have a plan that coordinates our resources, our programs and the people who run them.

Our weapons in this strategy are: the law and criminal justice system; our foreign policy; our treatment systems, and our schools and drug prevention programs. So the basic weapons we need are the ones we already have, what has been lacking is a strategy to effectively use them.

Let me address four of the major elements of our strategy.

First, we are determined to enforce the law, to make our streets and neighborhoods safe. So to start, I'm proposing that we more than double Federal assistance to state and local law enforcement. Americans have a right to safety in and around their homes.

And we won't have safe neighborhoods unless we are tough on drug criminals—much tougher than we are now. Sometimes that means tougher penalties. But more often it just means punishment that is swift and certain. We've all heard stores about drug dealers who are caught and arrested—again and again—but never punished. Well, here the rules have changed: If you sell drugs, you will be caught. And when you're caught, you will be prosecuted. And once you're convicted, you will do time. Caught. Prosecuted. Punished.

I am also proposing that we enlarge our criminal justice system across the board—at the local, state and Federal levels alike. We need more prisons, more jails, more courts, more prosecutors. So tonight, I'm requesting—altogether—an almost billion-and-a-half dollar increase in drug-related Federal spending on law enforcement.

And while illegal drug use is found in every community, nowhere is it worse than in our public housing projects. You know, the poor have never had it easy in this world. But in the past, they weren't mugged on the way home from work by crack gangs. And their children didn't have to dodge bullets on the way to school. That is why I'm targeting $50 million to fight crime in public housing projects—to help restore order, and to kick out the dealers for good.

The second element of our strategy looks beyond our borders, where the cocaine and crack, bought on America's streets, is grown and processed. In Colombia alone, cocaine killers have gunned down a leading statesman, murdered almost 200 judges and seven members of their Supreme Court. The besieged governments of the drug-producing countries are fighting back, fighting to break the international drug rings. But you and I agree with the courageous President of Colombia, Virgilio Barco, who said that if Americans use cocaine, then Americans are paying for murder. American cocaine users need to understand that our nation has zero tolerance for casual drug use. We have a responsibility not to leave our brave friends in Colombia to fight alone.

The $65 million emergency assistance announced two weeks ago was just our first step in assisting Andean nations in their fight against the cocaine cartels. Colombia has already arrested suppliers, seized tons of cocaine and confiscated palatial homes of drug lords. But Colombia faces a long, uphill battle, so we must be ready to do more.

Our strategy allocates more than a quarter of a billion dollars for next year in military and law enforcement assistance for the three Andean nations of Colombia, Bolivia and Peru. This will be the first part of a five-year, $2 billion program to counter the producers, the traffickers and the smugglers.

I spoke with President Barco last week, and we hope to meet with the leaders of affected countries in an unprecedented drug summit, all to coordinate an inter-American strategy against the cartels. We will work with our allies and friends—especially our economic summit partners—to do more in the fight against drugs. I'm also asking the Senate to ratify the U.N. anti-drug convention concluded last December.

To stop those drugs on the way to America, I propose that we spend more than a billion-and-a-half dollars on interdiction. Greater interagency cooperation, combined with Defense Department technology can help stop drugs at our borders.

Our message to the drug cartels is this: The rules have changed. We will help any government that wants our help. When requested, we will for the first time make available the appropriate resources of America's armed forces. We will intensify our efforts against drug smugglers on the high seas, in international airspace and at our borders. We will stop the flow of chemicals from the United States used to process drugs. We will pursue and enforce international agreements to track drug money to the front men and financiers. And then we will handcuff these money launderers, and jail them—just like any street dealer. And for drug kingpins, the death penalty.

The third part of our strategy concerns drug treatment. Experts believe that there are two million American drug users who may be able to get off drugs with proper treatment. But right now, only 40 percent of them are actually getting help. This is simply not good enough.

Many people who need treatment won't seek it on their own. And some who do seek it are put on a waiting list. Most programs were set up to deal with heroin addicts. But today, the major problem is cocaine users. It's time we expand our treatment systems and do a better job of providing services to those who need them.

So tonight, I'm proposing an increase of $322 million in Federal spending on drug treatment.

With this strategy, we will do more. We will work with the states. We will encourage employers to establish employee assistance programs to cope with drug use. And, because addiction is such a cruel inheritance, we will intensify our search for ways to help expectant mothers who use drugs.

Fourth, we must stop illegal drug use before it starts. Unfortunately, it begins early—for many kids, before their teens. But it doesn't start the way you might think, from a dealer or an addict hanging around a school playground. More often, our kids first get their drugs free, from friends, or even from older brothers or sisters. Peer pressure spreads drug use. Peer pressure can help stop it.

I am proposing a quarter-of-a-billion-dollar increase in Federal funds for school and community prevention programs that help young people and adults reject enticements to try drugs. And I'm proposing something else. Every school, college and university—and every workplace—must adopt tough but fair policies about drug use by students and employees. Those that will not adopt such policies will not get Federal funds. Period.

The private sector also has a role to play. I spoke with a businessman named Jim Burke who said he was haunted by the thought—a nightmare really—that somewhere in America, at any given moment, there is a teen-age girl who should be in school, instead of giving birth to a child addicted to cocaine. So Jim did something. He led an anti-drug partnership, financed by private funds, to work with advertisers and media firms. Their partnership is now determined to work with our strategy by generating a million dollars worth of air time every day for the next three years—a billion dollars total. Think of it, a billion dollars of television time, all to promote the anti-drug message.

As President, one of my first missions is to keep the national focus on our offensive against drugs. So next week I will take the anti-drug message to the classrooms of America in a special televison address, one that I hope will reach every school, every young American. But drug education doesn't begin in class or on TV. It must begin at home and in the neighborhood. Parents and families must set the first example of a drug-free life. And when families are broken, caring friends and neighbors must step in.

These are the most important elements in our strategy to fight drugs. They are all designed to reinforce one another, to mesh into a powerful whole. To mount an aggressive attack on the problem from every angle. This is the first time in the history of our country that we truly have a comprehensive strategy.

As you can tell, such an approach will not come cheaply. Last February, I asked for a $700 million increase in the drug budget for the coming year. Over the past six months of careful study, we have found an immediate need for another billion-and-a-half dollars. With this added $2.2 billion, our 1990 drug budget totals almost $8 billion—the largest increase in history.

We need this program fully implemented—right away. The next fiscal year begins just 26 days from now. So tonight I'm asking the Congress—which has helped us formulate this strategy—to help us move it forward immediately.

We can pay for this fight against drugs without raising our taxes or adding to the budget deficit. We have submitted our plan to Congress that shows just how to fund it within the limits of our bipartisan budget agreement.

I know some will still say we are not spending enough money. But those who judge our strategy only by its price tag, simply don't understand the problem. Let's face it, we've all seen in the past that money alone won't solve our toughest problems.

To be strong and efficient, our strategy needs these funds. But there is no match for a united America, a determined America, an angry America. Our outrage against drugs unites us, brings us together behind this one plan of action, an assault on every front.

This is the toughest domestic challenge we've faced in decades. And it is a challenge we must face—not as Democrats or Republicans, liberals or conservatives—but as Americans. The key is a coordinated, united effort. We have responded faithfully to the request of the Congress to produce our nation's first national drug strategy. I'll be looking to the Democratic majority and our Republicans in Congress for leadership and bipartisan support. And our citizens deserve cooperation, not competition; a national effort, not a partisan bidding war.

To start, Congress needs not only to act on this national drug strategy, but also to act on our crime package announced last May; a package to toughen sentences, beef up law enforcement and build new prison space for 24,000 inmates.

You and I both know the Federal Government can't do it alone. The states need to match tougher Federal laws with tougher laws of their own—stiffer bail, probation, parole and sentencing.

And we need your help. If people you know are users, help them get off drugs. If you are a parent, talk to your children about drugs—tonight.

Call your local drug prevention program. Be a big brother or sister to a child in need. Pitch in with your local neighborhood watch program. Whether you give your time or talent, everyone counts.

Every employer who bans drugs from the workplace.

Every school that's tough on drug use.

Every neighborhood in which drugs are not welcome.

And most important, every one of you who refuses to look the other way. Every one of you counts.

Of course, victory will take hard work and time. But together we will win—too many young lives are at stake.

Not long ago, I read a newspaper story about a little boy named Dooney, who, until recently, lived in a crack house in a suburb of Washington, D.C. In Dooney's neighborhood, children don't flinch at the sound of gunfire. And when they play, they pretend to sell to each other small white rocks they call crack.

Life at home was so cruel that Dooney begged his teachers to let him sleep on the floor at school. And, when asked about his future, 6-year-old Dooney answered: "I don't want to sell drugs, but I will probably have to."

Well, Dooney does not have to sell drugs. No child in America should have to live like this. Together, as a people, we can save these kids. We have already transformed a national attitude of tolerance into one of condemnation. But the war on drugs will be hard-won, neighborhood by neighborhood, block by block, child by child.

If we fight this war as a divided nation, then the war is lost. But, if we face this evil as a nation united, this will be nothing but a handful of useless chemicals.

Victory. Victory over drugs is our cause, a just cause, and with your help, we are going to win.

Thank you, God bless you and good night.

David Boaz: The Legalization of Drugs: Decriminalization, 27 April 1988

Let me start this discussion of drug prohibition by reading the following quotation: "For thirteen years federal law enforcement officials fought the illegal traffic. State and local reinforcements were called up to help. The fight was always frustrating and too often futile. The enemy used guerrilla tactics, seldom came into the open to fight, blended easily into the general population, and when finally subdued turned to the United States Constitution for protection. His numbers were legion, his resources unlimited, his tactics imaginative. Men of high resolve and determination were summoned to Washington to direct the federal forces. The enemy was pursued relentlessly on land and sea and in the air. There were an alarming number of casualties on both sides, and, as in all wars, innocent bystanders fell in the crossfire."

Well, you may have guessed that although I read that recently, it wasn't written recently. It was written about the prohibition of alcohol in the 1920s, and it illustrates a very simple thesis of my talk: Alcohol didn't cause the high crime rates of the 1920s, prohibition did. Drugs don't cause today's alarming crime rates, drug prohibition does.

What are the effects of prohibition? (Specifically I'm talking here about drug prohibition, but the analysis applies to almost any prohibition of a substance or activity people want.) The first effect is crime. This is a very simple matter of economics. Drug laws reduce the number of suppliers and therefore reduce the supply of the substance, driving up the price. The danger of arrest for the seller adds a risk premium to the price. The higher price means that users often have to commit crimes to pay for a habit that would be easily affordable if it was legal. Heroin, cocaine, and other drugs would cost much less if they were legal.

Crime also results from another factor, the fact that dealers have no way to settle disputes with each other except by shooting each other. You don't see shoot-outs in the car business, you don't see shoot-outs even in the liquor or the tobacco business. But if you have a dispute with another drug dealer, if he rips you off, you can't sue him, you can't take him to court, you can't do anything except use violence.

And then the very illegality of the drug business draws in criminals. As conservatives always say about guns, if drugs are out-lawed, only outlaws will sell drugs. The decent people who would like to be selling drugs the way they might otherwise sell liquor will get squeezed out of an increasingly violent business.

The second effect of prohibition is corruption. Prohibition raises prices, which leads to extraordinary profits, which are an irresistible temptation to policemen, customs officers, Latin American officials, and so on. We should be shocked not that there are Miami policemen on the take, but that there are some Miami policemen not on the take. Policemen make $35,000 a year and have to arrest people who are driving cars worth several times that. Should we be surprised that some of this money trickles down into the pockets of these policemen?

A third effect, and one that is often underestimated, is bringing buyers into contact with criminals. If you buy alcohol you don't have to deal with criminals. If you buy marijuana on a college campus, you may not have to deal with criminals, but maybe the person you bought it from does deal with criminals. And if you are a high school student, there is a very good chance that the people you're buying drugs from— the people who are bringing drugs right to your doorstep, to your housing project, to your schoolyard—are really criminals; not just in the sense that they are selling drugs, but these are really criminal types. One of the strongest arguments for legalization is to divorce the process of using drugs from the process of getting involved in a criminal culture.

A fourth effect is the creation of stronger drugs. Richard Cowan in *National Review* has promulated what he calls the iron law of prohibition: The more intense the law enforcement, the more potent the drugs will become. If you can only smuggle one suitcase full of drugs into the United States or if you can only drive one car full of drugs into Baltimore, which would you rather be carrying— marijuana, coca leaves, cocaine, or crack? You get more dollars for the bulk if you carry more potent drugs. An early example of that is that a lot of people turned to marijuana when alcohol became more difficult to get during Prohibition. A few years after Prohibition began in the 1920s there began to be pressures for laws against marijuana. When you talk about drug legalization, one of the questions you will get is, "Well, marijuana is one thing, maybe even cocaine, but are you seriously saying you would legalize crack?" And the answer is that crack is almost entirely a product of prohibition. It probably would not have existed under a legalized system.

The fifth effect of prohibition is civil liberties abuses. I think the authorities actually overstepped their bounds recently when they seized a yacht because there was a quarter gram of marijuana on it, and there wasn't even anybody on the yacht except the crew, not one of whom could be connected to the marijuana. After a public uproar they actually had to back off. But I recall a time in this country when the government was only allowed to punish you after you got convicted in a court of law. It now appears that they can punish you by seizing your car or your boat, not even after an indictment—much less a conviction—but after a mere allegation by a police officer.

There is an inherent problem of civil liberties abuses in victimless crimes. Randy Barnett wrote about this in the Pacific Research Institute book *Dealing with Drugs;* the problem is that with victimless crimes like buying drugs there is no complaining witness. In most crimes, say robbery or rape, there is a person who in our legal system is called the complaining witness: the person who was robbed or raped, who goes to the police and complains that somebody has done something to him or her. When you buy drugs, neither party to the transaction complains. Now what does this mean? It means you don't have eyewitnesses complaining about the problem so the police have to get the evidence somewhere else. The policemen have to start going undercover, and that leads to entrapment, wiretapping, and all sorts of things that border on civil liberties abuses and usually end up crossing the border.

The sixth effect of prohibition is futility. The drug war simply isn't working. I was asked the other day by a *Washington Post* reporter, isn't a lot of the support for legalization that we're seeing from politicians and others merely a sign of frustration? And I said, frustration is a rational response to futility. It's quite understandable why people have gotten frustrated with the continuing failure of new enforcement policies.

If you are involved in a war and you're not winning, you have two basic choices. The first is escalation, and we've seen a lot of proposals for that.

New York Mayor Ed Koch has proposed to strip-search every person entering the United States from South America or Southeast Asia. Members of the D.C. City Council have called for the National Guard to occupy the capital city of the United States. Bob Dole has called for the death penalty for drug sellers. George Bush, trying to prove that he's no wimp, has upped the ante: he wants *swift* execution of drug dealers. Bush said, "Due process is fine, but we've got to find a way to speed it up." He was asked, how do you get around the due process problem? He responded, "I don't know the answer to that. I'm not a lawyer." Presumably his attorney general will be one, for a change.

On the other side of the political spectrum, Jesse Jackson wants to bring the troops home from Europe and use them to ring our southern border. The police chief of Los Angeles wants to invade Colombia.

The White House drug adviser and the usually sensible *Wall Street Journal* editorial page have called for arresting small-time users. The *Journal*, with its usual spirit, urged the government to "crush the users"; that's 23 million Americans.

The Justice Department wants to double our prison capacity even though we already have far more people in prison as a percentage of our population than any other industrialized country except South Africa. Ed Meese wants to drug test all workers.

The Customs Service has asked for authorization to "use appropriate force" to compel planes suspected of carrying drugs to land. It has clarified, in case there was any doubt, that yes, it means that if it can't find out what a plane is up to, it wants the authority to shoot the plane down and then find out if it's carrying drugs. These rather frightening ideas represent one response to the futility of the drug war.

The more sensible response, it seems to me, is to decriminalize—to de-escalate, to realize that trying to wage war on 23 million Americans who are obviously very committed to certain recreational activities is not going to be any more successful than Prohibition was. A lot of people use drugs recreationally and peacefully and safely and are not going to go along with this "zero tolerance" idea. They're going to keep trying to get drugs. The problems caused by prohibition are not going to be solved by stepped-up enforcement.

What would be the effects of decriminalization? The concern that most people have is that there would be more drug users. I'm not sure that's true. There are several factors that point in the other direction. One is the forbidden fruit aspect of drugs: because they're illegal, a lot of young people are tempted to give them a try. It's probably also true that both cultural and personality factors are more important than price or legality in determining whether people are going to use drugs. Similarly, consider how drugs would be sold. There would be only print advertising of legal drugs; we would surely ban television ads, as we do with liquor and tobacco. You would go to, say, a liquor store where you would find these drugs with a warning label on them and available only to adults. That system might well be less effective in getting drugs to young people than schoolyard pushers are—and you wouldn't have schoolyard pushers. Those are a number of reasons why drug use might fall after legalization.

Having said all that, I will say I think it is likely that there would be more users of drugs that are currently illegal. There would be somewhat more users, I suspect, using cleaner, safer drugs and dying less often. And of course to the extent that there is drug switchng, it's not at all clear that people switching from alcohol to marijuana are doing anything more dangerous; in fact, the medical evidence is almost overwhelming that if you switch from either alcohol or tobacco to marijuana and probably even to other illegal drugs you are more likely to live a long and healthy life.

Most people use drugs recreationally; they're not abusers. The National Institute of Drug Abuse survey of cocaine users under 25 years old found that 250,000 young people used cocaine weekly. But 2.5 million had used it in the past month, 5.3 million had used it in the past year, and more than 8 million had tried cocaine. Now the key point here is that 8 million young people have tried cocaine of which 250,000 used it weekly. Surely those who use it weekly are the only ones who could be considered to have a cocaine problem; and indeed many of those people don't have a problem that requires any kind of attention.

It is generally estimated that there are 100,000 deaths a year in the United States from alcohol, 300,000 deaths a year from tobacco,

and only 3,500 deaths from all illegal drugs—and of those, 80 percent
are a result of prohibition, not of the drugs themselves.

It's important to look at what's happening with both illegal and
legal drugs right now. Illegal drugs, for the reasons I explained, are
getting stronger. Crack is replacing cocaine and so on. But legal drugs
are getting weaker. We're seeing increased demand for low-tar cigarettes, a shift away from hard liquor toward beer and wine, a shift
from wine to wine coolers. In the long run there is a trend away from
dangerous drugs in the United States. Right now, despite all the
hysteria, there is probably less usage of marijuana and cocaine, as well
as alcohol and tobacco, than there was five years ago. And I don't
think that prohibition or legalization will have a whole lot of effect on
that, except that possibly under legalization health and safety warnings
will be taken more seriously because they will not be viewed as just a
way of justifying this political crusade. We'll actually listen to them the
way we listen to the surgeon general on tobacco.

In the long run, however, if you ask me what will happen to drug
use, I would simply say, as Bernard Baruch said of the stock market, it
will fluctuate. And there's not a lot that public policy can do about it
one way or the other. There will at some points in our future be more
drug use than there is today, there will at other points be less. My
guess is that there will be a general downward trend.

Finally, the clearest effect of legalization would be less crime. Estimates are that anywhere from 40 to 70 percent of the violent crime
in urban areas— robberies, burglaries, and killings—is related to
the prohibition of drugs. A lot of policemen will tell you this off the
record. A friend of mine, in a big-city prosecutor's office, told me just
the other day that her colleagues had talked a lot about Baltimore
Mayor Kurt Schmoke's proposal for decriminalizing drugs. She said
that a surprising number of people in the district attorney's office
think that he is right—including a lot of the cops on the beat. They
say he's right that it's futile, that it causes more crime, and that there
is no way around that problem.

Let me say just a word here about the shift in public opinion.
Over the last couple of months we have seen a lot of new interest in
legalization. We've seen Mayor Schmoke issue a very stirring call for a
national debate on the issue. If you read his reasons for why there
should be a national debate, it's very clear that he believes legalization
is preferable to continuing the drug war. We've seen D.C. Mayor
Marion Barry and Rep. Steny Hoyer (D-Md.) also saying that it's time
for a national debate.

Interestingly, a month ago, you would almost have said this was
more a conservative issue than a liberal issue. People like William F.
Buckley, Jr., and Ernest van den Haag, economists like Milton
Friedman and Gary Becker, and the British magazine the *Economist*

all had endorsed some kind of decriminalization or legalization. Only in the past month or so have we finally seen liberals—who are supposed to protect individual rights—stepping out on this issue. Mayor Schmoke and Mayor Barry have been joined by Rep. Pete Stark (D-Ca.) and Mayor Donald Fraser of Minneapolis. Now state senator Joseph Galiber, a liberal Democrat from the Bronx, has introduced a bill to legalize drugs in New York. Now we're seeing drug legalization discusssed on the front pages of both the *Washington Post* and the *New York Times,* in *Time* and *Newsweek,* on "Nightline," "This Week with David Brinkley," and the "CBS Evening News."

We are approaching the point where we're going to keep passing stricter drug laws until the day that we finally give up and decriminalize drugs. People recognize that what we're doing isn't working. So we're going to keep stepping up enforcement but at the same time, more and more people are going to be recognizing the futility of the drug war. And at some point in the not-too-distant future there will be a critical mass in favor of decriminalization. Not in favor of saying drugs are okay, not necessarily even endorsing the attitude that people have the right to do with their own bodies what they want to do, but recognizing on health and safety and economic grounds that this effort at prohibition is not going to be any more successful than the previous one.

The preceeding speech was delivered before the Drug Policy Forum, Washington, D.C. Reprinted with permission.

5

Organizations, Government Agencies, and Helplines

THE SCOPE OF THE DRUG PROBLEM in the United States has mobilized both government agencies and private groups. In this chapter, sources of help and information are listed: public and private helplines for treatment referrals and emergency information, clearinghouses and computer bulletin boards providing information on drugs and related issues, federal and state government agencies dealing with nonemergency requests, and private organizations.

Helplines

Helplines offer information and treatment referrals to drug abusers and to those who care about them. Helplines are operated by the federal government as well as by private organizations.

Government Helpline

Drug Abuse Information and Treatment Referral Line
5600 Fishers Lane
Rockville, MD 20857
(800) 662-HELP
(800) 66-AYUDA, Spanish-language hotline

Hours: Monday through Friday, 9 A.M. to 3 A.M. Eastern time, and Saturday and Sunday, 12 P.M. to 3 A.M. Eastern time.

Operated by the National Institute on Drug Abuse (NIDA), the referral line provides information about various drugs, types of treatment, support groups, and other services. Trained counselors will make referrals to state and local treatment programs (both nonprofit and profit). All calls are confidential.

Privately Operated Helplines

(800) COCAINE

This helpline, founded by Dr. Mark S. Gold, is operated as a public service by Fair Oaks Hospital in Summit, New Jersey. The helpline is operated 24 hours a day, every day. All calls are confidential. Callers may inquire about the effects of cocaine or ask for referrals to treatment programs. Although the service is not intended as a crisis hotline, the counselors will refer callers with immediate needs to someone who can help.

(800) NCA-CALL

The National Council on Alcoholism and Drug Dependence (NCADD) information line provides information about NCADD's state and local affiliates and makes referrals to families and individuals seeking help with alcohol and other psychoactive drug problems.

The Pride Helpline: (800) 241-9746

The PRIDE (Parents' Resource Institute for Drug Education) helpline refers concerned parents to parent groups in their area, answers questions on forming anti-drug groups, and provides telephone consultations and referrals to emergency health centers.

Information Helplines and Bulletin Boards

Public and private agencies provide telephone and computer bulletin board information services for those who are seeking statistics and other facts about drug abuse in American society.

Federal Clearinghouses

The federal government clearinghouses for information about drugs, crime, and health issues may be reached on toll-free phone numbers or by mail. Each clearinghouse is staffed with experts armed with statistics and a wealth of information. These services are free.

Drug Information and Strategy Clearinghouse
P.O. Box 6424
Rockville, MD 20850
(301) 251-5154, in Washington, D.C.
(800) 245-2691, outside Washington, D.C.
Hours: Monday through Friday, 9 A.M. to 6 P.M. Eastern time.

Under the auspices of the Office for Drug-Free Neighborhoods in the U.S. Department of Housing and Urban Development (HUD), this clearinghouse has information about the prevention and control of drug trafficking in public housing around the nation. Residents of housing projects may call for help with creating anti-drug plans, HUD regulations, and free brochures on prevention, management, and enforcement of anti-drug policies. Information specialists will search computer databases on programs, publications, news articles, and letters about public housing and drugs.

Drug-Free Workplace Helpline
(800) 843-4971
Hours: Monday through Friday, 9 A.M. to 8 P.M. Eastern time.

Operated by NIDA, the helpline assists business, industry, and the work force on the development and implementation of comprehensive drug-free workplace programs. Callers may consult with experts on the phone or receive referrals to other workplace resources.

Drugs and Crime Data Center and Clearinghouse
1600 Research Boulevard
Rockville, MD 20850
(800) 666-3332
Hours: Monday through Friday, 8:30 A.M. to 5:15 P.M. Eastern time.

This division of the Bureau of Justice Statistics provides telephone help to callers interested in information on the correlation between drugs and crime. Experts answer questions such as, How many arrestees in Washington, D.C., tested positive for cocaine last year? The clearinghouse also maintains a bibliographic database and a library of over 3,500 listings. Upon request, the clearinghouse will send callers free publications about drugs and crime; a catalogue is also available. The clearinghouse also refers callers to state anti-drug resources.

National AIDS Clearinghouse
P.O. Box 6003
Rockville, MD 20849-6003
(800) 458-5231
(800) 243-7012, TTY line
Hours: Monday through Friday, 9 A.M. to 7 P.M. Eastern time.

How many HIV-positive babies will be born this year to abusers of IV drugs? This kind of question can be answered by experts at the National AIDS Clearinghouse. Operated by the federal Centers for Disease Control, this clearinghouse is intended primarily for health professionals, but it also assists the general public with information about AIDS. The clearinghouse distributes educational materials and maintains a computerized database of materials, service organizations, funding, and conferences on AIDS. Information is also available in Spanish.

National Clearinghouse for Alcohol and Drug Information (NCADI)
P.O. Box 2345
Rockville, MD 20852
(301) 468-2600, in Washington, D.C.
(800) 729-6686, outside Washington, D.C.
Hours: Monday through Friday, 9 A.M. to 7 P.M. Eastern time.

NCADI, a division of the Office for Substance Abuse Prevention in the U.S. Department of Health and Human Services, provides every type of information about psychoactive drugs, including alcohol. Questions such as, How many teens took LSD last month? and Is cocaine use declining? may be answered here. Services of NCADI include telephone statistics and information as well as free fact sheets, posters, videotapes, and other materials; a catalogue is available upon request. NCADI also publishes *Prevention Pipeline,* a bimonthly with the latest research and information about psychoactive drugs. It maintains a library and a bibliographic network of drug information. NCADI also provides access to educational and medical databases like ERIC, MEDLINE, and DRUGINFO.

National Criminal Justice Reference Service (NCJRS)
National Institute of Justice
P.O. Box 6000
Rockville, MD 20850
(301) 251-5500, in Washington D.C.
(800) 851-3420, outside Washington, D.C.
Hours: Monday through Friday, 8:30 A.M. to 7 P.M. Eastern time.

NCJRS provides information on drugs and crime, including drug testing, drug-control enforcement, sentencing, and prevention and treatment offered in the justice system. Information specialists will supply such facts as the average sentence for drug-related crimes or the number of positive tests for marijuana among those arrested. NCJRS also conducts bibliographic searches and has a CD-ROM library on drugs and crime. Upon request, NCJRS will supply written reports of the Drug Use Forecasting program (DUF), which collects data on drug use among nondrug arrestees in 22 U.S. cities.

These six clearinghouses may also be reached by calling a single phone number: (800) 788-2800. This number is useful for obtaining information from more than one source or if a caller does not know which clearinghouse is appropriate.

Computer Bulletin Boards

Bureau of Justice Statistics (BJS)
(301) 738-8895, bulletin board number
(800) 732-3277, information number
Hours: 24 hours a day.

This electronic bulletin board offers seven options:

1. BJS press releases
2. Latest BJS findings
3. Justice Statistics Clearinghouse Information
4. BJS conferences
5. News from the Drugs and Crime Data Center and Clearinghouse
6. National Archive of Criminal Justice Data
7. News from State Statistical Analysis Centers

Center for Substance Abuse Research (CESAR)
(301) 403-8343, bulletin board number
(800) 84-CESAR, bulletin board number

CESAR provides information about drugs and alcohol in the state of Maryland, as well as information on national drug trends, research reports, and bibliographies. The bulletin board is sponsored by the Maryland Drug and Alcohol Abuse Commission.

SEARCH Group, Inc.
(916) 392-8440, bulletin board access number

This service, operated by the National Consortium for Justice Information and Statistics, offers criminal justice publications, workshop and training notices, shareware, and a database identifying criminal justice agencies and their computerized information statistics.

Government Agencies

Federal Agencies

Drug Enforcement Administration (DEA)
Demand Reduction Section
Washington, DC 20537
(202) 307-7936

The DEA was created in 1973 by President Richard Nixon. The DEA, part of the Department of Justice, is responsible for enforcing federal laws dealing with illicit drugs. The DEA investigates illegal drug traffic, distribution, and processing. It also operates the Demand Reduction Program, creating drug-prevention programs for high school athletes, school clubs, and businesses. The DEA Demand Reduction Program works with professional athletes in football, basketball, and baseball. Speakers include law enforcement agents as well as drug-free major league athletes.

National Institute on Drug Abuse (NIDA)
5600 Fishers Lane
Rockville, MD 20857
(301) 443-6245

NIDA was established in 1974. It is the leading federal agency for research into the incidence, causes, prevention, and treatment of drug abuse. NIDA makes grants to research institutions around the country for the investigation of the underlying biological and biochemical mechanisms of drug abuse and addiction, the specific effects of drugs of abuse, the prevalence of drug abuse, treatment and prevention strategies, causes and consequences of drug abuse in the workplace and during pregnancy, the role of drugs in the spread of AIDS, and the identification of risk factors in drug abuse. NIDA also conducts in-house studies through the Addiction Research Center (ARC) and coordinates epidemiological surveys of drug use.

PUBLICATIONS: *NIDA Capsules* are short, factual summaries on topics such as PCP, designer drugs, and mandatory guidelines for federal drug-testing programs.

Office for Substance Abuse Prevention (OSAP)
Alcohol, Drug Abuse, and Mental Health Administration
5600 Fishers Lane
Rockwall II Building
Rockville, MD 20857
(301) 443-0365
(301) 468-2600, for monographs
(800) 729-6686, for monographs

OSAP was created by the Anti–Drug Abuse Act of 1988 "to lead the federal government's efforts toward the prevention and intervention of alcohol and other drug problems among the nation's citizens, with special emphasis on youth and families living in high-risk environments." OSAP carries out demonstration projects, assists communities in developing local prevention programs, operates a clearinghouse for drug information, runs media campaigns, and supports a national training system for health professionals. OSAP collaborates with the U.S. Department of Education and Department of Transportation to prevent traffic safety problems caused by alcohol and other drugs.

PUBLICATIONS: Prevention monographs include *Stopping Alcohol and Other Drug Use before It Starts; Prevention of Mental Disorders; Alcohol and Drug Use in Children and Adolescents; Research, Action, and the Community: Experiences in the Prevention of Alcohol and Other Drug Problems;* and many more. OSAP also publishes a bimonthly magazine, *Prevention Pipeline,* with information on drug prevention efforts and the latest research on drug abuse ($20/year).

State Agencies

Besides the federal government, each state maintains an office for drug-abuse prevention called Regional Alcohol and Drug Awareness Resource (RADAR). RADAR offices often supply free educational materials to those seeking to create school or community prevention programs or to students seeking information. The states also have offices for HIV prevention, which provide information on AIDS, including AIDS contracted through IV drug use, and coordinators for drug-free schools, who assist teachers, administrators, and students. The addresses and phone numbers for these and other state agencies that deal with drug abuse are listed below.

Alabama

Alabama Division of Mental Illness and Substance Abuse
Community Programs
Department of Mental Health
200 Interstate Park Drive
P.O. Box 3710
Montgomery, AL 36193-5001
(205) 271-9253

Drug-Free Schools
State Department of Education
50 North Ripley Street
Montgomery, AL 36130
(205) 242-8083

HIV Prevention
Department of Public Health
AIDS/STD Program
434 Monroe Street
Montgomery, AL 36230
(205) 261-5838

RADAR
Alabama Department of Mental Health/Mental Retardation
P.O. Box 3710
200 Interstate Park Drive
Montgomery, AL 36193
(205) 271-9258

Alaska

Alaska Department of Education
Drug-Free Schools Program
801 West 10th Street, Suite 200
Juneau, AK 99801-1894
(907) 465-2824

Drug and Alcohol Agency
Division of Alcoholism and Drug Abuse
Department of Health and Social Services
P.O. Box 110607
Juneau, AK 99811-0607
(907) 586-6201

HIV Prevention
AIDS Program
Section of Epidemiology
Division of Public Health
3601 C Street, Suite 576
Anchorage, AK 99524-0249
(907) 561-4406

RADAR
Alaska Council on Prevention of Alcohol and Drug Abuse
3333 Denali Street, Suite 201
Anchorage, AK 99503
(907) 258-6021

Arizona

Arizona Drug and Alcohol Agency
Offices of Community Behavioral Health
Department of Health Services
2632 East Thomas Street
Phoenix, AZ 85016
(602) 255-1030

HIV Prevention
Department of Health Services
Division of Disease Prevention
3008 North 3rd Street
Phoenix, AZ 85012
(602) 230-5819

RADAR
Arizona Prevention Resource Center
Extended Education
Arizona State University
Tempe, AZ 85287-1708
(602) 965-9666

State Coordinator for Drug-Free Schools
Arizona Department of Education
Comprehensive Health Unit
400 West Congress Street
Tucson, Arizona 85701-1371
(602) 628-5883

Arkansas

HIV Prevention
Arkansas Department of Health
Sexually Transmitted Diseases
4815 West Markham, Room 455
Little Rock, AR 72205
(501) 661-2133

Office on Alcohol and Drug Abuse Prevention
Department of Human Services
1515 West 7th Street, Suite 310
Little Rock, AR 72201
(501) 371-2604

RADAR
Division of Alcohol and Drug Abuse Prevention
Seventh and Main Streets
400 Donaghey Plaza North
Little Rock, AR 72203
(501) 682-6653

State Coordinator for Drug-Free Schools
Arkansas Department of Education/Drug Education
4 Capitol Mall, Room 405-B
Little Rock, AR 72201-1071
(501) 682-5170

California

Department of Alcohol and Drug Programs
1700 K Street
Sacramento, CA 95814
(916) 445-0834

Los Angeles County Department of Health Services
AIDS Programs
600 South Commonwealth Avenue, 6th Floor
Los Angeles, CA 90005
(213) 351-8000

RADAR
Department of Alcohol and Drug Programs
1700 K Street
Sacramento, CA 95814
(916) 327-8447

State Coordinator for Drug-Free Schools
California Department of Education
Healthy Kids, Healthy California
P.O. Box 944272
Sacramento, CA 94244-2720
(916) 657-2810

Colorado

Alcohol and Drug Abuse Division
Department of Health
4210 East 11th Avenue
Denver, CO 80220
(303) 331-6530

Colorado Department of Education
High Risk Intervention
201 East Colfax Avenue
Denver, CO 80203
(303) 866-6766

Colorado Department of Health
STD/AIDS Section
4210 East 11th Avenue
Denver, CO 80220
(303) 331-8320

RADAR
Resource Department
Colorado Alcohol and Drug Abuse Division
4210 East 11th Avenue
Denver, CO 80220
(303) 331-8201

Connecticut

Connecticut Alcohol and Drug Abuse Commission
999 Asylum Avenue
Hartford, CT 06105
(203) 566-4145

Department of Health Services
AIDS Program
150 Washington Street
Hartford, CT 06106
(203) 566-1157

RADAR
Connecticut Clearinghouse
334 Farmington Avenue
Plainville, CT 06062
(203) 793-9791

State Coordinator for Drug-Free Schools
Connecticut Department of Education
P.O. Box 2219
Hartford, CT 06145
(203) 566-2931

Delaware

AIDS Program Office
Building G
3000 Newport Gap Pike
Wilmington, DE 19808
(302) 995-8422

Bureau of Alcoholism and Drug Abuse
CT Building
Delaware State Hospital
1901 DuPont Highway
New Castle, DE 19720
(302) 421-6101

RADAR
Office of Prevention Resource Clearinghouse
Delaware Youth and Family Center
1825 Faulkland Road
Wilmington, DE 19805-1195
(302) 633-2539

State Coordinator for Drug-Free Schools
Department of Public Instruction
Health Education and Services
Townsend Building
P.O. Box 1402
Dover, DE 19903
(302) 739-4886

District of Columbia

Alcohol and Drug Abuse Services Administration
1300 1st Street, NE, 3rd Floor
Washington, DC 20002
(202) 727-1762

Commission of Public Health
Office of AIDS Activities
1660 L Street, NW, 7th Floor
Washington, DC 20036
(202) 637-3675

District of Columbia Public Schools
Substance Abuse Prevention Education Program
Giddings Administrative Unit
315 G Street, SE
Washington, DC 20003
(202) 724-3610

RADAR
Washington Area Council on Alcoholism and Drug Abuse
1232 M Street, NW
Washington, DC 20005
(202) 682-1700

Florida

Department of Health and Rehabilitative Services
1317 Winwood Boulevard
Building 6, Room 182
Tallahassee, FL 32399-0700
(904) 488-0900

HIV Education and Prevention
Department of HRS
AIDS Program
1317 Winwood Boulevard
Building 2
Tallahassee, FL 32399-0700
(904) 487-2478

Prevention Center
Florida Department of Education
325 West Gaines Street, Suite 414
Tallahassee, FL 32399-0400
(904) 488-6304

RADAR
Florida Alcohol and Drug Abuse Association
1030 East Lafayette Street, Suite 100
Tallahassee, FL 32301-4547
(904) 878-6922

Georgia

Division of Mental Health, Mental Retardation, and Substance Abuse
Department of Human Resources
878 Peachtree Street, NE, Suite 319
Atlanta, GA 30309
(404) 894-4785

HIV Prevention
Department of Human Resources
Office of Infectious Diseases
878 Peachtree Street, NE, Suite 109
Atlanta, GA 30309
(404) 894-5304

RADAR
Georgia Prevention Resource Center
Division of Mental Health
878 Peachtree Street, NE, Suite 319
Atlanta, GA 30309
(404) 894-4204

State Coordinator for Drug-Free Schools
Georgia State Board of Education
Health and Physical Education
1952 Twin Towers East
Atlanta, GA 30334-5040
(404) 656-2414

Hawaii

HIV Prevention
State of Hawaii
Department of Health
3627 Kilauea Avenue, Suite 304
Honolulu, HI 96816
(808) 735-5303

RADAR
Drug-Free Hawaii Prevention Resource Center
1218 Waimanu Street
Honolulu, HI 96814
(808) 524-5509

State Coordinator for Drug-Free Schools
Assistant Superintendent
Department of Education
P.O. Box 2360
Honolulu, HI 96804
(808) 586-3446

Idaho

Drug Education Consultant
Idaho Department of Education
Len B. Jordan Building
Boise, ID 83720
(208) 334-2165

HIV Prevention
Department of Health and Welfare
Bureau of Preventive Medicine
450 West State Street, 4th Floor
Boise, ID 83720
(208) 334-4309

RADAR
Boise State University
College of Health Science
4162 North Lafontana
Boise, ID 83702
(208) 385-0577

Substance Abuse Program
Division of Family and Children's Services
Towers Building, 3rd Floor
450 West State Street
Boise, ID 83720
(208) 334-5935

Illinois

Department of Alcoholism and Substance Abuse
State of Illinois Center
100 West Randolph Street, Room 5-600
Chicago, IL 60601
(312) 917-3840

Illinois Department of Public Health
AIDS Activity Section
111 North Canal Street, Suite 135
Chicago, IL 60606
(312) 917-3840

Illinois State Board of Education
Program Support Office
100 North First Street
Springfield, IL 62777
(217) 782-3810

RADAR
Prevention Resource Center Library
822 South College Street
Springfield, IL 62704
(217) 525-3456

Indiana

Department of Education
Center for School Improvement
State House, Room 229
Indianapolis, IN 46204-2798
(317) 232-6984

Division of Mental Health
Addiction Services W-353
402 West Washington Street
Indianapolis, IN 46204-2739
(317) 232-7816

RADAR
Indiana Prevention Resource Center for Substance Abuse
Indiana University, Room 110
840 State Road, 46 Bypass
Bloomington, IN 47405
(812) 855-1237

State Board of Health
Division of Acquired Diseases
HIV/AIDS Program
1330 West Michigan Street
P.O. Box 1964
Indianapolis, IN 46202
(317) 633-0851

Iowa

Department of Public Health
Division of Substance Abuse and Health Promotion
Lucas State Office Building, 3rd Floor
321 East 12th Street
Des Moines, IA 50319
(515) 281-3641

HIV Prevention
Department of Public Health
Division of Health Protection
Lucas State Office Building
Des Moines, IA 50319
(515) 281-4936

RADAR
Iowa Substance Abuse Information Center
Cedar Rapids Public Library
500 1st Street, SE
Cedar Rapids, IA 52401
(319) 398-5133

Substance Education Consultant
Iowa Department of Education
Grimes State Office Building
Des Moines, IA 50319
(515) 281-3021

Kansas

HIV Prevention
Kansas Department of Health and Environment
Mills Building, Suite 605
109 Southwest 9th Street
Topeka, KS 66612
(913) 296-6036

Kansas Alcohol and Drug Abuse Services
Department of Social and Rehabilitation Services
300 Southwest Oakley
Topeka, KS 66606-1861
(913) 296-3925

RADAR
Kansas Alcohol and Drug Abuse Services
Department of Social and Rehabilitative Services
300 Southwest Oakley
Topeka, KS 66606-1861
(913) 296-3925

State Coordinator for Drug-Free Schools
Kansas State Department of Education
120 East 10th Street
Topeka, KS 66612
(913) 296-4946

Kentucky

Division of Substance Abuse
Cabinet for Human Resources
Health Services Building
275 East Main Street
Frankfort, KY 40601
(502) 564-2880

HIV Prevention
Cabinet for Human Resources
STD Control (CTS)
275 East Main Street
Frankfort, KY 40621
(502) 564-4804

RADAR
Drug Information Service for Kentucky
Division of Substance Abuse
275 East Main Street
Frankfort, KY 40621
(502) 564-2880

State Department of Education
Alcohol/Drug Unit
1720 Capitol Plaza Tower
Frankfort, KY 40601
(502) 564-6720

Louisiana

HIV/AIDS Services Program
Department of Health and Hospitals
P.O. Box 60630
New Orleans, LA 70160
(504) 568-5508

Office of Human Services
Division of Alcohol and Drug Abuse
1201 Capitol Access Road, Room 4-SA-1
Baton Rouge, LA 70821-3868
(504) 342-9354

RADAR
Division of Alcohol and Drug Abuse
1201 Capitol Access Road, 4th Floor East
Baton Rouge, LA 70821-3868
(504) 342-9352

State Coordinator for Drug-Free Schools
Louisiana Department of Education
Bureau of Student Services
P.O. Box 94064
Baton Rouge, LA 70804-9064
(504) 342-3388

Maine

HIV Prevention Program
Department of Human Services
State House, Station 11
Augusta, ME 04333
(207) 289-3747

Office of Alcoholism and Drug Abuse Prevention
State House, Station 11
Augusta, ME 04333
(207) 289-2781

RADAR
Maine Alcohol and Drug Abuse Clearinghouse
Office of Alcoholism and Drug Abuse Prevention
State House, Station 11
Augusta, ME 04333
(207) 289-2781

State Coordinator for Drug-Free Schools
Department of Education
State House, Station 57
Augusta, ME 04333
(207) 289-3876

Maryland

Alcohol and Drug Abuse Administration
201 West Preston Street
Baltimore, MD 21201
(410) 225-6925

Center for AIDS Education
Department of Health and Mental Hygiene
201 West Preston Street
Baltimore, MD 21201
(410) 225-6707

RADAR
Alcohol and Drug Abuse Administration
Department of Health and Mental Hygiene
201 West Preston Street, 4th Floor
Baltimore, MD 21201
(410) 225-6543

State Department of Education
Drug-Free Schools Program
200 West Baltimore Street
Baltimore, MD 21201
(410) 333-2307

Massachusetts

Bureau of Substance Abuse Services
Department of Public Health
150 Tremont Street, 6th Floor
Boston, MA 02111
(617) 727-1960

Governor's Alliance against Drugs
John W. McCormack State Office Building
One Ashburton Place, Room 611
Boston, MA 02108
(617) 727-0786

HIV Prevention Program
Department of Health
150 Tremont Street
Boston, MA 02111
(617) 727-0368

RADAR
The Psychological Centers Prevention Network
488 Essex Street
Lawrence, MA 01840
(508) 685-1337

Michigan

Comprehensive School Health Unit
Department of Education
P.O. Box 30008
Lansing, MI 48909
(517) 373-2589

Office of Substance Abuse Services
Department of Public Health
3500 North Logan Street
Lansing, MI 48909
(517) 335-8810

RADAR
Michigan Substance Abuse and Traffic Safety Information Center
2409 East Michigan Avenue
Lansing, MI 48912-4019
(517) 482-9902

Special Office on AIDS
Center for Health Promotion
P.O. Box 30195
Lansing, MI 48909
(517) 335-8371

Minnesota

AIDS/STD Prevention Services Section
Minnesota Department of Health
717 Southeast Delaware Street
Minneapolis, MN 55440
(612) 623-5698

Chemical Dependency Program Division
Department of Human Services
Space Center Building
444 Lafayette Road
St. Paul, MN 55155-3823
(612) 296-3991

Drug Abuse Program
State Department of Education
Learner Support Systems
994 Capitol Square Building
St. Paul, MN 55101
(612) 296-3925

RADAR
Minnesota Prevention Resource Center
2829 Verndale Avenue
Anoka, MN 55303
(612) 427-5310

Mississippi

Mississippi Department of Health
HIV/AIDS Prevention Program
P.O. Box 1700
Jackson, MS 39215
(601) 960-7723

Mississippi Department of Mental Health
Division of Alcohol and Drug Services
1101 Robert E. Lee Building
239 North Lamar Street
Jackson, MS 39201
(601) 359-1288

RADAR
Department of Mental Health
Division of Alcohol and Drug Services
1101 Robert E. Lee Building
239 North Lamar Street
Jackson, MS 39201
(601) 359-1288

State Coordinator for Drug-Free Schools
State Department of Education
550 High Street
Jackson, MS 39205
(601) 359-3598

Missouri

Missouri Department of Health
Bureau of AIDS Prevention
1730 East Elm Street
P.O. Box 570
Jefferson City, MO 65102
(800) 533-AIDS
(314) 751-6438

Missouri Division of Alcohol and Drug Abuse
Department of Mental Health
1706 East Elm Street
Jefferson City, MO 65102
(314) 751-4942

RADAR
Missouri Division of Alcohol and Drug Abuse
1915 Southridge Drive
Jefferson City, MO 65109
(314) 751-4942

State Coordinator for Drug-Free Schools
State Department of Elementary and Secondary Education
P.O. Box 480
Jefferson City, MO 65102
(314) 751-2641

Montana

Alcohol and Drug Abuse Division
Department of Institutions
1539 11th Avenue
Helena, MT 59620
(406) 444-2827

HIV Prevention Program
Montana Department of Health and Environmental Sciences
Cogswell Building
Helena, MT 59620
(406) 444-3565

RADAR
Department of Institutions
Chemical Dependency Bureau
1539 11th Avenue
Helena, MT 59620
(406) 444-2878

State Coordinator for Drug-Free Schools
State Department of Education
Office of Public Instruction
Capitol Building
Helena, MT 59620
(406) 444-4434

Nebraska

Department of Health AIDS Program
P.O. Box 95007
Lincoln, NE 68509
(402) 471-2937

Division on Alcoholism and Drug Abuse
Department of Public Institutions
Lincoln Regional Center Campus
West Van Dorn and Folsom Streets
Lincoln, NE 68509
(402) 471-2851

RADAR
Alcoholism and Drug Abuse Council of Nebraska
650 J Street, Suite 215
Lincoln, NE 68508
(402) 474-0930

State Coordinator of Drug-Free Schools
Administrator of Curriculum
Nebraska State Department of Education
301 Centennial Mall South
Lincoln, NE 68509-4987
(402) 471-4332

Nevada

Bureau of Alcohol and Drug Abuse
Department of Human Resources
Kinkead Building
505 East King Street, Suite 500
Carson City, NV 89710
(702) 687-4790

HIV Prevention
Nevada State Health Division
Bureau of Disease Control and Intervention Services
Capitol Complex
505 East King Street, Room 104
Carson City, NV 89710
(702) 687-4804

RADAR
Bureau of Alcohol and Drug Abuse
505 East King Street, Suite 500
Carson City, NV 89710
(702) 687-4790

State Coordinator for Drug-Free Schools
State Department of Education
Office of Public Instruction
Capitol Complex
Carson City, NV 89710
(702) 687-3100

New Hampshire

HIV Prevention
Division of Public Health Services
Bureau of Disease Control
6 Hazen Drive
Concord, NH 03301
(603) 271-4477

RADAR
New Hampshire Office of Alcohol and Drug Abuse Prevention
State Office Park South
105 Pleasant Street
Concord, NH 03301
(603) 271-6100

State Coordinator for Drug-Free Schools
Department of Education
State Office Park South
105 Pleasant Street
Concord, NH 03301
(603) 271-2632

New Jersey

Department of Health
AIDS Program
363 West State Street, CN 360
Trenton, NJ 08625
(609) 984-6000

RADAR
New Jersey State Department of Health
Division of Alcoholism, Drug Abuse, and Addiction Services
129 East Hanover Street
Trenton, NJ 08625
(609) 292-0729

State Coordinator for Drug-Free Schools
New Jersey State Department of Education
General Academic Education
225 West State Street, CN 500
Trenton, NJ 08625
(609) 292-5780

New Mexico

Health and Environment
AIDS Prevention Program
P.O. Box 968
Santa Fe, NM 87501
(505) 827-0086

RADAR
Department of Health
Division of Substance Abuse
Harold Runnels Building
1190 St. Francis Drive
Santa Fe, NM 87501
(505) 827-2601

State Coordinator for Drug-Free Schools
State Department of Education
300 Don Gaspar Avenue
Santa Fe, NM 87501
(505) 827-6648

New York

AIDS Institute
Corning Tower
1315 Empire State Plaza
Albany, NY 12237
(518) 486-1320

Division of Substance Abuse Services
Office of Alcoholism and Substance Abuse
Executive Park Tower South, 2nd Floor
Stuyvesant Plaza
Albany, NY 12203
(518) 457-2061

New York Division of Alcoholism and Alcohol Abuse
194 Washington Avenue
Albany, NY 12210
(518) 473-3460

RADAR
Narcotic and Drug Research, Inc.
Resource Center
11 Beach Street, 2nd Floor
New York, NY 10013
(212) 966-8700, ext. 107

State Education Department
Bureau of Health and Drug Education
Washington Avenue
Albany, NY 12234
(518) 474-1491

North Carolina

Alcohol and Drug Services Section
Division of MH/DD/SAS
325 North Salisbury Street
Raleigh, NC 27603
(919) 733-4670

Department of Environment, Health, and Natural Resources
Communicable Disease Control
HIV/STD Control Branch
P.O. Box 27687
Raleigh, NC 27611-7687
(919) 733-7301

Department of Public Instruction
Alcohol and Drug Defense Section
210 North Dawson Street, Education Annex 11
Raleigh, NC 27603-1712
(919) 733-6615

RADAR
North Carolina Alcohol/Drug Resource Center
3109-A University Drive
Durham, NC 27707-3703
(919) 493-2881

North Dakota

Department of Public Instruction
Guidance/Drug-Free Schools
State Capitol, 9th Floor
Bismarck, ND 58501-0440
(701) 224-2269

Division of Alcoholism and Drug Abuse
Department of Human Services
1839 East Capitol Avenue
Bismarck, ND 58501-2152
(701) 224-2769

HIV Prevention
Department of Health
State Capitol
Bismarck, ND 58505
(701) 224-2378

RADAR
North Dakota Prevention Resource Center
1839 East Capitol Avenue
Bismarck, ND 58501
(701) 224-3603

Ohio

HIV Prevention
Department of Health
Epidemiology Division
246 North High Street, 8th Floor
Columbus, OH 43266
(614) 466-5480

RADAR
Department of Alcohol and Drug Addiction Services
Two Nationwide Plaza, 12th Floor
Columbus, OH 43215
(614) 466-6379

State Coordinator for Drug-Free Schools
Department of Education
Division of Education Services
65 South Front Street, Room 719
Columbus, OH 43266-0308
(614) 466-3708

Oklahoma

Alcohol and Drug Abuse Programs
Programs Division
P.O. Box 53277
Oklahoma City, OK 73152
(405) 521-0044

Department of Health
AIDS Division
P.O. Box 53551
Oklahoma City, OK 73152
(405) 271-4636

RADAR
Oklahoma State Department of Mental Health
1200 NE 13th Street, 2nd Floor
Oklahoma City, OK 73117
(405) 271-8755

State Coordinator for Drug-Free Schools
Office of Federal Financially Assisted Programs
State Department of Education
2500 North Lincoln Boulevard
Oklahoma City, OK 73105-4599
(405) 521-2106

Oregon

AIDS Coordinator
Department of Human Resources
1400 Southwest 5th Avenue
Portland, OR 97201
(503) 229-5792

Office of Alcohol and Drug Abuse Programs
Department of Human Resources
Public Service Building, Room 301
Capitol Mall
Salem, OR 97310
(503) 378-2163

RADAR
Oregon Drug and Alcohol Information
100 North Cook Street
Portland, OR 97227
(800) 237-7808, ext. 3673
(503) 280-3673

State Coordinator for Drug-Free Schools
State Department of Education
Division of Special Student Services
700 Pringle Parkway, SE
Salem, OR 97310
(503) 378-2677

Pennsylvania

Department of Health
AIDS Education and Risk Education
P.O. Box 90
Harrisburg, PA 17108
(717) 787-5900

Office of Drug and Alcohol Programs
Department of Health
Health and Welfare Building, Room 809
Foster and Commonwealth Avenues
Harrisburg, PA 17108
(717) 787-9857

RADAR
PENNSAIC
Columbus Square
652 West 17th Street
Erie, PA 16502
(800) 582-7746
(814) 459-0245

State Coordinator for Drug-Free Schools
Division of Student Services
State Department of Education
333 Market Street
Harrisburg, PA 17126-0333
(717) 783-9294

Puerto Rico

Coordinator for Drug-Free Schools
Department of Education
Office of Federal Affairs
P.O. Box 759
Hato Rey, PR 00919
(809) 758-4949, ext. 6047

RADAR
Department of Anti-Addiction Services
414 Barbosa Avenue
Rio Piedras, PR 00928-1414
(809) 763-3133

Rhode Island

HIV Prevention
Department of Health
Disease Control
75 Davis Street
Providence, RI 02908
(401) 277-2362

RADAR
Office of Substance Abuse
Division of Community Development
P.O. Box 20363
Cranston, RI 02920
(401) 464-2379

State Coordinator for Drug-Free Schools
State Department of Education
School Support Services
22 Hayes Street
Providence, RI 02908
(401) 277-2638

South Carolina

HIV Prevention
Health and Environmental Control
2600 Bull Street
Columbia, SC 29201
(803) 734-5482

RADAR
South Carolina Commission on Alcohol and Drug Abuse
The Drug Store Information Clearinghouse
3700 Forest Drive, Suite 300
Columbia, SC 29204
(803) 734-9559

State Coordinator for Drug-Free Schools
Department of Education
At-Risk Youth Program
1429 Senate Street, Room 1206
Columbia, SC 29201
(803) 734-8097

South Dakota

HIV Prevention
Department of Health
Communicable Disease
523 East Capitol Avenue
Pierre, SD 57501
(605) 773-3357

RADAR
Division of Alcohol and Drug Abuse
East Highway 34
c/o 500 East Capitol Avenue
Pierre, SD 57501-5070
(605) 773-3123

State Coordinator for Drug-Free Schools
State Department of Education
700 Governors Drive
Pierre, SD 57501-3182
(605) 773-4670

Tennessee

Department of Health
AIDS Education Coordinator
100 Ninth Avenue, N
Nashville, TN 37219
(615) 741-7387

Division of Alcohol and Drug Abuse Services
Department of Mental Health and Mental Retardation
James K. Polk Building, 4th Floor
505 Deaderick Street
Nashville, TN 37219
(615) 741-1921

RADAR
Tennessee Alcohol and Drug Association
545 Mainstream Drive, Suite 404
Nashville, TN 37228
(615) 244-7066

State Coordinator for Drug-Free Schools
Tennessee Department of Education
Drug-Free Schools Program
140 Cordell Hull Building
Nashville, TN 37219
(615) 741-6055

Texas

Commission on Alcohol and Drug Abuse
1705 Guadalupe Street
Austin, TX 78701
(512) 463-5510

Drug-Free Schools Coordinator
Texas Education Agency
Drug Abuse Prevention Program
1701 North Congress Avenue, Room 5-123
Austin, TX 78701-1494
(512) 463-9501

RADAR
Texas Commission on Alcohol and Drug Abuse Resource Center
720 Brazos Street, Suite 307
Austin, TX 78729
(512) 867-8700

Texas Department of Health
AIDS Division
1100 West 49th Street
Austin, TX 78756
(512) 458-7207

Utah

Division of Alcoholism and Drugs
Department of Social Services
Social Services Building
150 West North Temple Street
Salt Lake City, UT 84145-0500
(801) 533-6532

HIV Prevention
Utah Department of Health
Bureau of Epidemiology
P.O. Box 16660
Salt Lake City, UT 84116
(801) 538-6191

RADAR
Utah State Division of Substance Abuse
120 North 200 West, 4th Floor
Salt Lake City, UT 84145-0500
(801) 538-3939

Utah State Office of Education
Drug-Free School Program
250 East 500 South
Salt Lake City, UT 84111
(801) 538-7713

Vermont

Department of Education
Drug-Free School Program
120 State Street
Montpelier, VT 05602-2703
(802) 828-3111

HIV Prevention
Department of Health
VD Control Program
P.O. Box 70
60 Main Street
Burlington, VT 05402
(802) 863-7245

RADAR
Office of Alcohol and Drug Abuse Programs
103 South Maine Street
Waterbury, VT 05676
(802) 241-2178

Virginia

HIV Prevention
VD Control Section
109 Governor Street
Richmond, VA 23219
(804) 786-6267

RADAR
Office of Substance Abuse Services
Department of Mental Health, Mental Retardation, and
   Substance Abuse
Madison Building
109 Governor Street
Richmond, VA 23214
(804) 786-3909

State Coordinator for Drug-Free Schools
Department of Education
Health and Physical Education
P.O. Box 6-Q
Richmond, VA 23216-2060
(804) 225-2733

Washington

Bureau of Alcohol and Substance Abuse
Office Building 2
12th Avenue and Franklin Street
Olympia, WA 98504
(206) 753-5866

Department of Public Instruction
Substance Abuse Education
Old Capitol Building, Mail Stop FG-11
Olympia, WA 98504
(206) 753-5595

HIV-AIDS Office of Prevention and Education Services
Airdustrial Park, Building 9
Mail Stop LJ-17
Olympia, WA 98504
(206) 586-0426

RADAR
Washington State Substance Abuse Coalition
14700 Main Street
Bellevue, WA 98007
(206) 747-9111

West Virginia

Division on Alcoholism and Drug Abuse
State Office Building 3, Room 451
1800 Washington Street, E
Charleston, WV 25305
(304) 348-2276

HIV Prevention
Department of Health
VD Control Section
151 11th Avenue
Charleston, WV 25303
(304) 348-2950

RADAR
West Virginia Library Commission
Cultural Center
Charleston, WV 25305
(304) 348-2041

State Coordinator for Drug-Free Schools
State Department of Education
Student Support Services
Capitol Complex, B-309
Charleston, WV 25305
(304) 348-8830

Wisconsin

AIDS-HIV Program
Bureau of Public Health
P.O. Box 309
Madison, WI 53701-0309
(608) 267-5287

Office of Alcohol and Drug Abuse
Wilson Street State Office Building, Room 434
One West Wilson Street
Madison, WI 53707
(608) 266-2717

RADAR
Wisconsin Clearinghouse
315 North Henry Street
Madison, WI 53703
(608) 263-2797

State Coordinator for Drug-Free Schools
Programs Development
Department of Public Instruction
Bureau for Pupil Services
125 South Webster Street
Madison, WI 53707
(608) 266-0963

Wyoming

Health and Human Services
AIDS Prevention Program
Hathaway Building, 4th Floor
2300 Capitol Avenue
Cheyenne, WY 82002
(307) 777-5800

Office of Substance Abuse Programs
Hathaway Building, Room 350
2300 Capitol Avenue
Cheyenne, WY 82002
(307) 777-7115

RADAR
Wyoming CARE Program
Biological Science Building, Room 135
Laramie, WY 82071
(307) 766-4119

State Coordinator for Drug-Free Schools
State Department of Education
Office of Public Instruction
Hathaway Building
2300 Capitol Avenue
Cheyenne, WY 82002
(307) 777-6202

Private Organizations

Al-Anon Family Groups

P.O. Box 862, Midtown Station
New York, NY 10018-0862
(212) 302-7240
(800) 356-9996
(212) 869-3757, Fax

The Al-Anon Family Groups are a support organization, "a fellowship of relatives and friends of alcoholics who share their experience, strength, and hope in order to solve their common problems." More than 32,000 groups meet throughout the world. Members practice the 12-step recovery program based on the 12 steps of Alcoholics Anonymous. Al-Anon Family Group was founded in 1951. Members try to "ease our emotional burdens by sharing" and "learn to deal with our obsession, our anxiety, our anger, our denial, and our feelings of guilt." Friends or relatives of alcoholics may join whether or not the alcoholic is in treatment. Alateen is a related organization for "young people whose lives have been affected by someone else's drinking." None of the three groups follow a set religion, but all describe themselves as spiritual programs. Al-Anon Family Groups are free of charge, though voluntary contributions from members are welcomed.

To locate an Al-Anon or Alateen meeting in your area, check in the Yellow Pages under Al-Anon or Alcoholics, Families of. You may also call the 24-hour toll-free number, (800) 356-9996, or (212) 245-3151 (New York State) and (613) 722-1830 (Canada). Families of drug abusers may be referred to Nar-Anon and Coke-Anon.

PUBLICATIONS: Al-Anon and Alateen have an extensive list of books, pamphlets, and related materials such as bookmarks, cards, banners, posters, and audiocassettes. Publications include *Al-Anon Faces Alcoholism, Alateen—A Day at a Time, Dilemma of the Alcoholic Marriage, First Steps,* and others. Alateen publishes a newsletter, *Alateen Talk* ($2/year for individuals, less for groups).

Alcohol Research Information Service (ARIS)

1106 East Oakland
Lansing, MI 48906
(517) 686-1100

ARIS collects, correlates, and disseminates information regarding alcohol and its products, and their relation to the well-being of Americans. ARIS operates a clearinghouse for information about alcohol abuse and provides teaching materials for elementary and secondary schools.

PUBLICATIONS: *The Bottom Line* ($20/year) and *Monday Morning Report* ($30/year) are newsletters published by ARIS.

Alcoholics Anonymous
P.O. Box 459, Grand Central Station
New York, NY 10163
(212) 686-1100

Alcoholics Anonymous (AA), established in 1935, is well respected in the field of alcohol-abuse treatment. Founded by Bill W. (AA members are always anonymous), Alcoholics Anonymous believes that members "can solve their common problem and help others achieve sobriety." AA is the originator of the 12-step approach, in which alcoholics admit that they are powerless over alcohol and that their lives have become unmanageable. AA has almost 1.8 million members worldwide; anyone who wishes to recover from alcoholism is welcome to join. Not affiliated with any religion, political view, or institution, AA charges no membership fee but accepts donations from members. To locate an AA group, look in the Yellow Pages under Alcoholics Anonymous or call the national number for a referral.

PUBLICATIONS: *AA Comes of Age, Alcoholics Anonymous, As Bill Sees It, Pass It On,* and *Twelve Steps and Twelve Traditions* are some of the many AA publications.

American Council on Alcoholism (ACA)
National Executive Offices
8501 LaSalle Road, Suite 301
Towson, MD 21204
(301) 296-5555

The realization that the entire country "desperately needed . . . a realistic, educational approach to alcoholism and alcohol abuse" led to the establishment in 1976 of the Maryland Society of Alcoholism, now called the American Council on Alcoholism. The ACA acts as a forum for issues of prevention, education, identification, and treatment of alcoholism and alcohol abuse. The organization stresses the importance of early detection of alcohol abuse and believes that "alcoholism cannot be controlled by restrictive measures that may appear to make beverage alcohol difficult to obtain." ACA maintains a resource center on alcoholism, conducts conferences to emphasize continuing education in the field of alcoholism, keeps its members informed of developments in the field, and serves as a national voice for its members in Washington, D.C. Current projects include an effort to inform "at least 90 percent of the American public" about youth and alcohol, moderate drinking, and the identification and treatment of alcoholism. The ACA is supported by contributions from individuals, foundations, and corporations.

PUBLICATIONS: The *ACA Journal* is published twice a year. Books available through the ACA include *Too Old To Cry, Straight Talk: Answers to Questions Young People Ask about Alcohol, Relapse: A Guide to Successful Recovery,* and others. The ACA also markets videotapes and pamphlets, including *The Most Frequently Asked Questions about Teenage Drinking and Their Answers* and *The Most Frequently Asked Questions about Alcoholism.*

Americans for Nonsmokers' Rights
2530 San Pablo Avenue, Suite J
Berkeley, CA 94702
(415) 841-3032

Americans for Nonsmokers' Rights is an advocacy group that pursues legislation to protect nonsmokers from involuntary exposure to second-hand tobacco smoke. The Americans for Nonsmokers' Rights Foundation is the educational arm of the organization, responsible for creating comprehensive educational programs for school children.

The organization has lobbied for limitations on smoking during airline flights, in restaurants, at work, in public transportation, and other places. It campaigns for stronger laws to regulate smoking and to "protect children from the advertising and promotional activities of the tobacco industry." Americans for Nonsmokers' Rights is also "working to promote nonsmoking as the norm in our society and to increase the social unacceptability of smoking in enclosed public places." Its ultimate goal is a smoke-free society by the year 2000. The organization sponsors Teens as Teachers, a program in which teens talk to younger children about the dangers of tobacco and give them the confidence to say no to substance abuse.

PUBLICATIONS: The group publishes *A Smokefree Workplace, Legislative Approaches to a Smokefree Society, National Matrix of Local Smoking Ordinances, Smokefree Travel Guide,* and *Tobacco Smoke and the Nonsmoker.* Also available are stickers, pins, desk signs, and related items.

Cocaine Anonymous World Services, Inc. (CA)
3740 Overland Avenue, Suite H
Los Angeles, CA 90034
(310) 559-5833
(310) 559-2554, Fax

Cocaine Anonymous (CA) is "a fellowship of men and women who share their experience, strength, and hope with each other that they may solve their common problem and help others recover from their addiction." Modeled on AA, CA uses the 12-step recovery program. There are about 1,200 CA meetings per week throughout the United States and Canada. Recovering addicts may attend as many as they wish. Through meetings and frequent phone calls, CA members help each other stay straight.

New arrivals are assisted by sponsors, members with longer sobriety and longer time in the CA program. All CA members are assured anonymity, and everyone "who wants to stop using cocaine and all other mind-altering substances (including alcohol and other drugs) is welcome." Although CA describes itself as a spiritual program, it is not affiliated with any specific religion. There are no membership dues, but voluntary contributions may be made. Donations from nonmembers are not accepted. For a list of meeting sites and times, look for Cocaine Anonymous in the Yellow Pages of the local telephone directory or call Cocaine Anonymous World Services at the number above.

PUBLICATIONS: CA publishes numerous pamphlets about recovery, including *A Higher Power*, . . . *And All Other Mind Altering Substances*, and *Tools of Recovery*.

Committees of Correspondence, Inc.
57 Conant Street, Room 113
Danvers, MA 01923
(508) 774-2641

The Committees of Correspondence takes its name from the group organized by Samuel Adams during the American Revolution. The new organization was formed in 1980 to exchange information and ideas on drug-prevention issues. The group maintains a national computer database to coordinate members' efforts to fight drug abuse. Through letters, phone calls, and exchange of publications, the Committees of Correspondence aims "to prevent youth alcohol and drug use through education, to promote drug-free communities, to support existing national and international laws governing the use and control of illicit drugs, and to discourage any efforts to legalize illicit drugs or escalate their use." The organization maintains a research library on "who's who in the drug culture" to identify "those who have infiltrated and influenced government, education, and the media."

PUBLICATIONS: The Committees of Correspondence publishes quarterly newsletters and *Action Alerts*. The group also has an extensive library of books, pamphlets, and videotapes published and issued by other organizations.

Cottage Program International (CPI)
736 South 500, East
Salt Lake City, UT 84102
(801) 532-6185

CPI, founded in 1972, consists of volunteers seeking to "implement substance abuse prevention programs involving modification of behavior patterns." CPI, which has more than 7,000 members, provides trained volunteers who work with church, school, and community groups. CPI also operates the Families in Focus program, in which volunteers help family members communicate more clearly and make decisions more responsibly. In addition, CPI maintains a speakers' bureau.

PUBLICATIONS: The *Families in Focus Home Learning Guide* and other audiovisual programs for prevention training are available.

Daytop
Administrative Headquarters
54 West 40th Street
New York, NY 10018
(212) 354-6000

Daytop was founded in 1963 by Msgr. William O'Brien, a Catholic priest. Daytop, with centers in New York, California, Pennsylvania, and Texas, treats addicts by means of a therapeutic community, which is described as a caring, family approach to recovery from drugs. The name is an acronym for drug addicts treated on probation. In inpatient treatment, addicts are given increasing responsibilities within the community. Positive peer pressure is exerted in group meetings, in which members learn to be honest about their feelings and problems. Daytop's programs also include outpatient treatment and family therapy. Daytop has developed special programs for women and adolescents. The organization also aims to work with the criminal justice system, exerts effort to influence governmental policymakers, and trains counselors for therapeutic communities.

Daytop treatment is paid for with insurance, governmental funds, and private donations. Fees are set on a sliding scale in accordance with income. No one is rejected because of inability to pay.

PUBLICATIONS: Daytop publishes a newsletter, *Daytopics*.

Do It Now Foundation (DINF)
P.O. Box 27568
Tempe, AZ 85285
(602) 491-0393

The Do It Now Foundation (DINF) was created in 1968 at the height of the 1960s drug epidemic. DINF works to provide factual information to students and adults about all types of drugs, including over-the-counter and prescription drugs. DINF assists organizations engaged in alcohol- and drug-abuse education and maintains a library of information about drugs and health.

PUBLICATIONS: *Newservice* is a bimonthly newsletter ($15/year). DINF also publishes a series of pamphlets titled *Straight Talk, Recovery Talk,* and *Street Talk.* Books include *Drug Free: Staying off Alcohol and Drugs, Intoxication: Life in Pursuit of Artificial Paradise,* and *Diseasing of America.*

Drug Policy Foundation
4801 Massachusetts Avenue, NW, Suite 400
Washington, DC 20016-2087
(202) 895-1634
(202) 537-3007, Fax

The Drug Policy Foundation is an advocacy group formed in 1987 "to combat drug-war hysteria and to advocate sensible ways to curb drug abuse" while preserving individuals' constitutional rights. The foundation opposes the current tactics of the war on drugs, calling it a disaster that does little to control the use of illicit drugs and that creates "government corruption, overcrowded jails, drug dealing to children, and inadequate treatment for legal and illegal drug abuse." Essentially, the foundation wants to treat drug abuse as a medical, rather than a criminal, problem. The foundation lobbies for a change in federal laws to allow doctors to prescribe marijuana to patients who need it and to prescribe heroin for terminally ill cancer patients. Its Medical-Legal Advocacy Project coordinates legal assistance for those who cannot afford a lawyer in cases involving medicine and law. The foundation has staged monthly drug-policy forums on Capitol Hill, organized annual conferences on drug-policy reform, and held seminars dealing with specific issues such as drug testing. The foundation accepts no government funding and is supported by private donations. Membership fees begin at $25.

PUBLICATIONS: Members receive two newsletters, the *Drug Policy Letter* and *Drug Policy Action*, and discounts on publications. The foundation's *Drug Policy Collection* is an extensive catalogue of books and videotapes from various companies. Works include *On Liberty and Drugs* edited by Arnold S. Trebach and Kevin B. Zeese; *Natural Health, Natural Medicine* by Andrew M. Weil, M.D.; *Steal This Urine Test* by Abbie Hoffman; *Our Right to Drugs: The Case for a Free Market* by Thomas Szasz; and many others.

Institute for a Drug-Free Workplace
1301 K Street, NW
East Tower, Suite 1010
Washington, DC 20005
(202) 842-7400
(202) 842-0011, Fax

The Institute for a Drug-Free Workplace, a coalition of businesses and business organizations, was formed in 1989 by four members of the U.S. Chamber of Commerce. Based on the belief that the business community has an important role in preventing drug abuse, the institute's mission is to provide a clearinghouse for information on drug abuse, prevention programs, drug testing, and rehabilitation programs. The institute aims to "help educate employers and employees about the dangers of drug abuse . . . options for corporate policies and programs, and their respective rights and responsibilities." It issues media information and lobbies against state and federal legislation that would restrict drug testing by employers.

PUBLICATIONS: The institute publishes the *Drug-Free Workplace Report* ($45/year) and the *Employee Drug Education Bulletin,* a four-page quarterly newsletter ($1/single copy, less for bulk orders). A series of moderately priced pamphlets includes *What Every Employee Should Know about Drug Abuse—Answers to 20 Good Questions, Does Drug Testing Work?,* and *Courts Give Green Light to Drug Testing.* Books include *A Guide to State Drug Testing Laws and Legislation, Digest of Drug-Free Workplace Laws and Regulations,* and *Drug-Free Workplace Source Book.* The institute has also compiled a series of fact sheets on employee attitudes toward drugs and drug testing ($.60 each).

Institute on Black Chemical Abuse, Inc. (IBCA)
2616 Nicollet Avenue
Minneapolis, MN 55408
(612) 871-7878

IBCA, founded in 1975, is the nation's only resource center with a specific focus on African Americans and substance abuse. IBCA provides nonprofit, community-based services to African Americans, principally through its own treatment programs, training of drug-treatment counselors of other programs, and work with churches, schools, and businesses. IBCA aims to improve service delivery to African-American clients. IBCA supports culturally specific programs and an environment that "encourages and supports the exploration, recognition, and acceptance of African-American identity and experience." Client services include intervention and assessment, outpatient treatment and after-treatment care, programs on black codependency, home-based treatment, and maternal and child early intervention.

PUBLICATIONS: IBCA publishes a newsletter, *Scope,* and provides packets of articles and research papers on such topics as *Advertising and Drugs, Counseling for Minorities, Prevention for Blacks, Minorities and AIDS,* and many others ($15–$30). The institute also markets a half-hour videotape titled *A Thin Line* on the unique clinical needs of African Americans ($325) and several books, including *Marketing Booze to Blacks,* a look at alcoholic beverage advertisements targeting African Americans.

International Commission for the Prevention of Alcoholism and Drug Dependency (ICPA)
6830 Laurel Street, NW
Washington, DC 20012
(202) 722-6729

The International Commission for the Prevention of Alcoholism and Drug Dependency (ICPA), an arm of the U.N. World Health Organization (WHO), was established in 1950. ICPA operates in more than 100 countries, "working to reach thought leaders with principles, policies, and programs for prevention of drugs," including alcohol, tobacco, heroin, marijuana, cocaine, PCP, and others. ICPA conducts drug-prevention workshops and conventions, and encourages government and nongovernment bodies, such as local educational, religious, community, and professional groups, to work together on prevention ideas. ICPA is funded through individual donations and corporate or public grants. Specific programs include People for Prevention, a group plan that can be adapted to a particular community (starter kit available free upon request) and a speakers' bureau.

PUBLICATIONS: ICPA publishes news sheets for administrators, reports from world congresses, and the *ICPA Quarterly Bulletin*. ICPA also produces *Dispatch International* (short articles on drug issues), catalogues of educational aids, and brochures about drug-abuse prevention.

Licensed Beverage Information Council
1225 I Street, NW, Suite 500
Washington, DC 20005
(202) 682-4776

The Licensed Beverage Information Council was formed in 1979 by ten alcohol-industry trade associations representing manufacturers, importers, distributors, and sellers of alcoholic beverages, including beer, wine, and spirits. As a nonpolitical, nonadvocacy group, the council is devoted to the proposition that education is the best method available to address alcohol abuse. The council finances educational mailings to physicians, television broadcasts, and advertising campaigns including commercials, posters, and information cards. Council representatives participate in public and government forums on issues related to drinking. The council also awards educational grants to organizations working against underage drinking, drunken driving, drinking during pregnancy, and alcoholism.

PUBLICATIONS: The council publishes pamphlets titled *What Students Should Know about Drinking and Pregnancy, Employee Assistance Programs: Value and Impact,* and others. Videos financed by the council include the award-winning *New Frontiers: Understanding and Treating Alcoholism.*

Marijuana Study Group
P.O. Box 16054
Washington, DC 20041

The Marijuana Study Group, whose motto is "There is no justice without knowledge and truth," was established by a former president of the National Organization for the Reform of Marijuana Laws (NORML) to "research, publish, and distribute educational materials about marijuana and about public policies concerning marijuana's recreational, medicinal, and economic use." The study group monitors government publications and other sources for data on marijuana. The group, a nonprofit corporation supported by memberships, subscriptions, and donations, plans a research network to track criminal justice data. Membership, which includes a subscription to the newsletter, costs $25.

PUBLICATIONS: *Marijuana Digest,* newsletter.

Mothers Against Drunk Driving (MADD)
511 East John Carpenter Freeway, Suite 700
Irving, TX 75062
(214) 744-6233

Mothers Against Drunk Driving (MADD) was founded in 1980 by Candy Lightner, whose daughter was killed by a drunken driver. MADD's members include victims of drunken-driving accidents, members of their families, and concerned citizens. MADD "acts as the voice of victims of drunk driving crashes." It provides speakers and materials for medical facilities, health courses, and driver-education programs. MADD supports changes in laws on drunken driving and monitors court cases involving drunken driving.

PUBLICATIONS: *MADD in Action, MADD National Newsletter,* and *MADDvocate* are newsletters. MADD markets pamphlets on alcohol and drugs such as *About Drinking and Driving* and *Why You Should Say No! to Alcohol/Other Drugs and Driving.* MADD's books include *America Gets Madd!* and *No Time for Goodbyes.* MADD also sells curriculum kits, posters, banners, certificates, and the like.

Narcotics Anonymous (NA)
P.O. Box 9999
Van Nuys, CA 91409
(818) 780-3951
(818) 785-0923, Fax

Narcotics Anonymous (NA) was founded in 1953 by several drug addicts in southern California. NA groups now number 22,000 worldwide. NA group meetings follow the 12-step model originated by Alcoholics Anonymous. The NA philosophy is "not to focus on problems associated with any specific drug; instead, we focus on the disease of addiction itself."

Many NA members are cross-addicted; that is, they have problems with more than one drug. There are no membership dues; the only requirement is a desire to stop using all drugs, including alcohol. In addition to group meetings, Narcotics Anonymous members sponsor community awareness meetings, attend health fairs and conferences, and make informational presentations to judges and parole officers to inform the public about NA services. To those wishing to establish a group, the NA World Service Office distributes starter kits free upon request. To find an established group, check in the Yellow Pages under Narcotics Anonymous or call the number listed above.

PUBLICATIONS: NA has published a book, *Narcotics Anonymous—The Basic Text,* several pamphlets, and periodicals, *The NA Way Magazine, Newsline,* and *Meeting by Mail.* NA literature is available in several languages. NA sells medallions, key chains, posters, wallet cards, and audiotapes in which recovering addicts speak of their experiences.

National Asian Pacific American Families against Substance Abuse (NAPAFASA)
420 East Third Street, Suite 909
Los Angeles, CA 90013-1602
(213) 617-8277
(213) 617-2012, Fax

NAPAFASA is a nonprofit membership organization "dedicated to promoting culturally competent prevention and treatment for Asians and Pacific Islanders." The group represents the interests of Asians and Pacific Islanders at the local, state, and national levels, assisting members in applying for grants for drug treatment and prevention, and advising existing programs "to promote a clearer understanding of Asian and Pacific Islander cultures and their relationship to alcohol and other drug problems." The group holds national conferences in Washington, D.C., and runs 18 community-based drug-prevention programs for youth throughout the United States and the Pacific Islands.

National Council on Alcoholism and Drug Dependence, Inc. (NCADD)
12 West 21st Street
New York, NY 10010
(800) NCA-CALL
(212) 645-1690, Fax

The National Council on Alcoholism and Drug Dependence, (NCADD) was founded in 1944 to prevent the disease of alcoholism, other drug addictions, and related problems. NCADD seeks to educate the public about drugs; to encourage scientific research in prevention, diagnosis, and treatment of addictions; to advocate for policies that aim to reduce alcohol and other drug problems; and to promote treatment of drug abuse. NCADD has more than 200 affiliates around the nation, served by thousands of volunteers. NCADD hosts an annual national conference for leaders in the field of drug prevention. It also sponsors Alcohol Awareness Month in April and Alcohol- and Other Drug-Related Birth Defects Awareness Week beginning on Mother's Day each year.

PUBLICATIONS: NCADD publishes fact sheets, pamphlets, and posters with information on the use, effects, and problems of alcohol and other drugs, including *Alcohol-Related Birth Defects, Ten Answers to Your Questions about Ice,* and *Alcohol and Your Health.*

National Families in Action
2296 Henderson Mill Road, Suite 204
Atlanta, GA 30345
(404) 934-6364
(404) 934-7137, Fax

National Families in Action, founded in 1977 in Atlanta, created a nationwide, volunteer, grass-roots movement to prevent drug abuse in families and communities. The national organization helps interested parents form local groups "to inoculate families and communities against drug abuse with accurate information." The organization assists local groups to form committees and task forces and runs the National Drug Information Center, a library of 500,000 documents on drug abuse. (The information center may be reached at the phone number listed above.) National Families in Action is developing the National Drug Corps, patterned on the Peace Corps, to expand the prevention movement.

PUBLICATIONS: *Drug Abuse Update* is a quarterly digest of current articles from medical literature and the news media ($25/year). *Drug Abuse Update for Kids,* also a quarterly, is aimed at African-American, inner-city, elementary schoolchildren ($5/year). The organization publishes a series titled *You Have the Right To Know,* which explains the effects of specific drugs.

National Organization for the Reform of Marijuana Laws (NORML)
1636 R Street, NW
Washington, DC 20009
(202) 483-5500
(202) 483-0057, Fax
(900) 97-NORML ($2.95/minute)

NORML, founded in 1970, calls itself the largest and oldest drug law—reform organization. It has lobbied extensively for legalization of marijuana; failing full legalization, it supports decriminalization and legal medical prescription of marijuana. NORML also opposes drug testing to detect the use of marijuana. "The underlying premise of NORML," according to founder Keith Stroup, is that "recreational drug users should not be criminalized." Membership fees begin at $15 for low-income families; regular memberships cost $25/year.

PUBLICATIONS: *The Leaflet* is a quarterly magazine containing news about drug laws, medical uses of marijuana, drug policy, and the like. *Potpourri* is a newsletter for frequent contributors to NORML.

National Parents' Resource Institute for Drug Education (PRIDE)
50 Hurt Plaza, Suite 210
Atlanta, GA 30303
(404) 577-4500
(800) 67-PRIDE

Founded in 1977, the National Parents' Resource Institute for Drug Education (PRIDE) emphasizes prevention of drug abuse through education. PRIDE disseminates current research information and facilitates the organization of parent groups, parent-school teams, and community groups. PRIDE is most concerned with drug abuse among young people. It conducts the Community Action Plan and Parent Training Program for adults and offers junior youth programs. PRIDE also sponsors a yearly conference to bring parents, youth, and the public into contact with experts in the field of drug abuse. PRIDE operates a speakers' bureau, compiles statistics, and maintains a library.

PUBLICATIONS: The *PRIDE Quarterly* newsletter covers legal, social, physiological, and psychological effects of drugs and updates of research and current events in the field ($25/year).

Partnership for a Drug Free America
666 Third Avenue
New York, NY 10017
(212) 922-1560

Founded in 1986, the Partnership for a Drug Free America produces media campaigns to "unsell" illegal drugs. Its most famous ad is the TV commercial showing an egg frying, accompanied by the voice-over: "This is your brain. . . . This is your brain on drugs." The partnership aims to "denormalize" drug use in the United States and "reinforce positive factors of life without drugs."

PUBLICATIONS: *Partnership for a Drug Free America Newsletter* is published quarterly.

Phoenix House Foundation
164 West 74th Street
New York, NY 10023
(212) 595-5810

Phoenix House is the largest private, nonprofit, drug-abuse service organization in the United States. It has treated more than 50,000 people since its founding in 1967, and it currently cares for 1,800 adults and adolescents in New York, New Jersey, and California. Phoenix House programs include long-term residential treatment lasting from 18 months to 2 years. Clients participate in a therapeutic community in which all drugs are strictly prohibited. Phoenix House also provides short-term inpatient treatment (9–11 months) with outpatient support groups afterward. Fully accredited boarding schools known as Phoenix Academies combine drug treatment with academic instruction. Phoenix House also runs day schools and family programs. Phoenix House's Drug Education and Prevention Unit provides educational and prevention services for public and private schools, as well as government, business, and industry. The unit visits more than 100 schools a year and reaches more than 20,000 other individuals at health fairs and civic events.

Phoenix House is funded by government, corporate, and private funds. Programs are covered under medical insurance plans. No one is denied treatment because of inability to pay.

Smoking Policy Institute
914 East Jefferson
P.O. Box 20271
Seattle, WA 98102
(206) 324-4444

The Smoking Policy Institute is a nonprofit corporation that helps organizations create healthy, smoke-free environments. The institute provides information on sidestream smoke, smoking legislation, and labor/management issues related to smoking rules. For a fee, the institute consults with employers about smoking in the workplace and conducts presentations for management and employees.

PUBLICATIONS: The institute publishes a number of pamphlets and has produced several videos including *Let's Clear the Air* and *90 Days to a Smoke-Free Workplace*.

Students Against Driving Drunk (SADD)
P.O. Box 800
Marlboro, MA 01752
(508) 481-3568

Students Against Driving Drunk (SADD) is an organization of middle school, high school, and college students. SADD was established in 1981 by Robert Anastas, a Massachusetts teacher, after two of his students were killed in separate auto accidents. SADD chapters operate in thousands of schools in all 50 states and in Canada, Europe, Australia, New Zealand, and Africa. The group aims "to improve young people's knowledge and attitudes about alcohol and drugs to help save their lives and the lives of others." SADD provides lesson plans on drinking and driving, mobilizes students to exert peer pressure against driving while drinking, and promotes frank dialogue about drinking between teenagers and their parents. The SADD Contract for Life contains a promise from the student to call his or her parents "at any hour, from any place if I am ever in a situation where I have had too much to drink, or a friend or date who is driving has had too much to drink." The parent agrees to "seek safe, sober transportation home" in a similar situation and also to pay for a taxi or to pick up the teen who needs a sober ride. The parent promises "no questions asked and no argument," although the parent and teen can talk about the problem at a later time.

Student Athletes Detest Drugs is a related organization at the same address that promotes peer pressure to encourage athletes to remain drug-free. Student Athletes Detest Drugs asks members to take the Athlete's Pledge, a written document in which the athlete promises not to use illegal substances.

Both groups hold assemblies, rallies, and other events to educate their fellow students about the dangers of using drugs and alcohol, especially while driving. Students who would like to form a SADD program in their schools should contact the organization for a starter kit ($35 for high schools and colleges, $25 for middle schools).

PUBLICATIONS: SADD publishes *The Contract for Life* by Robert Anastas, which tells the SADD story; *Bob Anastas Talks to Parents* (pamphlet); *Celebrate Life* (a prom and activities guide); and various curriculum guides. The organization also sells T-shirts, sweatshirts and sweatpants, water bottles, and related merchandise.

Target/National Federation of State High School Associations
P.O. Box 20626
11724 NW Plaza Circle
Kansas City, MO 64195
(816) 464-5400
(800) 366-6667
(816) 464-5571, Fax

Target is a service component of the National Federation of State High School Associations. It was established in 1984 "to assist America's youth, K–12, in coping with tobacco, alcohol, and other drugs." Target runs a national resource center that supplies free and low-cost materials to schools, students, and parents. It offers four-day workshops to train leaders who return to their home schools. Through the Target Ambassadors Program, a two-day workshop, students, parents, and school personnel form cooperative partnerships to fight drug abuse.

PUBLICATIONS: Target publishes *Teaming for Prevention,* a discussion guide for parent-student meetings; *On Target,* an eight-page monthly newsletter "designed to educate students about tobacco, alcohol, and other drugs" (free to schools, $25/year to individuals); *On Target: Developing Chemically Free Student Leadership*, ideas for beginning or enhancing a drug-prevention program; *On Target: A Road Map to Healthy and Drug Free Lifestyles*, a curriculum development guide; and *Operation Prom/ Graduation*, a planning guide for drug-free activities. It also produces videos: *Let's Connect*, three scenes for discussion among parents and students; *No Matter How You Say It . . . Say No*, a film featuring pro basketball player Isaiah Thomas discussing the pressures to use drugs and how he dealt with them; *Go for Your Dreams*, featuring Nancy Hogshead, Olympic gold medal swimmer; and others.

6

Selected Print Resources

Bibliographies

AIDS Prevention

The National AIDS Clearinghouse publishes a free bibliography of publications by the America Responds to AIDS program. Order number B499 from:

National AIDS Clearinghouse
P.O. Box 6003
Rockville, MD 20849-6003
(800) 458-5231
(800) 243-7012, TTY

Alcohol: Private Sources for Bibliographies

The Center for Alcohol Studies at Rutgers University publishes an extensive series of bibliographies on all aspects of alcohol use and abuse. Each bibliography costs $17 and is updated yearly. Bibliography topics include

Alcohol and Drug Addiction/Polydrug Use

Blacks

Children of Alcoholics

Crime and Alcohol, Alcoholism

Economic Aspects

Heredity and Alcoholism

Hispanics

Military

Native Americans

Women and Alcohol

Youth

Another set of valuable bibliographies from the center is **Alcohol Education Materials: An Annotated Bibliography** by Gail Gleason Milgram, some with Penny Page. Volumes of this bibliography are as follows:

Literature of 1950–1973 (published in 1975). 304p. $20. Order number BBK–115.

Literature of 1973–1978 (published in 1980). 257p. $20. Order number BBK–116.

Literature of 1978–1979 (published in 1979). 107p. $10. Order number BBK–117.

Literature of 1979–1980 (published in 1980). 80p. $10. Order number BBK–118.

Literature of 1980–1981 (published in 1981). 84p. $10. Order number BBK–119.

A catalogue may be obtained by writing to:

Center for Alcohol Studies
Smithers Hall, Busch Campus
Rutgers University
New Brunswick, NJ 08903
(908) 932-4317

Alcohol: Additional Bibliography

Keller, Mark, ed. **International Bibliography of Studies on Alcohol.** New Brunswick, NJ: Center for Alcohol Studies, 1966. $150 for three volumes. Vol. 1, 631p. ISBN 0-911290-34-6. Vol. 2, 134p. ISBN 0-911290-35-4. Vol. 3, 320p. ISBN 0-911290-40-0.

This bibliography lists the scientific literature in all languages. It includes journal articles as well as books and conference proceedings.

Alcohol and Illicit Drugs: Abuse and Prevention

Derivan, William J., and Natalie Anne Silverstein. **Prevention Education: A Guide to Research.** New York: Garland, 1990. 400p. $34. ISBN 0-8240-3716-2.

The book presents more than 600 sources for information on prevention of the abuse of illicit drugs and alcohol. The sources are divided into three categories: prevention prior to abuse, prevention during the early stages of abuse, and education in the later phases of abuse. Citations include articles, books, journals, government publications, pamphlets, reports, and curriculum guides. Although most of the literature cited was published during the 1970s and early 1980s, the bibliography is a valuable source of information about substance-abuse prevention.

Myers, Sally, and Blanche Woolls. **Substance Abuse: A Resource Guide for Secondary Schools.** Englewood, CO: Libraries Unlimited, 1991. 300p. $28.50. ISBN 0-87287-805-8.

This annotated bibliography includes works of fiction as well as nonfiction and lists books, periodicals, databases, filmstrips, videos, and computer software. Several chapters list resources especially valuable for schools and for parents. The bibliography covers alcohol abuse as well as the abuse of illicit drugs.

Illicit Drugs: Federal Sources for Bibliographies

The Drugs and Crime Data Center and Clearinghouse provides the following bibliographies free of charge:

Amphetamines, Methamphetamines, and Crime (published in 1990). Order number 999121.

Asset Forfeiture/Asset Seizure (published in 1990). Order number 999127.

Crack Cocaine (published in 1990). Order number 999124.

Designer Drugs/Clandestine Labs (published in 1990). Order number 999122.

Drug Testing (published in 1991). Order number 999160.

Drug Testing in the Workplace (published in 1991). Order number 999161.

Drug Trafficking and Distribution (published in 1990). Order number 999126.

Drug Treatment in Correctional Settings (published in 1990). Order number 999123.

Drug Use and Crime (published in 1990). Order number 999103.

Drug Use Epidemiology: General and Special Populations (published in 1990). Order number 999125.

Gangs, Drugs, and Violence (published in 1991). Order number 999162.

Juveniles and Drugs (published in 1991). Order number 999128.

Minorities, Drugs, and Crime (published in 1991). Order number 999120.

Women, Drugs, and Crime (published in 1991). Order number 999129.

To order these bibliographies, or to receive a listing of all current publications available from the clearinghouse, write or call:

Drugs and Crime Data Center and Clearinghouse
1600 Research Boulevard
Rockville, MD 20850
(800) 666-3332

Illicit Drugs: Private Sources for Bibliographies

The National Organization for the Reform of Marijuana Laws (NORML) publishes a free bibliography, updated regularly, of books, monographs, articles, and government documents on marijuana covering the following topics:

The Drug Enforcement Juggernaut

Marijuana Prohibition Resurgent

The Myth of Marijuana's Threat to Public Health

Origins and Development of Marijuana Prohibition

Rise of Marijuana Use and the Origins of Decriminalization

The Second Wave of Reform

To obtain these bibliographies, write to:

NORML
1636 R Street, NW
Washington, DC 20009

Periodicals

The following periodicals might be helpful to researchers seeking further information on drug abuse in society.

Alcoholism and Drug Abuse Weekly
P.O. Box 3357
Wayland Square
Providence, RI 02906-0357
Weekly. $345/year (individuals) and $395/year (institutions).

The *Alcoholism and Drug Abuse Weekly* covers drug testing, AIDS and drugs, drug abuse prevention, treatment, and education. It reports new state and federal legislation on drugs and alcohol and discusses issues of importance to administrators of drug and alcohol abuse programs.

American Journal of Drug and Alcohol Abuse
Marcel Dekker, Inc.
P.O. Box 11305, Church Street Station
New York, NY 10249
Quarterly. $315/year.

This journal is co-sponsored by the American Academy of Psychiatrists in Alcoholism and Addictions and the American Medical Society on Alcoholism and Other Drug Dependencies. The latest research in the psychological and biological aspects of drug and alcohol abuse is discussed.

Contemporary Drug Problems
Federal Legal Publications, Inc.
157 Chamber Street
New York, NY 10007
Quarterly. $45/year.

This publication covers the legal aspects of drug and alcohol abuse, including the impact on law enforcement officers, the courts, and the penal system.

Crime and Delinquency
National Council on Crime and Delinquency
411 Continental Plaza
Hackensack, NJ 07601
Quarterly. $32/year.

Crime and Delinquency works to improve the criminal justice system, publishing articles on drug-related issues of law enforcement, the court system, correctional programs, and rehabilitation. A special area of interest is that of youthful drug offenders.

Drug Abuse and Alcoholism Newsletter
Vista Hill Foundation
3420 Camino del Rio North, Suite 100
San Diego, CA 92108
Six times a year. Free.

Published by the Vista Hill Hospital, this newsletter contains articles on rehabilitation and treatment issues.

Drug Abuse Update
National Families in Action
2296 Henderson Mill Road
Suite 300
Atlanta, GA 30345
Quarterly. $25/year.

Published by National Families in Action, a grass-roots movement of citizens concerned about drug and alcohol abuse, the *Drug Abuse Update* provides abstracts of the latest research in a simple, readable form. Topics include the medical, criminal, social, and cultural aspects of drug abuse. Each issue contains clear charts and graphs that are easily accessible to students.

Drugs and Society: A Journal of Contemporary Issues
Center for Alcohol and Addiction Studies
University of Alaska
3211 Providence Drive
Anchorage, AK 99508
Quarterly. $38/year (individuals) and $50/year (institutions).

Directed toward researchers, professionals in the field, and students, this journal discusses all aspects of drug and alcohol abuse: treatment, prevention, impact on society, etc.

Journal of Drug Education
Baywood Publishing Company
120 Marine Street
Farmingdale, NY 11735
Quarterly. $36/year (individuals) and $102/year (institutions).

For those interested in the prevention and treatment of drug and alcohol abuse, the *Journal of Drug Education* contains current, practical articles on the latest preventative strategies and trends in drug education and addiction management.

Journal of Drug Issues
P.O. Box 4021
Tallahassee, FL 32315-4021
Quarterly. $70/year.

This journal provides critical commentary on a wide range of drug abuse issues. The psychology, sociology, legislation, and history of drug abuse and treatment are all considered.

Journal of Psychoactive Drugs
409 Clayton Street
San Francisco, CA 94117
Quarterly. $70/year (individuals) and $120/year (institutions).

The *Journal of Psychoactive Drugs* was originally published as the current findings of the Haight-Asbury Free Medical Clinic, a noted drug treatment center in San Francisco, California. The journal contains the latest, authoritative information on the abuse of alcohol and other drugs. It considers related medical issues such as drug-related AIDS and sexually transmitted diseases.

Journal of Studies on Alcohol
Alcohol and Drug Abuse Research Center
McLean Hospital
Harvard Medical School
115 Mill Street
Balmont, MA 02178
Bimonthly. $95/year.

Published by the Rutgers Center of Alcohol Studies, this is an interdisciplinary journal of original research. It explores the use and misuse of alcohol: the biomedical, behavioral, social, and cultural aspects of this legal drug.

Journal on Alcohol and Drug Education
1120 East Oakland
P.O. Box 10212
Lansing, MI 48901
Three times per year. $40/year.

A scholarly journal for professionals in the field of alcohol and drug prevention education. Topics include attitudes of young people toward psychoactive drugs, user characteristics, prevention strategies, and so forth.

Periodical Reprint

Daedalus, the Journal of the American Academy of Arts and Sciences, devoted its entire summer 1992 issue to drug policy. Back issues (while available) may be obtained for $6.95 plus $2 for shipping and handling from:

Daedalus
Business Office
136 Irving Street, Suite 100
Cambridge, MA 02138

Monographs, Reports, Encyclopedias, and Pamphlets

Drug Abuse in the Family and in the Neighborhood

Berger, Gilda. **Violence and Drugs.** New York: Franklin Watts, 1989. 112p. $12.90. ISBN 0-531-10818.

In this readable volume, suitable for junior high school and older students, Berger discusses the effects of the use of drugs on society. She considers gang and cartel violence as well as the effects of the drug trade on law enforcement. Berger examines the pros and cons of various solutions to the drug war, including increased interdiction, law enforcement, and legalization.

Bureau of Justice Statistics. **Violent Crime in the United States.** Washington, DC: Bureau of Justice Statistics, 1991. 20p. Free. Order number NCJ127855.

This report summarizes national statistics on violent crime, including the relationship between violent crime and drugs. Useful for professionals in the field, most of the statistics are also easy for the general reader to understand.

Currie, Elliott. **Dope and Trouble: Portraits of Delinquent Youth.** New York: Pantheon, 1992. 294p. $22. ISBN 0-394-56151-1.

The children whose authentic voices pervade this book tell tales of drug use and dealing, gangs and crime, as well as abuse, neglect, and despair. The true stories of Lucifer, Loca, and Blaster, among others, are told in street language and are almost unbearably sad. This book gives the statistics on drug abuse a human face.

Drugs and Crime Data Center and Clearinghouse. **Drugs & Crime Facts, 1990.** Washington, DC: Drugs and Crime Data Center and Clearinghouse, 1991. 30p. Free. Order number NCJ128662.

Statistics about drugs and drug-related crime are listed in this book, which was compiled by the Bureau of Justice Statistics, a division of the U.S. Department of Justice.

Office for Substance Abuse Prevention. **Getting It Together: Promoting Drug-Free Communities.** Washington, DC: U.S. Department of Health and Human Services, Office for Substance Abuse Prevention, 1991. 71p. Free. Order number 1822.

This valuable book explains how to organize a community anti-drug program. It describes the characteristics of effective prevention programs and explores the relationship between community actions or attitudes and drug use. The book also suggests strategies for building life skills, giving information, providing alternatives for young people, and intervening when a problem is found. Community organizers will find directions for assessing their neighborhood's needs, applying for grants, influencing public officials, and evaluating program results. The book also includes a bibliography of drug information and prevention sources.

Stutman, Robert M., and Richard Esposito. **Dead on Delivery: Inside the Drug Wars, Straight from the Street.** New York: Warner, 1992. 274p. $22.95. ISBN 0-446-51558-2.

Stutman, the former head of the New York office of the Drug Enforcement Agency, describes life on the front lines of the war on drugs. The book details hair-raising encounters with criminals but also seriously considers the limitations of a law enforcement approach to the drug problem. Stutman advocates a mixture of social programs and law enforcement initiatives.

U.S. Department of Education. **What Works: Schools without Drugs.** Washington, DC: U.S. Department of Education, 1989. 96p. Free. Order number PHD006.

This concise handbook is essential to any effort to combat drug abuse in the educational system. Success stories from schools around the country are interwoven with factual information on various drugs, legislation relating to a school's right to search and seize drugs, students' rights, alternatives to drug use, and related topics. The book contains extensive notes and a recommended bibliography for further information.

Williams, Terry. **Cocaine Kids.** Reading, MA: Addison-Wesley, 1989. 140p. Hardcover, $16.95. ISBN 0-201-09360-X. Paper, $7.64. ISBN 0-201-57003-3.

The author, a sociologist, spent more than 1,000 hours in New York City's Washington Heights, a neighborhood pervaded by poverty and drug abuse. He interviewed and observed a gang composed of teenage drug dealers. He portrays the members as criminals who deal in violence as well as drugs, but also as "struggling young people trying to make a place for themselves in a world few care to understand and many wish would go away." In Williams's view, the drug trade, though deplorable, is a natural response by people who see no other avenues for their talents. *Cocaine Kids* is told primarily in the words of the young dealers and therefore contains street language. It has been criticized as nonjudgmental and soft-pedaling the violence and harm involved. The book has also been praised as a valuable look at the drug problem—from the inside.

Drug Policy

Benjamin, Daniel K., and Roger Leroy Miller. **Undoing Drugs: Beyond Legalization.** New York: Basic Books, 1991. 304p. $23. ISBN 0-465-08853-8.

Benjamin and Miller analyze what they deem the failure of the 1970 federal law regulating psychoactive drugs, the Controlled Substances Act. Using Prohibition as a model for why current drug laws fail, they advocate state control of dangerous drugs, much as alcohol is now regulated. In the authors' view, local control would ensure that people would live under laws that more closely matched their views. The authors also believe that local legal options would reduce the crime and violence of the inner cities.

Kleiman, Mark A. R. **Against Excess—Drug Policy for Results.** New York: Basic Books, 1992. 336p. $26. ISBN 0-465-01103-9.

Although this nearly 500-page book contains 60 pages of notes, it is not a compendium of statistics on drug abuse. Instead it is a philosophical consideration of drug policy. Kleiman, associate professor of public policy at Harvard University and a former drug policy analyst at the Department of Justice, argues that we should work for the regulation of drugs, not the eradication, which he considers impossible. He believes that regulations should be tailored to each drug, taking into account a cost-benefit analysis. That is, complete prohibition and a large amount of our anti-drug resources are appropriate for crack cocaine, in Kleiman's view, since the benefits to society of a reduction in the use of this drug are so desirable. Conversely, Kleiman feels that too much money and energy are devoted to a reduction in the use of marijuana, a drug he believes causes less harm. Kleiman discusses alcohol, tobacco, marijuana, heroin, and cocaine.

Lusane, Clarence, and Dennis Desmond. **Pipe Dream Blues: Racism and the War on Drugs.** Boston: South End Press, 1992. 293p. Hardcover, $30. ISBN 0-89608-411-6. Paper, $12. ISBN 0-89608-410-8.

Is the war on drugs racist? Yes, says the author of *Pipe Dream Blues.* In his view minority neighborhoods suffer the most from drug abuse and related crime, but they receive the smallest amount of assistance in coping with the problem. The author proposes more treatment centers, better police methods, and increased economic and political power for minority communities.

Mothers Against Drunk Driving. **Impaired Driving Issues—A How-To Manual.** Dallas: Mothers Against Drunk Driving, 1992. $9.75. Order number 6003, from MADD, Dallas, TX 75303-0124.

This excellent resource manual, updated regularly, comes in two versions, one for students and one for adults. The manual describes initiatives to reduce driving by people impaired by alcohol and other drugs through legislation, community programs, public education, lobbying, and other means.

Terkel, Susan Neiburg. **Should Drugs Be Legalized?** New York: Franklin Watts, 1990. 160p. Hardcover, $12.95. ISBN 0-531-15182-4. Public Library Binding, $13.90. ISBN 0-531-10944-5.

Terkel takes a calm, statistical approach to this hotly debated topic, examining and explaining both sides of the issue and giving equal weight to each. Topics include law as deterrent, the safety of street drugs, violence, and foreign policy. The book, suitable for teens, contains an extensive bibliography and a brief chronology of drugs in history.

White, Larry C. **Merchants of Death: The American Tobacco Industry.**
New York: Beech Tree Books, 1988. 256p. $17.95. ISBN 0-688-06706-9.

White tackles the politics of smoking in America, including chapters on
the history of the habit, discoveries of the medical effects of the drug,
and the response to these discoveries by government, the tobacco industry, and the advertising industry. He includes a chapter on advertising,
one on lawsuits, and one on government price supports paid to tobacco
growers. White has a great sense of the political clout of the industry, and
this book is nothing less than an indictment of public policy toward
smoking in America. The introduction is by Dr. C. Everett Koop, former
U.S. surgeon general and an outspoken critic of the tobacco industry.

Zimring, Franklin E., and Gordon Hawkins. **The Search for Rational Drug Control.** New York: Cambridge, 1992. 219p. $24.95. ISBN
0-521-41668-X.

Zimring and Hawkins see the debate about the legalization of drugs as "a
tug of war between . . . two powerful sentimental forces." Instead of a
war on drugs with broad goals, the authors advocate focusing energy and
money on the most vexing problems: street crime and the access of
children to dangerous drugs. The authors believe that a serious assessment should be made of the chance for success of each anti-drug program. Those programs likely to produce the greatest benefit for the
smallest investment should be promoted heavily; those yielding few
benefits should be dropped.

Drug Testing

Jussim, Daniel. **Drug Tests and Polygraphs, Essential Tools or Violations of Privacy?** New York: Messner, 1988. 128p. Hardcover, $12.98.
ISBN 0-671-64438-6. Paper, $5.95. ISBN 0-671-65977-4.

Although only half of this volume is relevant to the topic, it is still a
valuable resource. The author describes the legal issues in drug testing
and clearly explains the court decisions on the topic. He also discusses the
accuracy of the tests and spells out positions on both sides of the controversy over drug testing.

National Institute on Drug Abuse (NIDA). **Comprehensive Procedures
for Drug Testing in the Workplace: A Process Model of Planning,
Implementation, and Action.** Washington, DC: National Institute on
Drug Abuse, 1991. 20p. Free. Order number PHD548.

Intended for employers and others interested in drug testing in the
workplace, this book describes the necessary steps for urine testing.

———. **Employee Drug Screening: Detection of Drug Use by Urinalysis.** Rev. ed. Washington, DC: National Institute on Drug Abuse, 1988. 17p. Free. Order number PHD09.

This booklet answers employers' and employees' most frequently asked questions about urine screening for the detection of drug use.

———. **Urine Testing for Drugs of Abuse: NIDA Research Monograph 73.** Washington, DC: National Institute on Drug Abuse, 1988. 121p. Free. Order number M73.

This monograph explains the technology involved in a urine-testing program.

Drug Treatment and Prevention

Al-Anon. **Al-Anon Faces Alcoholism.** 2d ed. New York: Al-Anon Family Group Headquarters, Inc., 1990. 265p. $7.50. ISBN 0-910034-559.

This book contains a collection of articles written by professionals in the field of alcoholism and by Al-Anon members, who relate their personal experiences. The principles, practices, and programs of alcoholism recovery are described.

DeGregorio, Patrick, and Ralph Blumenthal. **Once through the Heart.** New York: Simon & Schuster, 1992. 352p. $21.95. ISBN 0-671-70750-7.

This is the moving story of a New York City police detective, Patrick DeGregorio, who discovers that his own daughter is addicted to drugs. Mary Anne began smoking cigarettes at the age of 11; progressed to whiskey, marijuana, and hallucinogens; and began selling drugs while still in high school. DeGregorio first denies his daughter's problem, but upon discovering her with a bag of drugs, he realizes that he can no longer ignore what is happening in his family. The book describes Mary Anne's entrance into drug treatment and her eventual recovery.

Donohew, Lewis, Howard E. Sypher, and William J. Bukowski. **Persuasive Communication and Drug Abuse Prevention.** Hillsdale, NJ: L. Erlbaum Associates, 1991. 334p. $49.95. ISBN 0-8058-0693-8.

The editors brought together some of the most successful drug-prevention researchers at a conference in 1989 and collected the documents from that conference in this book. The volume contains information about community, school, and personal prevention. While somewhat difficult to read, this book is a valuable consideration of the current status of drug prevention.

Hubbard, Robert L. **Drug Abuse Treatment, a National Study of Effectiveness.** Chapel Hill, NC: University of North Carolina Press, 1991. 213p. Hardcover, $34.95. ISBN 0-8078-1864-X. Paper, $12.95. ISBN 0-8078-4313-X.

This book considers a sample of publicly funded U.S. drug treatment programs, analyzing the success of each in the years 1979–1981. The book considers type of treatment, outcome, and cost effectiveness. Although this book contains research gathered before the advent of crack and AIDS, it is still a useful discussion of drug treatment and its results.

National Institute on Drug Abuse (NIDA). **Drug Abuse Curriculum for Employee Assistance Program Professionals.** Washington, DC: National Institute on Drug Abuse, 1989. 525p. Free. Order number BKD37.

This book provides a complete curriculum for people involved in employee assistance programs and health professionals dealing with employees who abuse drugs.

————. **Drugs in the Workplace: Research and Evaluation Data: NIDA Research Monograph 91.** Washington, DC: National Institute on Drug Abuse, 1989. 340p. Free. Order number M91.

For those who set policy about drug abuse by employees, this book contains papers presented at a 1988 NIDA conference on drugs in the workplace.

Office for Substance Abuse Prevention. **Citizen's Alcohol and Other Drug Prevention Directory: Resources for Getting Involved.** Washington, DC: Office for Substance Abuse Prevention, 1990. 276p. Free. Order number BK171.

Concerned citizens who wish to get involved in the effort to prevent drug abuse in their communities may consult this directory of more than 3,000 local, state, and federal agencies dealing with drug- and alcohol-related problems.

————. **Prevention Plus II: Tools for Creating and Sustaining a Drug-Free Community.** Washington, DC: Office for Substance Abuse Prevention, 1989. 541p. Free. Order number BK159.

Geared to community leaders, this book provides a framework for integrating prevention efforts aimed at young people into each community.

————. **Prevention Research Findings: 1988: OSAP Prevention Monograph 3.** Washington, DC: Office for Substance Abuse Prevention, 1990. 265p. Free. Order number BK162.

This monograph contains the proceedings from the First National Conference on Prevention Research Findings, held in 1988. Papers contained in the monograph cover topics such as the role of state and federal governments in prevention, prevention research, and school- and community-based prevention.

————. **Safer Streets Ahead: A Community Handbook To Prevent Impaired Driving.** Washington, DC: Office for Substance Abuse Prevention, 1991. 51p. Free. Order number PH292.

Prepared by the National Highway Traffic Safety Administration and the Office for Substance Abuse Prevention, this book is useful for people who would like to form a community action group to combat impaired driving. It explains how to enlist members of the community and how to educate the public about impaired driving. The book includes suggestions for safe parties and other substance-free youth activities.

U.S. Department of Education. **Profiles of Successful Drug Prevention Programs.** Washington, DC: U.S. Department of Education, 1990. 64p. Free. Order number BKD53.

For teachers, parents, and concerned citizens who would like to set up drug-prevention programs in schools, this book describes 51 successful plans. Details on assessment of drug use, rule enforcement, and drug-prevention curricula are included, as are strategies to involve parents, students, and the community.

Wright, Bob, and Deborah George Wright. **Dare To Confront! How To Intervene When Someone You Care about Has an Alcohol or Drug Problem.** New York: MasterMedia, 1990. $17.95. ISBN 0-942361-21-0.

The authors focus on intervention as "readily learned, easily applied, and dramatic in its results." This book is easy to read and is a valuable how-to guide for teens and adults who want to help someone they love stop the abuse of drugs or alcohol.

Drug Use: Past and Present

Courtwright, David T., Herman Joseph, and Don DesJarlais. **Addicts Who Survived, an Oral History of Narcotic Abuse in America 1923–1965.** Knoxville: University of Tennessee Press, 1989. 416p. $29.95. ISBN 0-87049-587-9.

This book is a compilation of oral histories of 60 elderly addicts, male and female, from all races and various walks of life. Divided into sections on becoming an addict, living the drug life, and treatment, the book gives an excellent picture of the realities of drug use. Most of the subjects have fascinating stories; the last section provides comments from law enforcement and treatment professionals. A brief history of drug use and drug legislation from 1920 to 1960 is included.

Foster, Carol D., ed. **Illegal Drugs and Alcohol—America's Anguish.** 5th ed. Wylie, TX: Information Plus Services, 1991. 136p. $20.95. ISBN 0-936474-94-7.

This fact-filled book is updated every two years to reflect the latest research and surveys on the use of drugs and alcohol in American society. Topics include alcohol and youth, drug trafficking, intravenous drug use and AIDS, smoking, drug testing, and drug-related laws.

Hawley, Richard A. **Think about Drugs and Society: Responding to an Epidemic.** Rev. ed. New York: Walker, 1991. 160p. $15.85. ISBN 0-8027-8114-4.

Suitable for junior high school students, Hawley's book focuses on the effects on society of cocaine, marijuana, and alcohol. Hawley discusses the history and current abuse of these drugs. An appendix covers legislation, government reports, and other primary sources.

Lender, Mark E., and James K. Martin. **Drinking in America: A History.** New York: Free Press, 1987. 222p. Hardcover, $27.95. ISBN 0-02-918530-0. Paper, $14.95. ISBN 0-02-918570-X.

This volume traces the use and abuse of alcohol from colonial days through the present. The ambivalent American attitude toward alcohol, which glorifies drinking but at times sanctions prohibition, is explored.

McKenna, Terence. **Food of the Gods: The Search for the Original Tree of Knowledge.** New York: Bantam, 1992. 311p. $21.50. ISBN 0-553-07868-2.

The author, an ethnobotanist, documents the evolution of human attitudes toward drugs. Originally, plants were viewed as sacred sources of wisdom intended to enhance sensory perception. Today's psychoactive drugs, on the other hand, are intended to numb or destroy perception.

McWilliams, John C. **The Protectors: Harry J. Anslinger and the Federal Bureau of Narcotics.** Newark, DE: University of Delaware Press, 1990. 251p. $37.50. ISBN 0-87413-352-1.

Harry J. Anslinger, the first commissioner of the Federal Bureau of Narcotics, shaped American policy toward dangerous drugs for decades; to some extent his influence is still felt today. Anslinger was committed to the crime-control approach to drug policy. In this serious study of

Anslinger's work, historian John McWilliams analyzes antinarcotics laws and American attitudes toward drugs from 1914, when the Harrison Narcotics Act was passed, through 1962, when Anslinger retired. Despite citing some flaws, the *American Historical Review* called the book a "well-balanced examination of a significant figure in U.S. political history."

Musto, David F. **The American Disease: Origins of Narcotics Control.** New York: Oxford University Press, 1988. 400p. $13.95. ISBN 0-19-505211-0.

An exhaustive and readable history of narcotics legislation in the United States with some discussion of the patterns of popularity of each drug. The history begins with colonial times and extends through the early 1980s, but concentrates on the late nineteenth and early twentieth centuries. Musto explains the political forces behind each swing in public opinion and details the cyclical nature of attitudes toward drugs.

Schivelbusch, Wolfgang. **Tastes of Paradise: A Social History of Spices, Stimulants, and Intoxications.** Translated from the German by David Jacobson. New York: Pantheon, 1992. 236p. $25. ISBN 0-394-57984-4.

Mixing historical documents, statistics, and anecdotes, the author describes the chemicals we use to change the way we feel. He considers spices, coffee, tea, chocolate, alcohol, and narcotics, linking them to the customs of the society in which they are consumed. Although the juxtaposition of harmless compounds with dangerous drugs is alarming, the book is entertaining and thought-provoking.

Smith, Mickey C. **A Social History of the Minor Tranquilizers: The Quest for Small Comfort in the Age of Anxiety.** Binghamton, NY: Haworth Press, 1991. 265p. $14.95. ISBN 1-56024-142-X.

During the 1950s, Miltown and Equanil and other minor tranquilizers were developed. The author describes how these drugs were promoted, prescribed, and abused from the 1950s through the 1980s. Smith links the use of these drugs to the nature of American society. Accessible to the general reader, this book is also of interest to professional health care workers.

Stuck, M. F. **Adolescent Worlds: Drug Use and Athletic Activity.** Westport, CT: Praeger, 1990. 184p. $45. ISBN 0-275-93647-3.

Stuck sets out to answer two questions: What are the place and the meaning of sports in the lives of teenagers? Do psychoactive drugs play a significant role in the lives of young people involved in sports? While the author does not provide definitive answers, he does supply excellent quotations from young people who discuss their perceptions of drugs and sports.

Wadler, Gary L., and Bryan Hainline. **Drugs and the Athlete.** Philadelphia: Davis, 1989. 353p. Hardcover, $49. ISBN 0-8036-9008-8. Paper, $35. ISBN 0-8036-9009-6.

The authors discuss the pressures that might lead athletes to take drugs, and they examine the usefulness of drug testing of athletes. Both legal and illicit drugs are discussed, and the chemistry, physiology, and use patterns of each are described. The appendices give the drug-testing policies of all major sports.

Drugs and Health

Cozic, Charles P., and Karin Swisher. **Chemical Dependency.** San Diego, CA: Greenhaven Press, 1991. 288p. Hardcover, $15.95. ISBN 0-89908-1797. Paper, $8.95. ISBN 0-89908-154-1.

Another fine volume in Greenhaven's series describing the pros and cons of various issues. Topics in this book include, What are the causes of chemical dependency?, How harmful is alcohol?, Should pregnant women be prosecuted for drug abuse?, and How can chemical dependency be reduced? Original articles written for this book and reprints from other sources illustrate the complexity of each topic. The book also contains political cartoons and thought-provoking questions after each chapter.

Gold, Dr. Mark S. **The Facts about Drugs and Alcohol.** 3d ed. New York: Bantam, 1988. 144p. $3.95. ISBN 0-92-9162-00-5.

This book by the founder of the cocaine helpline (800) COCAINE describes the biological effects of the most popular drugs (alcohol, cocaine, marijuana, hallucinogens, heroin, and others) with particular attention to the effects of these drugs on adolescent bodies. The book includes material on drug dependency, testing, and treatment. Straightforward, factual, and easy to read, this is a valuable resource for teenagers seeking information about the medical and psychological effects of drug abuse.

McCormick, Michele. **Designer Drug Abuse.** New York: Franklin Watts, 1990. 128p. $12.90. ISBN 0-531-10660-8.

McCormick's well-researched book explains the differences between so-called designer drugs and other psychoactive substances. She describes the history of these drugs, including early efforts by underground labs to outwit law enforcement by inventing drugs that had not yet been banned. McCormick includes case studies, medical treatment, and the chemical makeup of each drug. This book is easy to read and a fine factual resource for adolescent researchers.

O'Brien, Robert, Morris Chafetz, and Glen Evans, eds. **Encyclopedia of Alcoholism.** 2d ed. New York: Facts on File, 1992. 346p. $45. ISBN 0-8160-1955-X.

An excellent reference on alcohol abuse, the encyclopedia covers the history of consumption, attitudes, treatment, prevention, and other topics. The book deals primarily with the United States but contains some information on alcohol abuse in other countries. Useful appendices present data and references to periodical literature and agencies providing help and information on alcohol.

O'Brien, Robert, Sidney Cohen, Glen Evans, and James Fine, eds. **Encyclopedia of Drug Abuse.** 2d ed. New York: Facts on File, 1992. 496p. $45. ISBN 0-8160-1956-8.

An excellent reference for information on all aspects of drug abuse. Items in the main body of the text are arranged alphabetically and cover the biology, social effects, regulation, and history of psychoactive drugs in the United States and several other countries. Useful appendices give statistics and the specific provisions of some drug laws. References to periodical literature and agencies providing help and information on drug abuse are included.

Office for Substance Abuse Prevention. **Alcohol, Tobacco, and Other Drugs May Harm the Unborn.** Washington, DC: Office for Substance Abuse Prevention, 1990. 80p. Free. Order number PH291.

This monograph presents the most recent research and clinical studies on the effects of alcohol, tobacco, and other drugs on the fetus, mother, and newborn baby.

Ryan, Elizabeth A. **Straight Talk about Drugs and Alcohol.** New York: Facts on File, 1989. 160p. $16.95. ISBN 0-8160-1525-2.

This book provides an extensive description of the physical and emotional effects of drug and alcohol abuse. The facts are interspersed with interviews with teens who are currently in recovery programs. The book explains recommended methods of confronting a drug or alcohol abuser, and provides references to other sources of information about this problem.

Snyder, Solomon H., ed. **The Encyclopedia of Psychoactive Drugs.** New York: Chelsea House, 1992. 25 vols., 3125p. $17.95 per volume or $473.75 for the set. ISBN 0-685-54587-3 (set).

An excellent series suitable for young adults, *The Encyclopedia of Psychoactive Drugs* contains information on the history, chemistry, patterns of use, social consequences, treatment, and biological and psychological effects of drugs of abuse. Individual volume titles include *Alcohol and Alcoholism, LSD, Marijuana, PCP, Heroin, Prescription Narcotics, Barbiturates, Inhalants, Valium, Amphetamines, Cocaine,* and *Nicotine.*

International Drug Trafficking

Lee, Rensselaer W. **The White Labyrinth: Cocaine and Political Power.** New Brunswick, NJ: Transaction Books, 1989. 262p. Hardcover, $32.95. ISBN 0-88738-285-1. Paper, $18.95, ISBN 1-56000-565-3.

The author discusses the economic and political aspects of the South American cocaine trade, showing why the illicit drug is such a valuable commodity for producing nations and why supply-side efforts to stop drug abuse are often futile. The author is an assoc ate scholar at the Foreign Policy Research Institute. He discusses the relationship between cocaine traffickers and political rebels, the organization of the cartels, and the so-called pro-coca elements of established South American governments. *Library Journal* calls this book "extremely well researched and organized" but warns that it is "scholarly in tone."

McCoy, Alfred W. **The Politics of Heroin: CIA Complicity in the Global Drug Trade.** Chicago: Lawrence Hill Books, 1991. 640p. Hardcover, $29. ISBN 1-55652-126-X. Paper, $19.95. ISBN 1-5565-2-1251.

This work is the revised and expanded edition of *The Politics of Heroin in Southeast Asia,* written in 1972 by Alfred W. McCoy and Cathleen B. Read and published by Harper & Row, New York. The author, a professor of Southeast Asian history at the University of Wisconsin at Madison, spent 20 years researching the heroin trade, visiting remote poppy-producing areas of Southeast Asia. Although the Central Intelligence Agency (CIA) has consistently denied any involvement in the heroin trade, the author claims that the agency, to further its political goals, has been actively involved. The book contains an impressive amount of documentation, including maps of CIA landing strips and heroin-smuggling routes.

Scott, Peter Dale, and Jonathan Marshall. **Cocaine Politics: Drugs, Armies, and the CIA in Central America.** Berkeley and Los Angeles: University of California Press, 1991. 279p. $24.95.

With a theme similar to that of Alfred McCoy's book, **Cocaine Politics** concentrates on Central and South America. The authors, employing extensive documentation, describe complicity between drug traffickers and U.S. intelligence agents. The book claims that the U.S. anticommunist agenda, particularly regarding the contras (rebels against the Communist government of Nicaragua), often overshadowed anti-drug goals.

The CIA has denied all charges of complicity with the drug trade, but the authors believe they have proved their assertions.

Swisher, Karin L. **Drug Trafficking: Current Controversies.** San Diego, CA: Greenhaven Press, 1991. 200p. Public Library Binding, $16.95. ISBN 0-89908-576-8. Paper, $9.95. ISBN 0-89908-582-2.

This volume is part of a fine series that presents opposing views by experts on specific aspects of each topic. Original work written just for this series is supplemented by reprints from books and periodicals. The book also contains political cartoons and thought-provoking exercises at the end of each chapter. Topics in this volume include, Can the war on drugs be won?, Should drugs be legalized?, Is the U.S. war against international drug trafficking effective?, and How has drug trafficking affected the United States? Views range from very liberal to extremely conservative, and the book serves as a catalyst for discussion and analysis.

Selected Nonprint Resources

VIDEOTAPES DEALING WITH DRUG PREVENTION, drug use, and drug treatment are listed in this chapter. For other nonprint sources of information on drug abuse in society, see Chapter 5.

Addiction: The Problems, the Solutions
Type: VHS Videocassette
Length: 31 min.
Date: 1991
Cost: Purchase $189, rental $75/1 week
Source: Sunburst Drug Education
              39 Washington Avenue, Box 40
              Pleasantville, NY 10570-9971
              (800) 431-1934; (914) 769-2109, Fax

The nature of addiction, often a controversial topic, is explored in this video, which won an award from the National Council on Family Relations. Addiction is defined by three Cs—loss of *control, compulsive* use, and *continued* use despite negative consequences. The video discusses types and signs of addiction and cross addiction. Five teens tell their stories, from the beginning of their addiction through recovery. This is an informative and honest look at a complex topic.

Alcohol Facts: For Teenagers Only
Type: VHS Videocassette
Length: 31 min.
Date: 1984

Cost: Purchase $145, rental $55/1 week
Source: Sunburst Drug Education
             39 Washington Avenue, Box 40
             Pleasantville, NY 10570-9971
             (800) 431-1934; (914) 769-2109, Fax

An informative, award-winning video, *Alcohol Facts* stresses the myths that teens often hold about this powerful drug and debunks them in a low-key, nonalarmist manner. The film focuses on the effects that teens might experience if they drink and explores the special problems of children of alcoholics. Peer education and alcohol counseling are also portrayed, as well as strategies for resisting peer pressure.

Cocaine/Crack: A Teenager's Story
Type: VHS Videocassette
Length: 28 min.
Date: 1989
Cost: Purchase $189, rental $75/1 week
Source: Sunburst Drug Education
             39 Washington Avenue, Box 40
             Pleasantville, NY 10570-9971
             (800) 431-1934; (914) 769-2109, Fax

Recommended by the Addiction Research Foundation, this video tells one teen's dramatic story of cocaine addiction, beginning with his first, curious experiment and proceeding through addiction and the realization that he needed help. Personality changes often associated with cocaine use, such as paranoia and denial, are shown as well as the medical consequences. Two psychiatrists who work with chemically dependent teens discuss the meaning of addiction, the nature of cocaine, and other issues.

Dirty Business
Type: VHS Videocassette
Length: 32 min.
Date: 1988
Cost: Purchase $169, rental $75/1 week
Source: Sunburst Drug Education
             39 Washington Avenue, Box 40
             Pleasantville, NY 10570-9971
             (800) 431-1934; (914) 769-2109, Fax

Nicotine is a drug, but production and sale of it is also a business. This highly praised film, which is also available in Spanish and Portuguese, explores the marketing of tobacco and tobacco products and alerts viewers to the strategies used by many companies in advertising cigarettes. The stories of six former Marlboro men, the models who portrayed the masculine Marlboro smoker, are presented; all are dying of tobacco-related ailments. Tobacco companies tried to block distribution of this film and for good reason: It is an extremely powerful indictment of smoking, especially for young people.

Drinking and Driving: The Toll, the Tears
Type: VHS Videocassette
Length: 58 min.
Date: 1986
Cost: Purchase $49.50
Source: Public Broadcasting Service
            1320 Braddock Place
            Alexandria, VA 22314-1698
            (800) 344-3337

After killing a young father in a drinking-related car crash, Kelly Burke produced this film as part of his sentence for driving under the influence. The film, narrated by talk show host Phil Donahue, shows real, alcohol-related automobile accidents throughout the United States. Drivers and victims, as well as their survivors, are profiled. The film is poignant and has the powerful appeal of truth.

Drug Abuse: Sorting It Out
Type: VHS Videocassette
Length: 20 min.
Date: 1988
Cost: Purchase $49.95
Source: Health Education Services
            10200 Jefferson Boulevard
            P.O. Box 802
            Culver City, CA 90232-0802
            (800) 421-4246; (310) 839-2249, Fax

Real teens who have been in trouble with drugs and alcohol and who have turned their lives around discuss their experiences in this candid and ultimately uplifting film. The teens pull no punches, describing why they began to use drugs and how they struggled to overcome their dependencies. The underlying message of the film is that rehabilitation and drug-free lives can be achieved.

Drug-Free Zones: Taking Action
Type: VHS Videocassette
Length: 30 min.
Date: 1991
Cost: Purchase $39.50

Source: Cal Image Marketing
             3034 Gold Canal Drive, Suite B
             Rancho Cordova, CA 95670
             (916) 638-8383; (800) 982-1420

Edward James Olmos, star of *Stand and Deliver* and *American Me,* narrates this film about neighbors uniting against drug abuse. The film is a how-to guide for community groups: how to identify areas of drug trafficking, how to mobilize residents, and how to create drug-free zones. The film describes several successful grass-roots efforts and concludes with a challenge to organize and fight drugs in one's own town.

Drugs: A Plague upon the Land
Type: VHS Videocassette
Length: 60 min.
Date: 1990
Cost: Purchase $19.98
Source: Health Education Services
           10200 Jefferson Boulevard
           P.O. Box 802
           Culver City, CA 90232-0802
           (800) 421-4246; (310) 839-2249, Fax

Originally broadcast as an "ABC News Special Report," this film explores the current drug crisis, focusing on cocaine and crack. Law enforcement, international strategies, drug treatment, and drug use among young people are highlighted. The film includes highlights from President Bush's inaugural address in which he comments on drugs, as well as an evaluation of the progress of anti-drug efforts during his administration.

Face to Face with Drugs in America
Type: VHS Videocassette
Length: 22 min.
Date: 1989
Cost: Purchase $29.95
Source: The Health Connection
           Narcotics Education, Inc.
           12501 Old Columbia Pike
           Silver Springs, MD 20904-6600
           (800) 548-8700

A live narrator walks in and out of animated scenes, interacting with characters, as he explains the consequences of even casual drug use— not only to the user but to our entire society. Crime, violence, medical problems, and other effects are linked to this so-called victimless crime. Those who do not use drugs are saluted as strong, even heroic figures.

Feeling Good: Alternatives to Drug Abuse
Type: VHS Videocassette
Length: 12 min.
Date: 1980
Cost: Purchase $49.95
Source: Health Education Services
10200 Jefferson Boulevard
P.O. Box 802
Culver City, CA 90232-0802
(800) 421-4246; (310) 839-2249, Fax

The Reverend Jesse Jackson narrates this short film, made in 1980, in which he says, "We must put hope in our brains, not dope in our veins." Jackson acknowledges the temptations of drugs, but urges viewers to look for other mood-altering experiences: gardening, teaching, talking, or achieving excellence in any field.

I Live in an Alcoholic Family
Type: VHS Videocassette
Length: 35 min.
Date: 1988
Cost: Purchase $199, rental $75
Source: Sunburst Drug Education
39 Washington Avenue, Box 40
Pleasantville, NY 10570-9971
(800) 431-1934; (914) 769-2109, Fax

Three Cs that apply to children of alcoholics are explained in this video: The child did not *cause* the alcoholism, the child cannot *control* the alcoholic's drinking, and the child cannot *cure* the alcoholic. The stories of three families help the viewer understand the dynamics of addiction from the family's point of view. The video also explores the healing process, particularly the strength that comes from living through adversity.

Icy Death
Type: VHS Videocassette
Length: 25 min.
Date: 1989
Cost: Purchase $49.95
Source: The Health Connection
Narcotics Education, Inc.
12501 Old Columbia Pike
Silver Springs, MD 20904-6600
(800) 548-8700

Ice, a drug gaining in popularity at a frightening rate, is surrounded by the usual myths, that it is not harmful, addictive, or understood. This video explains the chemical composition of the drug, the effects on the body, the dangers to the user, and the potential for addiction. Ice is compared with crack and other drugs.

Let's Connect
Type: VHS Videocassette
Length: 12 min.
Date: 1992
Cost: Purchase $39.95
Source: Target
P.O. Box 20626
11724 NW Plaza Circle
Kansas City, MO 64195-0626
(800) 366-6667; (816) 464-5571

The producers of this award-winning video say that it is not intended to provide answers but that it "provokes thought, encourages discussion, and promotes cooperative community action." They have succeeded admirably. The video contains three short scenes: A high school activities sponsor and his teenage children discuss the community problem of underage drinking; a father and son attempt to communicate about their relationship; a teen drinker confronts her parents about their indifference to her behavior. The video is supported by a package of questions and tips for discussion leaders. This program is a good start for a parent or school campaign to combat teen drug and alcohol abuse.

Lives in the Balance: Keeping Drinkers off the Road
Type: VHS Videocassette
Length: 30 min.
Date: 1992
Cost: Purchase $89
Source: Health Education Services
10200 Jefferson Boulevard
P.O. Box 802
Culver City, CA 90232-0802
(800) 421-4246; (310) 839-2249, Fax

You can make a difference: That's the message of this activist video that portrays the problem—drunken driving—and several solutions, including Students Against Driving Drunk (SADD) and other organizations. Students are challenged to become involved in the effort to keep impaired drivers out of the driver's seat. Advertisements for alcoholic drinks are analyzed to help viewers understand the life-style such ads are trying to sell.

Marijuana and Your Mind
Type: VHS Videocassette
Length: 31 min.

Date: 1985
Cost: Purchase $145, rental $55
Source: Sunburst Drug Education
            39 Washington Avenue, Box 40
            Pleasantville, NY 10570-9971
            (800) 431-1934; (914) 769-2109, Fax

This award-winning video explains what marijuana is and how it achieves its psychoactive effects. The video explores both immediate and long-term consequences of use, stressing that marijuana justifies serious concern. Not preachy or alarmist, the video nonetheless gets its anti-drug point across. The film presents the experiences of two high school students who use pot as a way to deal with their anxieties and suggests more constructive ways to cope with problems.

New Frontiers: Understanding and Treating Alcoholism
Type: VHS Videocassette
Length: 45 min.
Date: 1991
Cost: Free
Source: Licensed Beverage Information Council
            1225 I Street, NW, Suite 500
            Washington, DC 20005
            (202) 682-4776

Funded by the Licensed Beverage Information Council and produced by the American Medical Association, this video originally aired on the Discovery channel and CNBC. An award winner, the video explains the nature of the disease of alcoholism—what we currently know about its nature, its origins, and its most effective treatments. Several scenes depicting medical procedures might be a bit graphic for the youngest viewers, but the scientific information is sound and clearly presented. Doctors who research and treat alcoholism, as well as recovering alcoholics, present the material in a conversational way.

No Matter How You Say It . . . Say No
Type: VHS Videocassette
Length: 11 min.
Date: 1987
Cost: Purchase $19.95
Source: Target
            P.O. Box 20626
            11724 NW Plaza Circle
            Kansas City, MO 64195-0626
            (800) 366-6667; (816) 464-5571, Fax

In this short video, produced by the U.S. Department of Health and Human Services with the National Basketball Association, Detroit

Pistons' all-star guard Isaiah Thomas talks to a small group of students who have dealt with pressures to use drugs and alcohol. The message is firmly anti-drug; the emphasis is on coping with peer pressure. Thomas gives the students reasons for not using drugs and advises them on how to refuse without alienating their friends.

Straight at Ya
Type: VHS Videocassette
Length: 44 min.
Date: 1988
Cost: Purchase $27
Source: Health Education Services
            10200 Jefferson Boulevard
            P.O. Box 802
            Culver City, CA 90232-0802
            (800) 421-4246; (310) 839-2249, Fax

Television stars Kirk Cameron of "Growing Pains" and Dan Frischman of "Head of the Class" narrate this three-part video in which animation and live action alternate. Part 1 stresses decisions and the responsibility that each decision entails. Part 2 describes ways to say no, such as, "Drugs do not solve problems, people do." Part 3 explains that popularity and drugs do not go together. The messages are presented in a light, humorous manner.

These Kids Are Tough! True Stories of Real Teens Resisting Drugs
Type: VHS Videocassette
Length: 24 min.
Date: 1990
Cost: Purchase $169, rental $40/1 week
Source: HRM Video
            175 Tompkins Avenue
            Pleasantville, NY 10570-9973
            (800) 431-2050; (914) 747-1744, Fax

In this film, which won awards from the National Education Film and Video Festival and the National Council on Family Relations, several real teenagers explain why they decided not to take drugs. These kids have faced almost overwhelming difficulties, such as personal problems, poverty, family trouble, and neighborhood violence, and have chosen to remain drug-free. The video does not preach or talk down. It simply allows the teens to speak for themselves and to show that drugs are not the answer to their problems.

Tobacco and You
Type: VHS Videocassette

Length: 22 min.
Date: 1990
Cost: Purchase $149, rental $55/1 week
Source: Sunburst Communications
39 Washington Avenue, Box 40
Pleasantville, NY 10570-3498
(800) 431-1934; (914) 769-2109, Fax

Recommended by the *School Library Journal,* this video interweaves a talk show on the health problems of smokers with clips of teenagers talking about why they smoke. The video also examines tobacco advertising and the strategies used to entice teens to smoke.

Waking Up from Dope
Type: VHS Videocassette
Length: 39 min.
Date: 1984
Cost: Purchase $69.95
Source: Health Education Services
10200 Jefferson Boulevard
P.O. Box 802
Culver City, CA 90232-0802
(800) 421-4246; (310) 839-2249, Fax

This film focuses on alcohol, marijuana, and tobacco, the three most common gateway drugs for young people. The host, Jevon Thompson, is a former drug user who skillfully uses humor to show the audience the implications of their actions. The emphasis is on responsibility for one's actions. Strategies for withstanding peer pressure are presented in an amusing and informative way.

Glossary

acid A slang term for LSD, a hallucinogen.

active ingredient Of the many substances found in a plant or mixture, the one that produces the principal effect on the user.

addiction According to a 1957 World Health Organization (WHO) statement, addiction is "a state of periodic or chronic intoxication, detrimental to the individual and society, produced by the repeated consumption of a drug." WHO goes on to state that addiction is characterized by compulsion to obtain and use the drug, a tendency to increase the dose, and both psychological and physical dependence on the effects. By 1965, WHO had dropped the term *addiction* in favor of *drug dependence,* but *addiction* is still widely used to mean a physical and/or psychological need for a drug.

AIDS (Acquired Immune Deficiency Syndrome) An incurable illness in which the body's immune system is impaired, leaving the patient vulnerable to many diseases.

alcohol Ethyl alcohol is the active ingredient in beer, wine, and spirits. Alcohol is made by fermentation and may be distilled. A psychoactive drug, alcohol causes intoxication (a drunken state) in sufficient doses.

alcoholic A person who suffers from the disease of alcoholism, an addiction to alcohol. Even a person who has stopped drinking may be an alcoholic, because the basic craving for the drug still exists.

amphetamine A drug that stimulates the central nervous system. Amphetamines have few approved medical uses, principally the treatment of narcolepsy (uncontrolled periods of sleep).

analog (also spelled analogue) A drug that is synthesized to copy the effect or function of another.

antagonist A drug that blocks the effects of a psychoactive drug or, if taken first, produces undesirable effects when the psychoactive drug is taken. Antagonists are sometimes given to recovering addicts so that they will have more incentive to avoid the drug.

bad trip Slang term for a hallucinogen-induced state characterized by anxiety and mental or physical distress.

barbiturates A group of psychoactive drugs that depress or slow down the central nervous system. Barbiturates are often used in legitimate medical practice as sedatives.

basuco (also spelled bazuco) A highly addictive, smokeable paste of cocaine, popular in South America.

blood alcohol concentration (BAC) The amount of alcohol in the bloodstream. A BAC of 0.10 or more indicates intoxication as defined by law in most states.

boarder babies A term for children with no need for hospitalization but who have been left to live in hospitals because their parents are not able to care for them. Boarder babies are often the children of drug abusers.

breathalyzer A machine into which breath is exhaled so that the concentration of alcohol in the bloodstream may be measured.

carbon monoxide One of the harmful gases present in cigarette smoke. Carbon monoxide, in very high concentrations, can cause suffocation.

cartel A multinational drug-trafficking organization.

Coca Nostra Slang term for the cocaine traffickers of South America, derived from Cosa Nostra, a name for the Mafia.

cocaine A drug derived from the coca plant, used in medicine as a topical anesthetic, and prized on the street as a psychoactive drug.

crack A concentrated, smokeable form of cocaine.

craving A fierce desire for a food, a drug, or an action, characterized by disregard for negative consequences.

crop eradication An anti-drug policy in which the plants that supply the raw material of psychoactive drugs are destroyed in the field.

crop substitution An anti-drug policy in which farmers are given financial incentives to plant nondrug crops instead of opium, coca, hemp, or other drug crops.

cross-addiction Addiction to more than one drug, for example, alcohol and cocaine.

cut   To mix a street drug with other, cheaper substances in order to reduce potency and increase profits (e.g., heroin may be cut with sugar).

defoliant   A chemical that withers and destroys plants.

demand reduction   Term for anti-drug policies that concentrate on prevention and treatment (i.e., reducing the demand for drugs).

dependence   The World Health Organization (WHO), in a 1965 statement, defined dependence as "a state, psychic and sometimes also physical, resulting from the interaction between a living organism and a drug, characterized by behavioral and other responses that always include a compulsion to take the drug on a continuous or periodic basis in order to experience its psychic effects, and sometimes to avoid the discomfort of its absence. Tolerance may or may not be present." The terms *dependence* and *addiction* are sometimes used interchangeably.

designer drugs   Drugs whose chemical formulas are similar to those of popular psychoactive drugs, with slight alterations originally intended to circumvent the Controlled Substances Act. These artificially designed and manufactured drugs are now as illegal as the drugs they mimic.

detox   Slang term for detoxification. The process an addict goes through as the traces of drugs leave the body. Sometimes medical help is necessary to make the detoxification safe.

drive-by shootings   A tactic used by rival drug gangs in which bullets are sprayed at a target from a moving car.

drug abuse   Any use of an illegal drug or improper use of a legal drug (e.g., underage drinking and smoking, or use of prescription drugs without a prescription).

Drug Enforcement Administration (DEA)   A division of the U.S. Department of Justice devoted to the enforcement of the nation's drug-control laws.

drug testing   The testing of body fluids (e.g., blood or urine) for the presence of drug metabolites, which indicate that a drug has been taken. Exhaled breath may also be tested to determine the amount of alcohol that has been ingested. A positive test result means that drug traces have been found.

Ecstasy   Street name for MDMA.

employee assistance programs (EAPs)   Programs put in place by business and industry to help employees recover from drug or alcohol abuse and other problems.

fentanyl   A synthetic narcotic used in legitimate medical practice as an anesthetic and on the street as a psychoactive drug.

fetal alcohol effect (FAE)   Term for a cluster of symptoms, sometimes including learning disabilities or lowered intelligence, suffered by a child whose mother drank alcohol during pregnancy. FAE is less severe than fetal alcohol syndrome (FAS).

fetal alcohol syndrome (FAS)   Term for a cluster of symptoms, sometimes including retardation, suffered by a child whose mother drank alcohol during pregnancy. FAS is more severe than fetal alcohol effect (FAE).

forfeiture   A tactic originally used centuries ago to seize the assets of pirates. In 1984, forfeiture was revived as a way for U.S. law enforcement agencies to confiscate the assets of drug traffickers. By law the proceeds of the forfeiture must be devoted to increased law enforcement.

French Connection   A drug ring, immortalized in a movie of the same name, that transported heroin from Southwest Asia through France to the United States.

gas chromatography   A test for drugs considered to be the most accurate, and the only drug-screening test accepted in most courts as proof of drug use. Gas chromatography checks urine for the presence of drug metabolites.

gateway drug   A drug that tends to act as the starting point for the use of more powerful and dangerous drugs or the more frequent use of any drug. Alcohol, tobacco, and marijuana are the most common gateway drugs.

Golden Crescent   A major opium-producing region in Southwest Asia encompassing parts of Afghanistan, Turkey, and Iran.

Golden Triangle   A major opium-producing region in Southeast Asia encompassing parts of Myanmar (formerly Burma), Laos, and Thailand.

halfway house   A community of recovering addicts who live together after their release from residential drug treatment and before their return home. A halfway house generally supervises work and study programs for recovering addicts.

hallucinogens   A group of psychoactive drugs, both organic and synthetic, capable of altering the user's perceptions of reality and causing hallucinations.

hashish   A drug derived from the hemp plant, related to but more concentrated than marijuana.

helpline   A telephone line that primarily aims to provide information, including treatment referrals, to drug users.

hepatitis   An inflammation of the liver that may be fatal.

heroin   A powerful narcotic drug, diacetylmorphine, derived from the opium poppy.

hit   A slang term for an inhalation of marijuana or another drug. The term *hit* also refers to a positive drug test.

hotline   A telephone line that helps drug users who are in crisis. Hotlines generally operate 24 hours a day every day.

ice   A smokeable form of methamphetamine.

illicit drug   A drug that is banned by law or taken in a manner that is banned (e.g., use of a sedative without a prescription or the underage consumption of alcohol).

immunoassay   A drug test to detect traces of drug metabolites in urine samples by adding antibiotics that bond with specific drugs.

inhalant   A gas that is inhaled in order to produce a psychoactive effect. Some inhalants, such as nitrous oxide, have legitimate medical functions. Others are common household substances like paint thinner or glue that are not intended for internal use.

interdiction   The interception of drugs while they are in transit, usually at the U.S. border.

intoxication   An excited mental state, often characterized by impaired judgment that may be produced by drugs or alcohol.

intravenous (IV)   Injected into a vein with a needle.

LSD   D-lysergic acid diethylamide, a hallucinogenic drug popularly known as acid.

marijuana   A drug derived from the hemp plant that is smoked or eaten. The active ingredient is tetrahydrocannabinol (THC).

mass spectrometry   A test to detect the presence of drug metabolites in urine. This test is used in combination with gas chromatography.

MDMA   A designer drug that is an analog of amphetamines and hallucinogens. MDMA is also called Ecstasy, XTC, Adam, and Essence.

meperidine   A synthetic, extremely powerful narcotic drug.

mescaline   A crystalline substance extracted from the dried tops of the mescal cactus. Mescaline is a hallucinogen.

metabolites Chemicals produced as the result of natural body processes. Drug metabolites are the end product of the body's use of drugs.

methamphetamine A synthetic amphetamine.

money laundering A practice that disguises the source of income of drug traffickers. Since drug dealers take in large amounts of cash, they must launder it or make it clean, often by reporting it as the profit from a dummy corporation, before they can deposit it in bank accounts or make other investments with it.

MPTP A designer drug that is an analog of heroin. Also called *new heroin.*

mules Slang term for low-level drug smugglers.

mushrooms Term used by drug dealers to describe innocent bystanders who sprout up in the line of fire. The term also refers, often incorrectly, to organic hallucinogens.

narcotic Technically, a narcotic is a drug derived from opium or an analog of opium. In law, the term is often applied to any illicit psychoactive drug.

needle exchange Programs in which needles used by drug users are exchanged for sterile needles to help combat the spread of AIDS and other diseases.

nicotine A principal ingredient in tobacco. Nicotine is an addictive, poisonous substance.

NIDA (National Institute on Drug Abuse) A federal government agency that studies the problems of drug abuse as well as treatment and prevention strategies.

opiates Drugs such as codeine, morphine, and heroin that are derived from the opium plant.

organic Derived from plants.

outpatient treatment Treatment for drug addiction in which an addict lives at home and reports to a center at specific times. *Inpatient treatment* involves an addict living in a drug treatment facility.

PCP Abbreviated name of phencyclidine, an animal tranquilizer and a hallucinogen originally developed as an anesthetic for humans but discarded from legitimate medical practice because of its bizarre psychoactive effects.

peyote   The dried top of the mescal cactus, chewed for its hallucinogenic effect.

plata o plomo **(silver or lead)**   Slang term for the choice given by drug cartels to many anti-drug forces in South America—*plata* (bribe) or *plomo* (gunshot).

posses   Slang term for drug gangs from the island of Jamaica who have set up operations in the United States.

prohibition   In general, the banning of a drug. Prohibition also refers to the period, 1918–1933, during which the sale and manufacture of alcohol was banned in the United States.

psychedelic   Another term for hallucinogenic. Capable of altering perception or causing hallucinations.

psychoactive   Capable of changing mood, perception, or thought processes.

pusher   A drug seller or dealer.

random drug testing   Testing done without notice and without cause, that is, without suspicion of drug use or a precipitating incident such as an accident.

recovering addict (or recovering alcoholic)   A person, once addicted, who has stopped using drugs or alcohol. Because drug or alcohol addiction is a permanent condition, even people who have abstained for years speak of themselves as recovering rather than as cured.

residential treatment   Live-in treatment program for drug addiction.

safety-sensitive job   A job in which the safety of other workers or of the public is at stake (e.g., air traffic controller).

sedative   A drug that depresses or slows down the central nervous system. In medicine, sedatives are prescribed to relieve pain, produce relaxation, or promote sleep.

Sendero Luminoso (Shining Path)   A Communist guerrilla group waging war in Peru. The group's activities are financed by coca trafficking.

sexually transmitted disease (STD)   A disease, such as AIDS or herpes, that may be spread through sexual contact.

sidestream smoke   Smoke that escapes into the air (and thus may be inhaled by nonsmokers) from a burning cigarette or from a smoker's exhalation.

SIDS (Sudden Infant Death Syndrome) A poorly understood phenomenon in which a seemingly healthy infant dies suddenly.

skid row Slang term for poor areas in which homeless people congregate. At one time the term referred almost exclusively to places where many penniless alcoholics lived.

speedball Slang term for a mixture of heroin and cocaine.

steroid Drug often abused by athletes in order to increase muscle mass. Steroids may cause liver damage and other harmful side effects.

substance abuser Someone who takes illicit drugs or who uses any drug (including alcohol) to excess or in an improper way.

substitute A drug that satisfies the craving of an addict while producing fewer undesirable effects. For example, methadone is often a substitute for heroin.

supply side Anti-drug policies that concentrate on the producers, importers, and sellers of drugs.

syphilis A sexually transmitted disease.

syringe A hypodermic needle.

thin-layer chromatography A type of test to detect traces of drug metabolites in urine. (See **gas chromatography**.)

TNT (tactical narcotics team) A police force that floods an area plagued by drug dealers in order to clear it of drug traffic. TNT teams were used in New York City for several years but are now being phased out.

tobacco The leaves of the tobacco plant, dried and processed, then smoked or chewed. The active ingredient is nicotine.

trafficker A drug dealer. The term is generally applied to major distributors or importers, although street-level dealers are also traffickers.

tuberculosis A serious and sometimes fatal disease of the lungs.

12 steps A set of principles, first developed by Alcoholics Anonymous (AA), and now used by many self-help groups for overcoming addiction. (See Treatment in chapter 4 for the 12 steps of AA.)

underground lab An illegal drug-processing site.

uppers A slang term for amphetamines.

withdrawal Symptoms an addict experiences when deprived of a drug. Withdrawal symptoms may be both mental and physical.

works Slang term for the equipment needed for intravenous drug use—a syringe (needle), a spoon or container for dissolving the drug, and a tourniquet.

Index

Geraldine Woods is the author of more than 30 books for young people, several on the topic of drug abuse and some written in collaboration with her husband, Harold. She currently teaches English and directs the independent study program at the Horace Mann School in New York City. Ms. Woods lives in Manhattan with her husband and her son, Thomas. *Drug Abuse in Society* is her first book for ABC-CLIO.